Double Diamond edition

MICROSOFT

POWERPOINT 4

for Windows

Gary B. Shelly
Thomas J. Cashman
Sherry L. Green
Marvin M. Boetcher

SHELLY
CASHMAN
SERIES®

Special thanks go to the following reviewers of the Shelly Cashman Series Windows Applications textbooks:

Susan Conners, Purdue University Calumet; **William Dorin**, Indiana University Northwest; **Robert Erickson**, University of Vermont; **Roger Franklin**, The College of William and Mary; **Roy O. Foreman**, Purdue University Calumet; **Patricia Harris**, Mesa Community College; **Cynthia Kachik**, Santa Fe Community College; **Suzanne Lambert**, Broward Community College; **Anne McCoy**, Miami-Dade Community College/Kendall Campus; **Karen Meyer**, Wright State University; **Mike Michaelson**, Palomar College; **Michael Mick**, Purdue University Calumet; **Cathy Paprocki**, Harper College; **Jeffrey Quasney**, Educational Consultant; **Denise Rall**, Purdue University; **Sorel Reisman**, California State University, Fullerton; **John Ross**, Fox Valley Technical College; **Lorie Szalapski**, St. Paul Technical College; **Susan Sebok**, South Suburban College; **Betty Svendsen**, Oakton Community College; **Jeanie Thibault**, Educational Dynamics Institute; **Margaret Thomas**, Ohio University; **Carole Turner**, University of Wisconsin; **Diane Vaught**, National Business College; **Dwight Watt**, Swainsboro Technical Institute; **Melinda White**, Santa Fe Community College; **Eileen Zisk**, Community College of Rhode Island; and **Sue Zulauf**, Sinclair Community College.

1 2 3 4 5 6 7 8 9 10   BC   9 8 7 6 5

CONTENTS

PREFACE

▶ THE WINDOWS ENVIRONMENT

S ince the introduction of Microsoft Windows version 3.1, the personal computing industry has moved rapidly toward establishing Windows as the de facto user interface. The majority of software development funds in software vendor companies are devoted to Windows applications. Virtually all PCs purchased today, at any price, come preloaded with Windows and, often, with one or more Windows applications packages. With an enormous installed base, it is clear that Windows is the operating environment for both now and the future.

The Windows environment places the novice as well as the experienced user in the world of the mouse and a common graphical user interface between all applications. An up-to-date educational institution that teaches applications software to students for their immediate use and as a skill to be used within industry must teach Windows-based applications software.

▶ OBJECTIVES OF THIS DOUBLE DIAMOND EDITION

M *icrosoft PowerPoint 4 for Windows Double Diamond Edition* was specifically developed for an introductory course that covers the essentials of presentation graphics. No previous experience with a computer is assumed, and no mathematics beyond the high school freshman level is required. The objectives of this book are as follows:

FIGURE P-1

▶ To teach the fundamentals of Microsoft PowerPoint 4 for Windows
▶ To acquaint the student with the proper way to build a presentation
▶ To use practical problems to illustrate presentation graphics
▶ To take advantage of the many new capabilities of presentation graphics in a graphic environment (see Figure P-1)

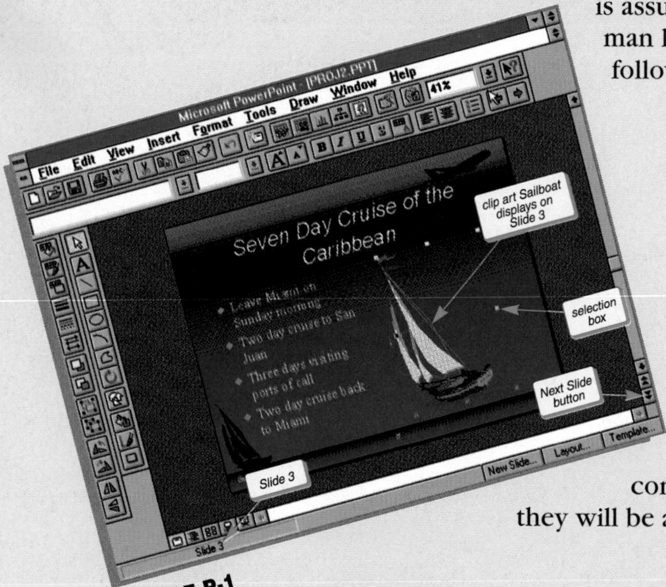

The textbook covers all essential aspects of Microsoft PowerPoint for Windows. When students complete a course using this Double Diamond Edition, they will be able to solve a variety of presentation graphics problems.

▶ THE SHELLY CASHMAN APPROACH

T he Shelly Cashman Series Windows Applications books present word processing, spreadsheet, database, programming, presentation graphics, and Windows itself by showing the actual screens displayed by Windows and the applications software. Because the student interacts with pictorial displays when using Windows, written words in a textbook does not suffice. For this reason, the Shelly Cashman Series emphasizes screen displays as the primary means of teaching Windows applications software. Every screen shown in the Shelly

Cashman Series Windows Applications books appears in color, because the student views color on the screen. In addition, the screens display exactly as the student will see them. The screens in this book were captured while using the software. Nothing has been altered or changed except to highlight portions of the screen when appropriate (see the screens in Figure P-2).

The Shelly Cashman Series Windows Applications books present the material using a unique pedagogy designed specifically for the graphical environment of Windows. The textbooks are primarily designed for a lecture/lab method of presentation, although they are equally suited for a tutorial/hands-on approach wherein the student learns by actually completing each project following the step-by-step instructions. Features of this pedagogy include the following:

▸ **Project Orientation:** Each project in the book solves a complete problem, meaning that the student is introduced to a problem to be solved and is then given the step-by-step process to solve the problem.

▸ **Step-by-Step Instructions:** Each of the tasks required to complete a project is identified throughout the development of the project. For example, a task might be to change the fill color of an object. Then, each step to accomplish the task is specified. The steps are accompanied by screens (see Figure P-2). The student is not told to perform a step without seeing the result of the step on a color screen. Hence, students learn from this book the same as if they were using the computer. This attention to detail in accomplishing a task and showing the resulting screen makes the Shelly Cashman Series Windows Applications textbooks unique.

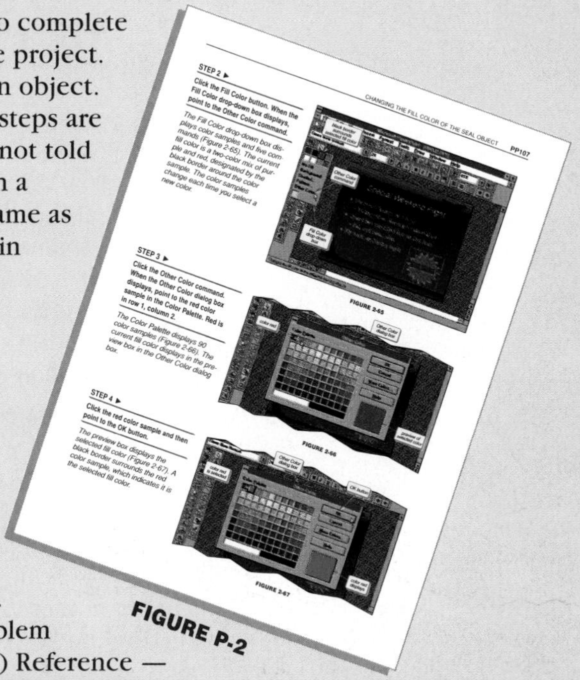

▸ **Multiple Ways to Use the Book:** Because each step to accomplish a task is illustrated with a screen, the book can be used in a number of ways, including: (a) Lecture and textbook approach — The instructor lectures on the material in the book. The student reads and studies the material and then applies the knowledge to an application on a computer; (b) Tutorial approach — The student performs each specified step on a computer. At the end of the project, the student has solved the problem and is ready to solve comparable student assignments; (c) Reference — Each task in a project is clearly identified. Therefore, the material serves as a complete reference because the student can refer to any task to determine how to accomplish it.

▸ **Windows/Graphical User Interface Approach:** Windows provides a graphical user interface. All of the examples in the book use this interface. Thus, the mouse is used for the majority of control functions and is the preferred user communication tool. When specifying a command to be executed, the sequence is as follows: (a) If a button invokes the command, use the button; (b) If a button is not available, use the command from a menu; (c) If a button or a menu cannot be used, only then is the keyboard used to implement a Windows command.

▸ **Emphasis on Windows Techniques:** The most general techniques to implement commands, enter information, and generally interface with Windows are presented. This approach allows the student to move from one application software package to another under Windows with a minimum amount of relearning with respect to interfacing with the software. An application-specific method is taught only when no other option is available.

FIGURE P-2

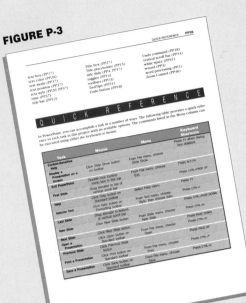

▶ **Reference for All Techniques:** Even though general Windows techniques are used in all examples, a Quick Reference chart (see Figure P-3) at the end of each project details not only the mouse and menu methods for implementing a command, but also contains the keyboard shortcuts for the commands presented in the project. Therefore, students are exposed to all means for implementing a command.

▶ ORGANIZATION OF THIS DOUBLE DIAMOND EDITION

*M*icrosoft PowerPoint 4 for Windows Double Diamond Edition provides detailed instruction on how to use Microsoft PowerPoint 4 for Windows. The material is divided into three projects as follows:

Project 1 – Building a Slide Presentation   In Project 1, students are introduced to PowerPoint terminology; the PowerPoint window; and the basics of creating a bulleted list presentation. Topics include starting PowerPoint; establishing the foundation of a presentation using the Pick A Look Wizard; selecting a template; displaying information on every slide; changing text style; decreasing font size; saving a presentation; changing line spacing; checking spelling; printing a presentation; exiting PowerPoint and opening an existing presentation; correcting errors; and obtaining online Help.

Project 2 – Creating a Presentation in Outline View   In Project 2, students create a presentation in Outline view and learn how to insert clip art. Topics include arranging text using the Promote and Demote butons; changing slide layouts; adding clip art; drawing an object and adding text to the object; changing text color and fill color; rearranging slide order; copying and pasting; reversing the last edit using the Undo button; and printing an outline.

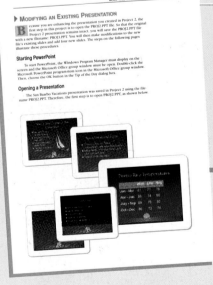

Project 3 – Enhancing a Presentation and Adding Graphs and Tables   In Project 3, students enhance the presentation created in Project 2 by adding a graph, a table, and transition and build effects, and running an automatic slide show (see Figure P-4). Topics include saving the presentation with a new name; changing templates; deleting objects; adding a graph using Microsoft Graph 5; adding a table using Microsoft Word 6; adding slide transition effects; adding build effects; establishing slide show timings; and running an automatic slide show.

End-of-Project Student Activities

Each project ends with a wealth of student activities including these notable features:

- A list of key terms for review
- A Quick Reference that lists the ways to carry out a task using the mouse, menu, or keyboard shortcuts
- Six Student Assignments for homework and classroom discussion
- Three Computer Laboratory Exercises that usually require the student to load and manipulate a PowerPoint presentation from the Student Diskette that accompanies this book
- Four Computer Laboratory Assignments (see Figure P-5) that require the student to develop a complete project assignment; the assignments increase in difficulty from a relatively easy assignment to a case study

FIGURE P-5

PP66 PROJECT 1 BUILDING A SLIDE PRESENTATION

COMPUTER LABORATORY ASSIGNMENT 2
Building a Presentation Using the Pick a Look Wizard and Changing Paragraph Line Spacing

Purpose: To become familiar with building a presentation, applying a template, changing paragraph line spacing, printing a presentation, and saving a presentation.

Problem: You are the assistant manager of Maximum Savings and Loan. Your area of responsibility is the loan department. Maximum Savings and Loan is starting its annual home improvement loan campaign. You have been asked to develop a presentation on consumer credit for the home improvement loan campaign.

Instructions: Perform the following tasks:

1. Using the Pick a Look Wizard, choose the Blue Diagonal template and add company name, date, and page number, as shown in Figure CLA1-2.
2. Create a title slide using your name as the presenter.
3. Create a bulleted list for the slide shown in Figure CLA1-2.
4. Adjust the paragraph line spacing to one line after each paragraph.
5. Save the presentation on your data disk with the filename CLA1-2.
6. Print the presentation slides choosing the Print command from the File menu.
6. Exit PowerPoint.

FIGURE CLA1-2

COMPUTER LABORATORY ASSIGNMENT 3
Building a Presentation Using a Template, Changing Paragraph Line Spacing, and Spell Checking

Purpose: To become familiar with designing and building a presentation, applying a template using the Pick a Look Wizard, changing paragraph line spacing, spell checking a presentation, printing a presentation, and saving a presentation.

Problem: You are the assistant director of admissions at Western State University. You have been asked by the chancellor to give a presentation on Western State University. Create a title slide and the bulleted list of the issues you plan to discuss (Figure CLA1-3). Create at least three more slides to complete the presentation. The paragraphs on the next page are excerpts from the Western State University catalog. Use the underlined passages to complete your presentation.

FIGURE CLA1-3

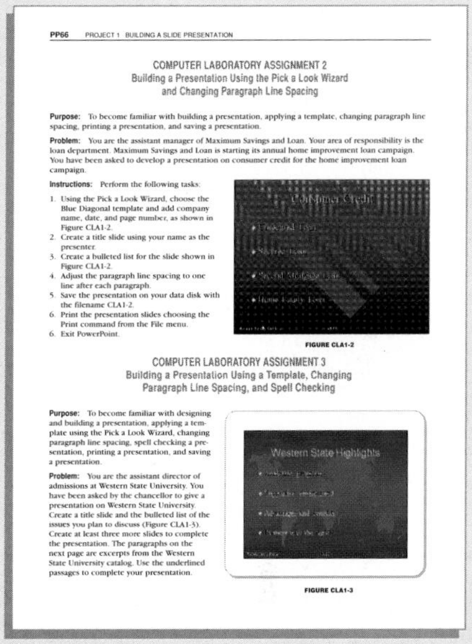

Ancillary Materials for Teaching from the Shelly Cashman Series Windows Applications Textbooks

A comprehensive instructor's support package accompanies all textbooks in the Shelly Cashman Series.

Computer-Based LCD Lecture Success System The Shelly Cashman Series proudly presents the finest LCD learning material available in textbook publishing. The Lecture Success System diskette, together with a personal computer and LCD technology, are used in lieu of transparencies. The system enables you to explain and illustrate the step-by-step, screen-by-screen development of a project in the textbook without entering large amounts of data, thereby improving your students' grasp of the material. The Lecture Success System leads to a smooth, easy, error-free lecture.

The Lecture Success System diskette comes with files that correspond to key figures in the book. You load the files that pertain to a project and display them as needed. If the students want to see a series of steps a second time, simply reopen the file you want to start with and redo the steps. This presentation system is available to adopters without charge.

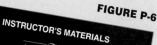

Instructor's Materials This instructor's ancillary (Figure P-6) contains the following:

- Detailed lesson plans including project objectives, the project overview, and a three-column outline of each project that includes page references and illustration references
- Answers to all student assignments at the end of the projects
- A test bank of True/False, Multiple Choice, and Fill-In questions
- An Instructor's Diskette that includes the projects and solutions to the Computer Laboratory Assignments at the end of each project
- A Lesson Plans and Test Bank Diskette that includes the detailed lesson plans and test bank for customizing to individual instructor's needs

FIGURE P-6

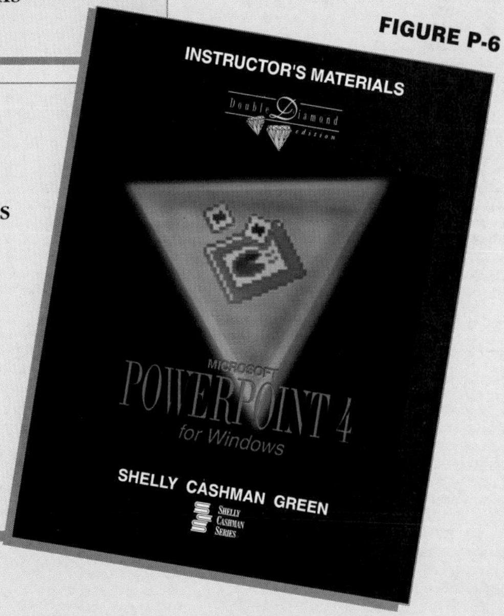

MicroExam IV   MicroExam IV, a computerized test-generating system, is available free to adopters of any Shelly Cashman Series textbooks. It includes all of the questions from the test bank just described. MicroExam IV is an easy-to-use, menu-driven software package that provides instructors with testing flexibility and allows customizing of testing documents.

NetTest IV   NetTest IV allows instructors to take a MicroExam IV file made up of True/False and Multiple Choice questions and proctor a paperless examination in a network environment. The same questions display in a different order on each PC. Students have the option of instantaneous feedback. Tests are electronically graded, and an item analysis is produced.

► ACKNOWLEDGMENTS

The Shelly Cashman Series would not be the success it is without the contributions of outstanding publishing professionals. First, and foremost, among them is Becky Herrington, director of production and designer. She is the heart and soul of the Shelly Cashman Series, and it is only through her leadership, dedication, and untiring efforts that superior products are produced.

Under Becky's direction, the following individuals made significant contributions to these books: Peter Schiller, production manager, Ginny Harvey, series administrator and manuscript editor; Ken Russo, senior illustrator and cover art; Anne Craig, Mike Bodnar, Greg Herrington, Dave Bonnewitz, and Dave Wyer, illustrators; Jeanne Black, Betty Hopkins, and Rebecca Evans, typographers; Tracy Murphy, series coordinator; Sue Sebok and Melissa Dowling LaRoe, copy editors; Marilyn Martin and Nancy Lamm, proofreaders; Henry Blackham, cover and opener photography; and Dennis Woelky, glass etchings.

Special recognition for a job well done must go to James Quasney, who, together with writing, assumed the responsibilities as series editor. Particular thanks go to Thomas Walker, president and CEO of boyd & fraser publishing company, who recognized the need, and provided the support, to produce the full-color Shelly Cashman Series Windows Applications textbooks.

We hope you will find using the book an enriching and rewarding experience.

Gary B. Shelly
Thomas J. Cashman

PRESENTATION GRAPHICS

USING MICROSOFT POWERPOINT 4 FOR WINDOWS

Microsoft PowerPoint 4 for Windows

BUILDING A SLIDE PRESENTATION

OBJECTIVES You will have mastered the material in this project when you can:

▸ Start PowerPoint
▸ Describe the PowerPoint window
▸ Use the PowerPoint Pick a Look Wizard
▸ Select a template
▸ Create a title slide
▸ Create a bulleted list
▸ Italicize text
▸ Change font size

▸ Save a presentation
▸ Create a new slide
▸ Use the PowerPoint spelling checker
▸ Print a transparency presentation
▸ Exit PowerPoint
▸ Open a saved presentation
▸ Edit a presentation
▸ Use PowerPoint online Help

▸ WHAT IS POWERPOINT?

PowerPoint is a complete **presentation graphics program** that allows you to produce professional-looking presentations. PowerPoint gives you the flexibility to make an informal presentation in a small conference room using overhead transparencies (Figure 1-1a), to make an electronic presentation using a projection device attached to a personal computer (Figure 1-1b), or to make a formal presentation to a large audience using 35mm slides (Figure 1-1c).

PowerPoint contains several features to assist in the creation of a presentation. The following list describes these PowerPoint features.

▸ **_Word processing_**   **Word processing** allows you to create automatic bulleted lists, combine words and images, check spelling, find and replace text, and use multiple fonts and type sizes.
▸ **_Outlining_**   **Outlining** allows you to quickly create your presentation by using an outline format. You can import outlines from Microsoft Word or other word processors.
▸ **_Graphing_**   **Graphing** allows you to create and insert charts into your presentations. Graph formats include two-dimensional (2-D) graphs: area, bar, column, combination, line, pie, xy (scatter), and three-dimensional (3-D) graphs: area, bar, column, line, and pie.

FIGURE 1-1a

Overhead transparencies

FIGURE 1-1b

Projection device connected to a personal computer

35mm slides

FIGURE 1-1c

▶ *Drawing*   **Drawing** allows you to create diagrams using shapes, such as arcs, arrows, cubes, rectangles, stars, and triangles. Drawing also allows you to modify shapes without redrawing.

▶ *Clip art*   **Clip art** allows you to insert artwork into your presentation without creating it yourself. There are over 1000 graphic images in the Microsoft ClipArt Gallery.

▶ *Presentation management*   **Presentation management** allows you to control the design and arrangement of your presentation.

▶ *Wizards*   A **wizard** is a tutorial approach to quickly and efficiently create a presentation. PowerPoint wizards make it easy to create quality presentations by prompting you for specific content and design criteria. The AutoContent Wizard asks you what are you going to talk about and what type of presentation are you going to give, such as recommending a strategy or selling a product. The Pick a Look Wizard asks you questions about the type of presentation media you are using for your presentation, such as color overheads or video screen. The Pick a Look Wizard asks you to select a format for your presentation and to select printing options. You may also select footer options, such as date, page number, and company name, or other text you might want to include on the bottom of every slide. With either wizard, just answer the questions that display in the windows. After completing the wizard steps, your presentation is well on its way to completion.

▶ PROJECT ONE — TIPS AND TECHNIQUES FOR FINDING THE RIGHT JOB

his book presents a series of projects using PowerPoint to produce slides similar to those you would develop in an academic or business environment. Project 1 uses PowerPoint to create the overhead presentation shown in Figures 1-2a through 1-2d. The objective is to produce a presentation on Tips and Techniques for Finding the Right Job that will be presented using an overhead projector. As an introduction to PowerPoint, this project steps you through the most common type of presentation, a **bulleted list**. A bulleted list is a list of paragraphs, each preceded by a bullet. A **bullet** is a symbol (usually a heavy dot) that precedes text when the text warrants special emphasis. The first of the four slides is called the title slide (Figure 1-2a). The **title slide** introduces the presentation to the audience.

Slide Preparation Steps

The following preparation steps give you an overview of how to create the slides in Figures 1-2a, 1-2b, 1-2c, and 1-2d. If you are creating

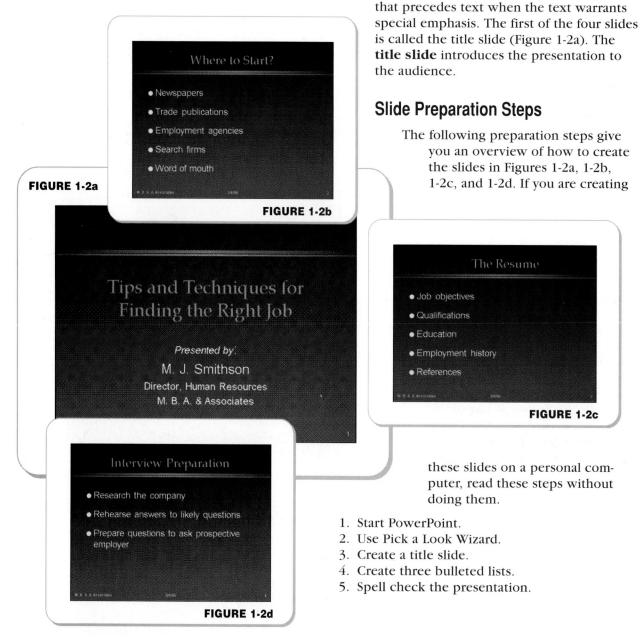

FIGURE 1-2a

FIGURE 1-2b

FIGURE 1-2c

FIGURE 1-2d

these slides on a personal computer, read these steps without doing them.

1. Start PowerPoint.
2. Use Pick a Look Wizard.
3. Create a title slide.
4. Create three bulleted lists.
5. Spell check the presentation.

6. Save the presentation.
7. Print the presentation.
8. Exit PowerPoint.
9. Open PowerPoint.
10. View Quick Preview.
11. Make a transparency.

▶ STARTING POWERPOINT

To start PowerPoint, the Windows Program Manager must display on the screen and the Microsoft Office group window must be open. Perform the following steps to start PowerPoint or ask your instructor how to start PowerPoint on your system.

TO START POWERPOINT ▼

STEP 1 ▶

Point to the Microsoft PowerPoint program-item icon (📇) in the Microsoft Office window (Figure 1-3).

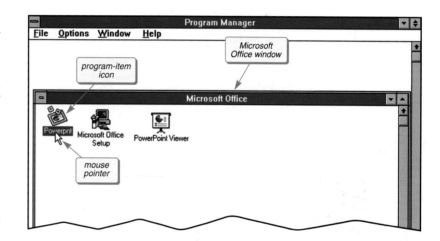

FIGURE 1-3

STEP 2 ▶

Double-click the left mouse button. When the Tip of the Day dialog box displays, point to the OK button (OK).

PowerPoint displays an empty slide and the Tip of the Day dialog box (Figure 1-4). The Tip of the Day changes each time you start PowerPoint.

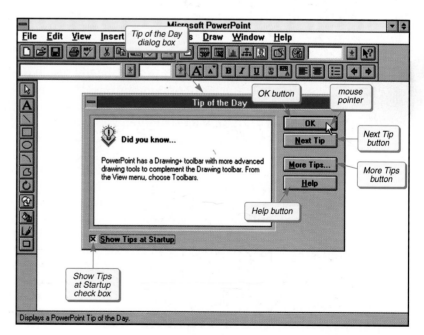

FIGURE 1-4

STEP 3 ▶

Choose the OK button.

The PowerPoint startup dialog box displays (Figure 1-5). The option button selected at startup depends on the option chosen the last time PowerPoint was started.

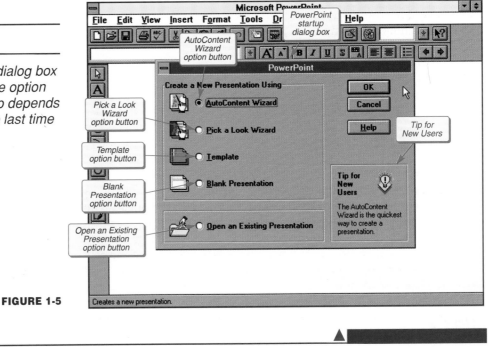

FIGURE 1-5

The Tip of the Day (Figure 1-4 on the previous page) displays each time you start PowerPoint. These tips provide helpful hints for designing and building presentations. The Next Tip button (**Next Tip**) in the Tip of the Day dialog box displays the next tip in the Tip of the Day library. The More Tips button (**More Tips...**) displays the Tip of the Day Help window where you may select the topic for which you want more information. The Help button (**Help**) displays the PowerPoint Help window. To discontinue the Tip of the Day dialog box at startup, click the Show Tips at Startup check box to remove the x. To reactivate the Tip of the Day at startup, choose the Tip of the Day command from the Help menu and then click the Show Tips at Startup check box to add an x.

▶ THE POWERPOINT STARTUP DIALOG BOX

Each time you start PowerPoint, the PowerPoint startup dialog box displays (Figure 1-5 above). The PowerPoint startup dialog box contains a list of option buttons. You may select only one option button from the list. The option button choices are AutoContent Wizard, Pick a Look Wizard, Template, Blank Presentation, and Open an Existing Presentation. The PowerPoint startup dialog box helps you create a new presentation or open an existing presentation.

When creating a new presentation, the AutoContent Wizard helps you decide content and order, whereas the Pick a Look Wizard helps you decide appearance and attitude. If you choose either the AutoContent Wizard or the Pick a Look Wizard option button, additional dialog boxes display. You determine the design of your slides through the selections made in these dialog boxes. The Template options allow you to choose a template. A **template** provides consistency in design and color throughout the entire presentation. The template determines the color scheme, font style and size, and layout of your presentation. The Blank Presentation option displays a blank PowerPoint slide after prompting you to choose a layout. The Open an Existing Presentation option displays the Open dialog box, where you choose the presentation you wish to open.

▶ PICK A LOOK WIZARD

The Pick a Look Wizard presents a series of dialog boxes that prompt you for design criteria to customize the Slide Master for your presentation. The **Slide Master** is a "control" slide that holds the title and text place-holders, as well as background items that display on all your slides in the presentation. As you move from step to step in the Pick a Look Wizard, you are asked for the type of output you are using for this presentation. Your choices are black-and-white overheads, color overheads, on-screen presentation, and 35mm slides. Project 1 uses the on-screen presentation format. On-screen presentation allows you to develop your presentation in color for an on-screen slide show, yet allows you to print your presentation as either color overheads or black-and-white overheads.

In another step, you are prompted to select a template. PowerPoint designed templates specifically for the type of presentation output. The templates for on-screen presentations and 35mm slides have the most color. Color overhead templates use some color, but black-and-white overhead templates use no color. Templates may be changed at anytime during the development of your presentation. Dialog boxes display in subsequent Pick a Look Wizard steps for printing options and footer options.

By choosing option buttons and selecting check boxes, you can quickly create the look and feel of your presentation. Perform the following steps to use the Pick a Look Wizard.

TO USE THE PICK A LOOK WIZARD ▼

STEP 1 ▶

Choose the Pick a Look Wizard option button in the PowerPoint startup dialog box by pointing to it and clicking the left mouse button. Then, point to the OK button (Figure 1-6).

The black dot in the Pick a Look Wizard option button denotes it is selected. The other option buttons in the PowerPoint startup dialog box are white. You may select only one option button.

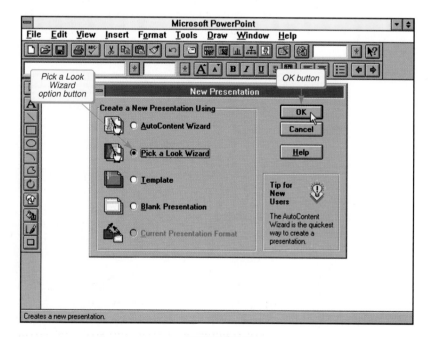

FIGURE 1-6

STEP 2 ▶

Choose the OK button. When the Pick a Look Wizard – Step 1 of 9 dialog box displays, point to the Next button ([Next>]).

The Pick a Look Wizard – Step 1 of 9 dialog box displays (Figure 1-7).

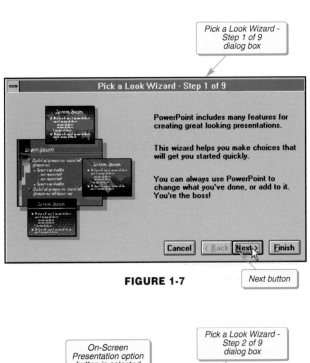

FIGURE 1-7

STEP 3 ▶

Choose the Next button. When the Pick a Look Wizard Step 2 of 9 dialog box displays, point to the Next button.

The Pick a Look Wizard – Step 2 of 9 dialog box displays (Figure 1-8). The On-Screen Presentation option button is selected.

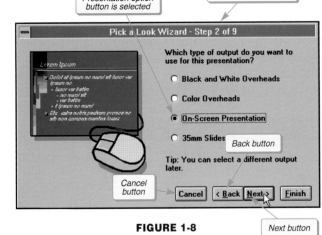

FIGURE 1-8

STEP 4 ▶

Choose the Next button.

The Pick a Look Wizard – Step 3 of 9 dialog box displays (Figure 1-9). The Multiple Bars option button is selected. To help you select the best template for your presentation, a preview of the Multiple Bars template displays in the dialog box. Microsoft artists designed the Multiple Bars template to display white text on a cyan (light blue-green) background.

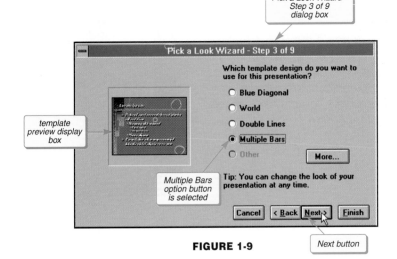

FIGURE 1-9

STEP 5 ▶

Select the Double Lines option button by clicking the left mouse button. Then, point to the Next button.

The Double Lines option button is selected. A preview of the Double Lines template displays in the dialog box (Figure 1-10). The Double Lines template was selected because it was designed to display light colored text on a dark background. Light text on a dark background provides a stronger contrast than light text on a light background. Recall that the Multiple Bars template displayed white text on a cyan background.

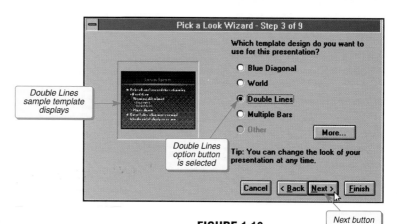

FIGURE 1-10

STEP 6 ▶

Choose the Next button. When the Pick a Look Wizard – Step 4 of 9 dialog box displays, point to the Speaker's Notes check box.

The Pick a Look Wizard – Step 4 of 9 dialog box displays (Figure 1-11). All four check boxes display with an x. The check boxes are used to select the different ways to print your presentation.

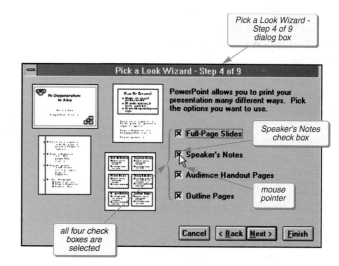

FIGURE 1-11

STEP 7 ▶

Click the Speaker's Notes check box to remove the x.

The Speaker's Notes check box is blank, which designates you will not be prompted to add Pick a Look Wizard slide options to the speaker's notes pages (Figure 1-12).

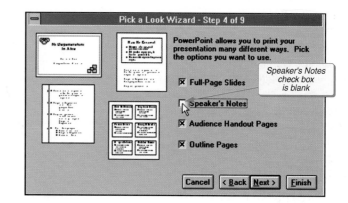

FIGURE 1-12

STEP 8 ▶

Remove the x from the Audience Handout Pages check box and the Outline Pages check box by clicking them one at a time. Then, point to the Next button.

The Audience Handout Pages check box is blank and the Outline Pages check box is blank, which designate you won't be prompted to add Pick a Look Wizard hand-out options or outline options (Figure 1-13).

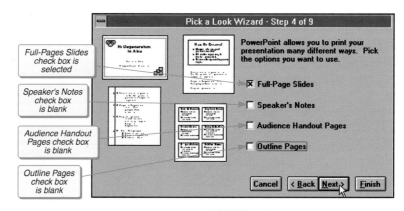

FIGURE 1-13

STEP 9 ▶

Choose the Next button.

The Pick a Look Wizard – Slide Options dialog box displays (Figure 1-14). The check boxes for Name, company, or other text, Date, and Page Number are not selected. The Pick a Look Wizard – Slide Options dialog box gives you the opportunity to add text, a date, or page numbers to the footer of the Slide Master. The name used during the PowerPoint installation, M.B.A. & Associates, displays in the text box (Figure 1-14). Your screen will display the name that was used during the installation of PowerPoint on your computer. The text box is blank if PowerPoint was installed without entering a company name.

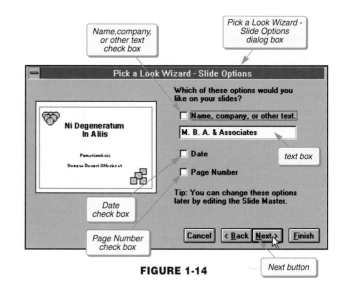

FIGURE 1-14

STEP 10 ▶

Choose the Name, company, or other text check box, the Date check box, and the Page Number check box and point to the Next button.

The Name, company, or other text check box, the Date check box, and the Page Number check box each contain an x (Figure 1-15).

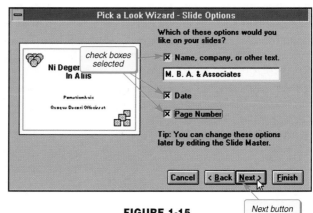

FIGURE 1-15

STEP 11 ▶

Choose the Next button. When the Pick a Look Wizard – Step 9 of 9 dialog box displays, point to the Finish button (Finish).

The Pick a Look Wizard – Step 9 of 9 dialog box displays (Figure 1-16).

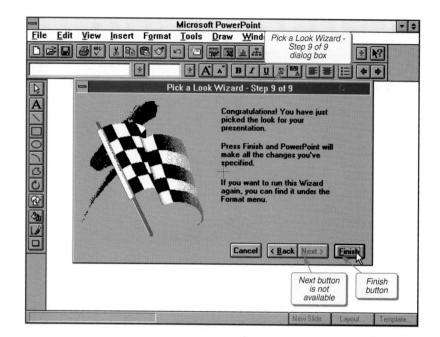

FIGURE 1-16

STEP 12 ▶

Choose the Finish button to exit Pick a Look Wizard and go to the first slide in your presentation.

The first slide of the presentation displays the Double Lines template and the slide options selected in the Pick a Look Wizard (Figure 1-17).

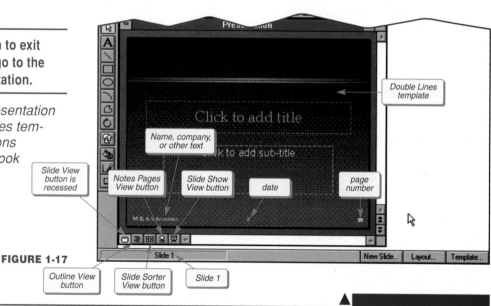

FIGURE 1-17

Recall earlier in the Pick a Look Wizard — Slide Options dialog box you selected options to display on every slide (Figure 1-15 on the previous page). Because you selected options for Name, company, or other text, Date, and Page Number, they display at the bottom of the slide.

In the Pick a Look Wizard — Step 3 of 9 dialog box (Figure 1-10 on page PP9), you selected a template from a list of four option buttons. To see all possible templates, choose the More button (More...). Choosing the More button displays the Presentation Template dialog box. Then, choose the desired template from the drop-down file list in the \powerpnt\template\sldshow directory by selecting the template of choice. When you highlight the template name by clicking it, a preview of the template displays in the lower right corner of the Presentation Template dialog box. Once you select a template, choose the **Apply button** (Apply) to apply it to your presentation.

▶ THE POWERPOINT WINDOW

T he basic unit of a PowerPoint presentation is a **slide**. **Objects** are the building blocks for a PowerPoint slide. A slide contains one or many objects, such as title, text, graphics, tables, charts, and drawings. In PowerPoint, you have the option of using the PowerPoint default settings or establishing your own settings. A **default setting** is a particular value for a variable that is assigned automatically by PowerPoint and that remains in effect unless canceled or overridden by the user. These settings control the placement of objects, the color scheme, the transition between slides, and other slide attributes. **Attributes** are the properties or characteristics of an object. For example, if you underline the title of the slide, the title is the object and the underline is the attribute.

PowerPoint Views

PowerPoint has five views. You may use any or all views while creating your presentation. You change views by clicking one of the view buttons found on the **View Button Bar** at the bottom of the PowerPoint screen (Figure 1-17 on the previous page). The PowerPoint window display is dependent on the view. Some views are graphical, while others are textual. The views are:

▶ **Slide view**   Slide view displays a single slide as it appears in your presentation. When creating a presentation in Slide view, you type the text and add graphic art, utilizing buttons on the toolbars.

▶ **Outline view**   Outline view displays a presentation in an outline format, showing all slide titles and text.

▶ **Slide Sorter view**   Slide Sorter view displays miniatures of the slides in your presentation. You can then copy, cut, paste, or change slide position to modify your presentation.

▶ **Notes Pages view**   Notes Pages view displays the current note page. Notes Pages view allows you to create speaker's notes to use when you give your presentation. Each notes page corresponds to a slide and includes a reduced slide image.

▶ **Slide Show view**   Slide Show view displays your slides as an electronic presentation on your computer, using the full screen.

In Project 1, you create a presentation in Slide view.

PowerPoint Window

The **PowerPoint window** in Slide view contains the title bar, the menu bar, the toolbars: Standard toolbar, Formatting toolbar, and Drawing toolbar; the status bar, the AutoLayout object area, the mouse pointer, the scroll bars, and the view buttons.

TITLE BAR   The **title bar** (Figure 1-18a) displays the name of the current PowerPoint file. Until you save your presentation, PowerPoint assigns the name Presentation.

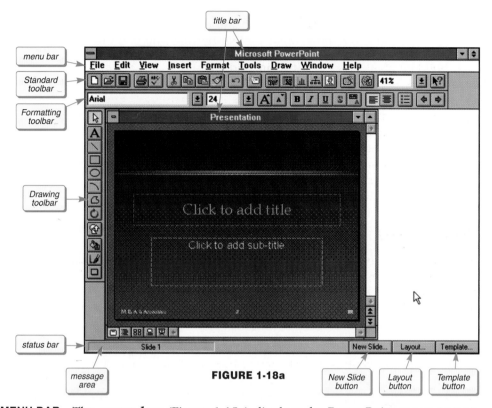

FIGURE 1-18a

MENU BAR The **menu bar** (Figure 1-18a) displays the PowerPoint menu names. Each menu name represents a list of commands that allows you to retrieve, store, print, and change objects in your presentation. To display a menu, such as the File menu, point to the name File on the menu bar and click the left mouse button.

STATUS BAR Located at the bottom of the PowerPoint window, the **status bar** consists of three buttons: New Slide button (New Slide...), Layout button (Layout...), and Template button (Template...), and an area to display messages (Figure 1-18a). Most of the time, the current slide number displays in the status bar. However, when you choose a command, the status bar provides a short message about that command.

NEW SLIDE BUTTON Choosing the **New Slide button** (Figure 1-18a) inserts a new slide into a presentation after the current slide.

LAYOUT BUTTON Choosing the **Layout button** (Figure 1-18a) displays the Slide Layout dialog box. Select a slide layout from the options in the dialog box.

TEMPLATE BUTTON Choosing the **Template button** (Figure 1-18a) displays the Presentation Template dialog box. You may select a template anytime during the creation of your presentation.

TOOLBARS PowerPoint **toolbars** consist of buttons that allow you to perform tasks more quickly than using the menu bar. For example, to save, you choose the Save button (⊟) on the Standard toolbar. Each button face has a graphical representation that helps you remember its function. Figure 1-18b, Figure 1-18c, and Figure 1-18d on the next page illustrate the buttons on each of the three toolbars that display each time you start PowerPoint and open a presentation in Slide view. They are the Standard toolbar, the Formatting toolbar, and the Drawing toolbar. Each button will be explained in detail when it is used in the projects. PowerPoint allows you to customize all toolbars and to add toolbar buttons you use most often. Likewise, you can remove those toolbar buttons you don't use. Choose the **Customize command** in the Tools menu to alter toolbars to meet your requirements.

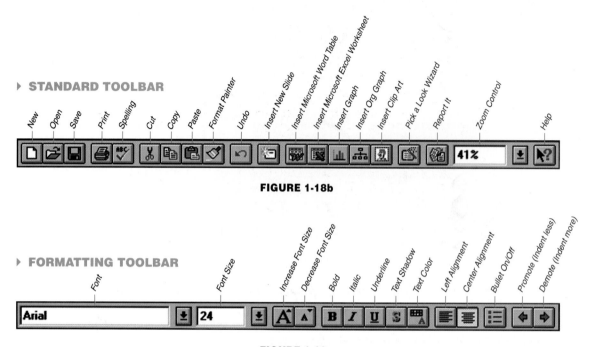

▸ **STANDARD TOOLBAR**

FIGURE 1-18b

▸ **FORMATTING TOOLBAR**

FIGURE 1-18c

▸ **DRAWING TOOLBAR**

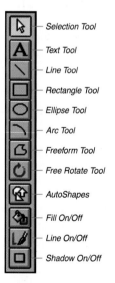

FIGURE 1-18d

STANDARD TOOLBAR The **Standard toolbar** (Figure 1-18b) contains tools to execute the most common commands found in the menu bar, such as open, print, save, copy, cut, paste, and many more. The Standard toolbar also has a button for the **Zoom Control**. You control how large or small a document appears on the PowerPoint window with the Zoom Control.

FORMATTING TOOLBAR The **Formatting toolbar** (Figure 1-18c) contains tools for changing text attributes. The Formatting toolbar allows you to quickly change font, font size, and alignment. It also contains tools to bold, italicize, underline, shadow, color, and bullet text. The five **attribute buttons**, Bold, Italic, Underline, Text Shadow, and Bullet, are on/off switches, or **toggles**. You choose the button once to turn the attribute on; then, you choose it again to turn the attribute off.

DRAWING TOOLBAR The **Drawing toolbar** (Figure 1-18d) is a collection of tools for drawing lines, circles, and boxes. The Drawing toolbar also contains tools to alter the objects once you have drawn them.

SCROLL BARS The **vertical scroll bar** (Figure 1-19), located on the right side of the PowerPoint window, allows you to move forward or backward through your presentation.

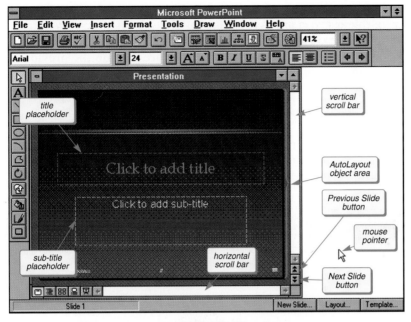

FIGURE 1-19

Choosing the **Next Slide button** (⯆) (Figure 1-19), located on the vertical scroll bar, advances you to the next slide in the presentation. Clicking the **Previous Slide button** (⯅) (Figure 1-19), located on the vertical scroll bar, backs you up to the slide preceding the current slide.

The **horizontal scroll bar** (Figure 1-19), located on the bottom of the PowerPoint window, allows you to display a portion of the window when you magnify the slide, such that you cannot display it in the PowerPoint window.

It should be noted that in Slide view, both the vertical and horizontal scroll bar actions are dependent upon Zoom Control. If you are in Slide view and Zoom Control is set, such that the entire slide is not visible in the Slide window, clicking the up arrow on the vertical scroll bar will display the next portion of your slide, not the previous slide. Therefore, to go to the previous slide, click the Previous Slide button. To go to the next slide, click the Next Slide button.

AUTOLAYOUT OBJECT AREA   The **AutoLayout object area** (Figure 1-19) is a collection of placeholders for title, text, clip art, graphs, or charts. These placeholders display when you create a new slide. You can change the AutoLayout anytime during the creation of your presentation by selecting the Layout button located on the status bar and then choosing another layout.

PLACEHOLDERS   Surrounded by a dotted line, **placeholders** are the empty objects on a new slide. Depending on the AutoLayout selected, placeholders display for title, text, graphs, tables, organization charts, and clip art. Once you place contents in a placeholder, the placeholder becomes an object. For example, text typed in the placeholder becomes a text object.

TITLE PLACEHOLDER   Surrounded by a dotted line, the **title placeholder** is the empty title object on a new slide (Figure 1-19). Text typed in the title placeholder becomes the title object.

SUB-TITLE PLACEHOLDER   Surrounded by a dotted line, the **sub-title placeholder** is the empty sub-title object that displays below the title placeholder on a title slide (Figure 1-19).

MOUSE POINTER   The **mouse pointer** can become one of several different shapes, depending on the task you are performing in PowerPoint and the pointer's location on the screen. The different shapes will be discussed when they display in subsequent projects. The mouse pointer in Figure 1-19 on the previous page has the shape of a left-pointing block arrow (⬉).

▶ MAXIMIZING THE POWERPOINT WINDOW

T he PowerPoint window is not maximized when you start PowerPoint. Maximizing the PowerPoint window makes it easier to see the contents of the window. Perform the following steps to maximize the PowerPoint window.

TO MAXIMIZE THE POWERPOINT WINDOW ▼

STEP 1 ▶

Point to the Maximize button (▲) in the upper right corner of the PowerPoint window (Figure 1-20).

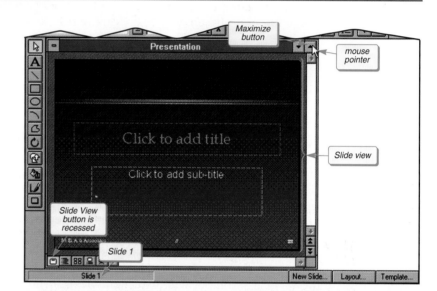

FIGURE 1-20

STEP 2 ▶

Click the left mouse button.

The PowerPoint window fills the desktop (Figure 1-21). The **Restore button** *(⬍) replaces the Maximize button at the right side of the menu bar. Choosing the Restore button returns the PowerPoint window to its original size.*

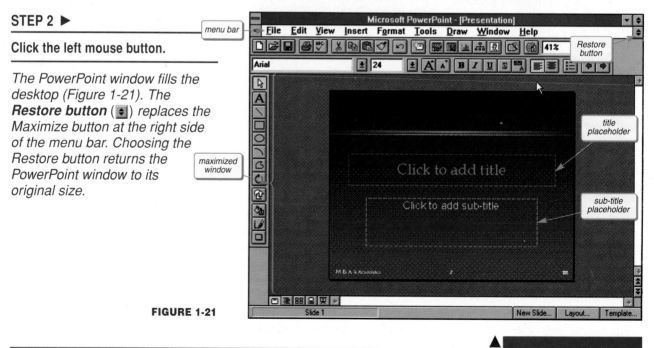

FIGURE 1-21

▶ CREATING THE TITLE SLIDE

T he purpose of the title slide is to introduce the presentation to the audience. PowerPoint assumes the first slide in a new presentation is the **title slide**. With the exception of a blank slide, PowerPoint assumes every new slide has a title. To make creating your presentation easier, any text you type after a new slide displays becomes the title object. In other words, you do not have to first select the title placeholder before typing text. The AutoLayout for the title slide has a title placeholder near the middle of the window and a sub-title placeholder directly below the title placeholder (Figure 1-21 on the previous page).

Entering the Presentation Title

The presentation title for Project 1 is Tips and Techniques for Finding the Right Job. You type the presentation title in the title placeholder on the title slide. Perform the following steps to explain how to create the title slide for Project 1.

TO ENTER THE PRESENTATION TITLE ▼

STEP 1 ▶

Type Tips and Techniques for Finding the Right Job

Tips and Techniques for Finding the Right Job displays in the title text box (Figure 1-22). When you type the first character, a slashed outline, called the **selection box,** *displays around the title place-holder. A small vertical line (|), called the* **insertion point,** *indicates where the next character displays. The highlighted (colored) box is the* **text box,** *and it indicates you are in* **text mode.**

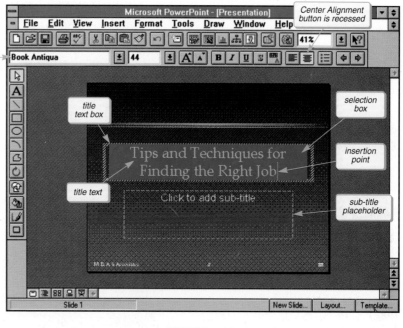

FIGURE 1-22

Notice that you do not press the ENTER key after the word Job. If you press the ENTER key after typing the title, PowerPoint creates a new paragraph. A **paragraph** is a segment of text with the same format that begins when you press the ENTER key and ends when you press the ENTER key again. Pressing the ENTER key creates a new line in a new paragraph. Therefore, do not press the ENTER key unless you want to create a two-paragraph title. Additionally, PowerPoint **line wraps** text that exceeds the width of the placeholder. Tips and Techniques for Finding the Right Job exceeds the width of the title placeholder. PowerPoint wrapped the text into two lines (Figure 1-22).

The title is centered in the window because the Double Lines template alignment attribute is centered. The Center Alignment button () is recessed on the Formatting toolbar.

> **PRESENTATION TIP**
>
> When designing your slide title, keep in mind that uppercase letters are less distinct, making them more difficult to read than lowercase letters. For emphasis, it is acceptable to use all uppercase letters in short titles. Capitalize only the first letter in all words in long titles, except for short articles such as or, the, or an, unless the article is the first word in the title (i.e., The Road to Success).

Correcting a Mistake While Typing

If you type the wrong letter and notice the error before typing the next word, use the BACKSPACE key to erase all the characters back to and including the one that is wrong. If you mistakenly pressed the ENTER key after entering the title and the cursor is on the new line, simply press the BACKSPACE key to return the insertion point to the right of the letter b in the word Job.

You can reverse the last change made by clicking the **Undo button** (🔄) on the Standard toolbar or by choosing the **Undo command** from the Edit menu.

Entering the Presentation Sub-title

The next step is to enter Presented by: M. J. Smithson, Director, Human Resources, M. B. A. & Associates into the sub-title placeholder.

TO ENTER THE PRESENTATION SUB-TITLE ▼

STEP 1 ▶

Position the mouse pointer on the label, Click to add sub-title, located inside the sub-title placeholder. Then, click the left mouse button.

The insertion point is in the sub-title text box (Figure 1-23). The mouse pointer displays as an I-beam (I). The I-beam mouse pointer indicates the mouse is within a text placeholder. The selection box indicates the sub-title placeholder is selected.

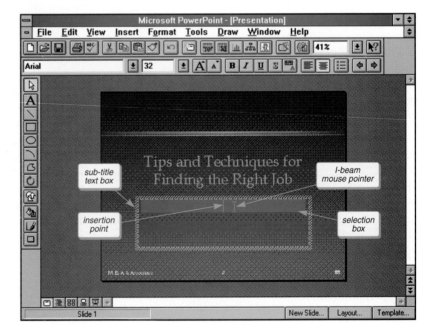

FIGURE 1-23

STEP 2 ▶

Type Presented by: **and press the ENTER key. Type** M. J. Smithson **and press the ENTER key. Type** Director, Human Resources **and press the ENTER key. Type** M. B. A. & Associates

The text displays in the sub-title object, as shown in Figure 1-24. The insertion point displays after the letter s in Associates.

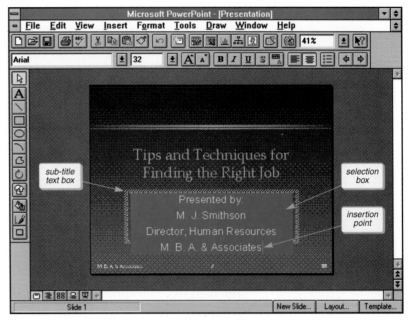

FIGURE 1-24

The previous section created a title slide using an AutoLayout for title slide. PowerPoint displayed the title slide layout because you created a new presentation. You entered text in the title placeholder without selecting the title placeholder because PowerPoint assumes every slide has a title. However, you could click the title placeholder to select it and then type your title. In general, to type text in any text placeholder, click on the text placeholder and type. You also added a sub-title that identifies the presenter. While this is not required, it is often useful information to the audience.

▶ TEXT ATTRIBUTES

T his presentation is using the Double Lines template that was selected through the Pick a Look Wizard. Each template has its own text attributes. A **text attribute** is a characteristic of the text, such as font (typeface), font size, font style, or font color. You can adjust text attributes anytime before, during, or after you type the text. Recall that a template determines the color scheme, font style and size, and layout of your presentation. Most of the time, you will use that template's text attributes and color scheme. However, there are times when you want to change the way your presentation looks and still keep a particular template. PowerPoint gives you that flexibility. You can use the template you want and change the text color, the text size, the text typeface, and the text style. Table 1-1 on the next page explains the different text attributes available in PowerPoint.

▶ **TABLE 1-1**

ATTRIBUTE	DESCRIPTION
Font	Defines the appearance and shape of letters, numbers, and special characters.
Text color	Defines the color of the text. Displaying text in color requires a color monitor. Printing text in color requires a color printer or plotter.
Font size	Specifies the size of the characters on the screen. Character size is gauged by a measurement system called points. A single **point** is about 1/72 of an inch in height. Thus, a character with a point size of eighteen is about 18/72 (or 1/4) inch in height.
Text style	Defines text characteristics. Text styles include plain, italic, bold, shadowed, and underlined. Text may have one or more styles at a time.
Subscript	Defines the placement of a character in relationship to another. A subscript character displays or prints slightly below and next to another character.
Superscript	Defines the placement of a character in relationship to another. A superscript character displays or prints slightly above and immediately to one side of another character.

The next two sections explain how to change the text style and font size attributes.

▶ CHANGING THE TEXT STYLE

Text styles include plain, italic, bold, shadowed, and underlined. PowerPoint allows you to use one or more text styles in your presentation. Perform the following steps to add emphasis to the title slide by changing plain text to italic text.

TO CHANGE THE TEXT STYLE ▼

STEP 1 ▶

Point to Presented by: and triple-click the left mouse button.

The paragraph Presented by: is highlighted (Figure 1-25).

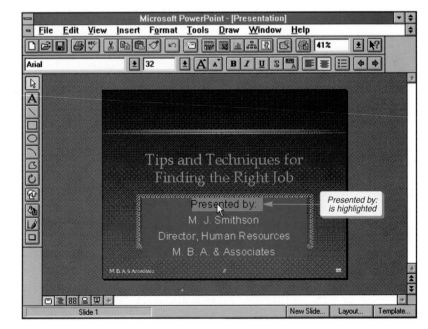

FIGURE 1-25

STEP 2 ▶

Position the mouse pointer on the Italic button (**I**) on the Formatting toolbar.

*When you point to a button on a toolbar, PowerPoint displays a yellow **ToolTips** box with the corresponding name of that tool. When pointing to the Italic button, the ToolTips box displays the word Italic (Figure 1-26).*

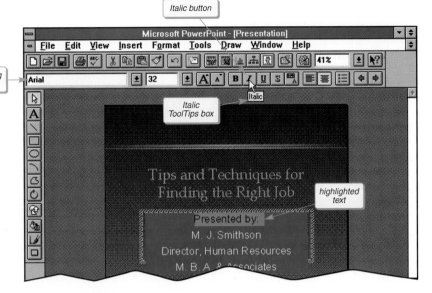

FIGURE 1-26

STEP 3 ▶

Choose the Italic button on the Formatting toolbar by clicking the left mouse button.

The text is italicized and the Italic button is recessed (Figure 1-27).

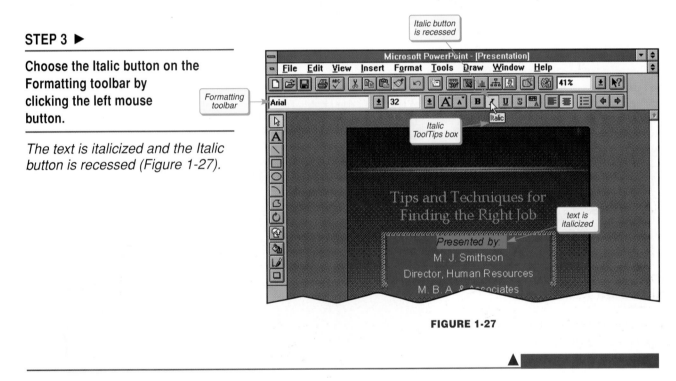

FIGURE 1-27

To remove italics from text, select the italicized text and then click the Italic button. The Italic button is recessed and the text does not have the italic text style.

▶ CHANGING THE FONT SIZE

The Double Lines template default font size is 32 points for body text and 44 points for title text. A point is 1/72 of one inch in height. Thus, a character with a point size of 44 is about 44/72, or 11/18 of one inch in height. Slide 1 requires you to decrease the font size for the following three paragraphs: (1) Presented by: (2) Director, Human Resources (3) M. B. A. & Associates. Perform the following steps on the next page to change font size.

TO CHANGE FONT SIZE ▼

STEP 1 ▶

With Presented by: highlighted, point to the Decrease Font Size button (▲) on the Formatting toolbar (Figure 1-28).

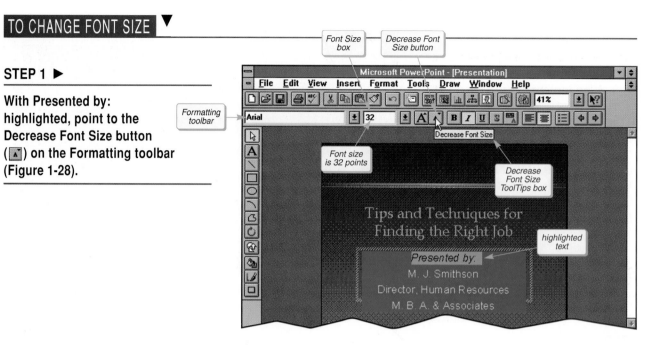

FIGURE 1-28

STEP 2 ▶

Click the Decrease Font Size button twice so 24 displays in the Font Size box on the Formatting toolbar.

The paragraph, Presented by:, reduces to 24 points (Figure 1-29). The Font Size box displays the new font size as 24 points.

FIGURE 1-29

STEP 3 ▶

Position the mouse pointer immediately in front of the letter D in Director.

The mouse pointer now displays as an I-beam because the pointer is positioned before the letter D in Director (Figure 1-30).

FIGURE 1-30

STEP 4 ▶

Drag the I-beam mouse pointer from the letter D in Director to the third letter s in Associates to highlight all characters in these two paragraphs (Figure 1-31).

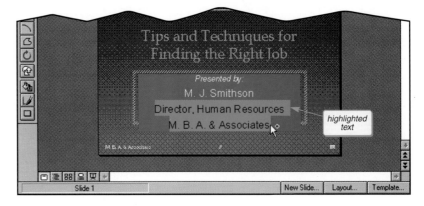

FIGURE 1-31

STEP 5 ▶

Click the Decrease Font Size button twice so 24 displays in the Font Size box.

The paragraphs, Director, Human Resources and M. B. A. & Associates, reduce to 24 points. The Font Size box displays the font size as 24 points (Figure 1-32).

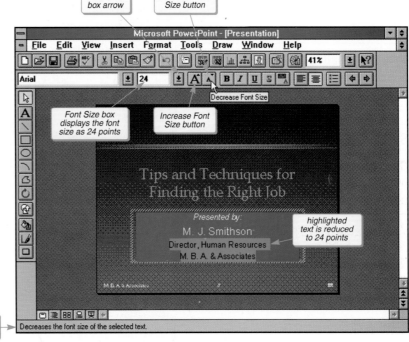

FIGURE 1-32

Instead of using the Decrease Font Size button, you can click the Font Size arrow on the Formatting toolbar to display a list of available font sizes and then click the desired point size. You may also click the Font Size box and type a font size between 1 and 999.

If you need to increase the font size, click the **Increase Font Size button** (A), located next to the Decrease Font Size button on the Formatting toolbar.

PRESENTATION TIP

When designing a presentation, use the following rules as guidelines:

▸ Short lines of text are easier to read than long lines.
▸ Use bold and italic sparingly for emphasis.
▸ Use no more than two types of fonts and styles.

▶ SAVING THE PRESENTATION

While you are building your presentation, the computer stores it in main memory. It is important to save your presentation frequently because if the computer is turned off or if you lose electrical power, the presentation is lost. Another reason to save is if you run out of lab time before completing your project, you may finish the project later without having to start over. Therefore, it is mandatory to save on disk any presentation you will use later. Before you continue with Project 1, save the work completed thus far. Perform the following steps to save a presentation to drive A, using the Save button on the Standard toolbar. (It is assumed that you have a formatted disk in drive A.)

TO SAVE THE PRESENTATION ▼

STEP 1 ▶

Insert a formatted diskette in drive A and point to the Save button on the Standard toolbar (Figure 1-33).

FIGURE 1-33

STEP 2 ▶

Choose the Save button.

PowerPoint displays the Save As dialog box (Figure 1-34). The default filename *.ppt displays in the File Name box. The default directory displays under Directories:. The current drive displays in the Drives box.

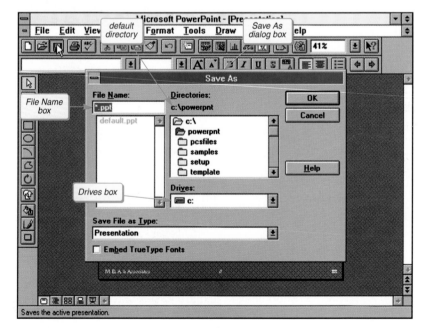

FIGURE 1-34

STEP 3 ▶

Type `proj1` in the File Name box. Do not press the ENTER key after typing the filename.

The name proj1 replaces *.ppt in the File Name box (Figure 1-35).

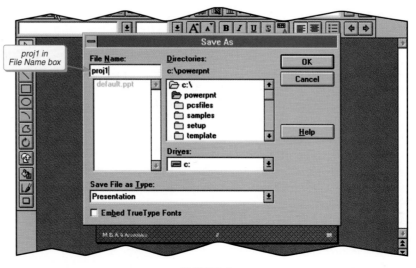

FIGURE 1-35

STEP 4 ▶

Choose the Drives box arrow and point to a:

A drop-down list of available drives displays (Figure 1-36).

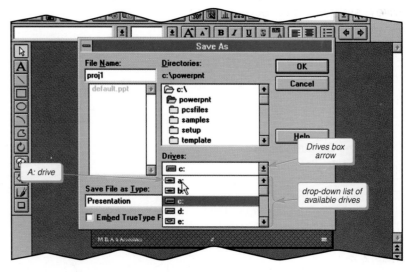

FIGURE 1-36

STEP 5 ▶

Select drive A by clicking the left mouse button.

Drive A becomes the current drive (Figure 1-37).

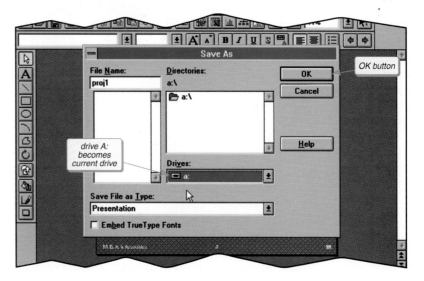

FIGURE 1-37

STEP 6 ▶

Choose the OK button in the Save As dialog box.

The Summary Info dialog box displays (Figure 1-38). The name displaying in the Author text box is the name of the person that was entered at the time PowerPoint was installed. Your screen will display a name other than M. J. Smithson. If a name was not entered during installation, the Author text box is blank. You may edit the information displayed in the Summary Info dialog box by pressing the TAB key to advance to the next text box. Pressing the ENTER key when text is highlighted clears the text box. To accept the information as it displays in the Summary Info dialog box, choose the OK button.

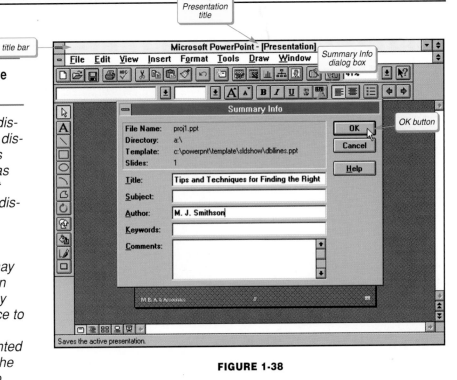

FIGURE 1-38

STEP 7 ▶

Choose the OK button in the Summary Info dialog box.

The presentation is saved to drive A under the filename PROJ1.PPT. The presentation title displays in the title bar as PROJ1.PPT (Figure 1-39).

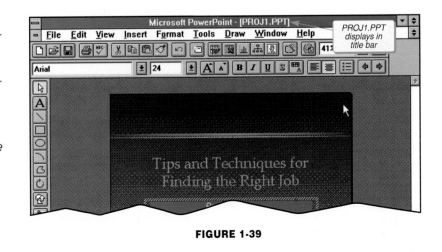

FIGURE 1-39

PowerPoint automatically appends to the filename PROJ1 the extension **.ppt**, which stands for **P**ower**P**oint. Although the presentation PROJ1 is saved on disk, it also remains in main memory and displays on the screen.

PowerPoint filenames follow the Windows naming conventions. When saving your presentation file, use no more than eight characters, no spaces, and no reserved characters, such as a period (.), quotation mark ("), slash (/), backslash (\), brackets ([ ]), colon (:), semicolon (;), vertical bar (|), equal sign (=), or comma (,).

The Summary Info dialog box provides you with an area to store information about your presentation. Table 1-2 lists the types of information contained in the Summary Info dialog box.

▸ **TABLE 1-2**

SUMMARY INFO TYPES	CONTENTS
Title box	The presentation title.
Subject box	The presentation subject. You can state a brief description of the presentation content.
Author box	The author's name.
Keywords box	Keywords used in the presentation. Used to associate keywords with a presentation when using the **Find File command** in the File menu.
Comments box	Comments about the presentation.

It is a good practice to save periodically while you are working on a project. By doing so, you protect yourself from losing all the work you have done since the last time you saved.

▸ ADDING A NEW SLIDE

T he title slide for your presentation is created. The next step is to add the first bulleted list slide in Project 1. The New Slide button adds a slide into the presentation, which is placed after the current slide. Usually when you create your presentation, you are adding slides with text, graphics, or charts. When you add a new slide, PowerPoint displays a dialog box for you to choose one of the AutoLayouts. These AutoLayouts have placeholders for various objects, such as title, text, graphics, graphs, and charts. Some placeholders provide access to other PowerPoint visuals by allowing you to double-click the placeholder. Figure 1-40 displays the twenty-one different AutoLayouts available in PowerPoint. More information about using AutoLayout placeholders to add graphics follows in subsequent projects. Perform the following steps on the next page to add a Bulleted List slide.

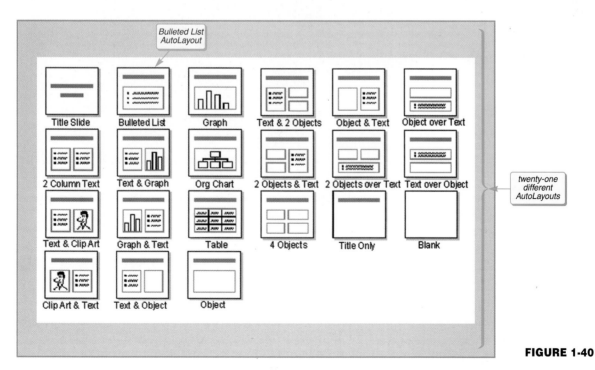

FIGURE 1-40

TO ADD A NEW SLIDE ▼

STEP 1 ▶

Position the mouse pointer on the
New Slide button on the status bar
(Figure 1-41).

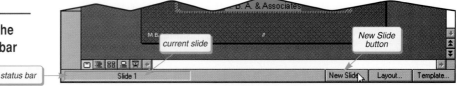

FIGURE 1-41

STEP 2 ▶

Choose the New Slide button.

*The New Slide dialog box displays
(Figure 1-42). The Bulleted List
AutoLayout is selected, and the
AutoLayout title, Bulleted List, dis-
plays at the bottom right corner of
the New Slide dialog box.*

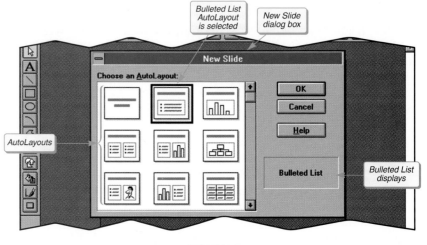

FIGURE 1-42

STEP 3 ▶

Choose the OK button in the New
Slide dialog box.

*Slide 2 displays, keeping the
attributes of the Double Lines template (Figure 1-43).*

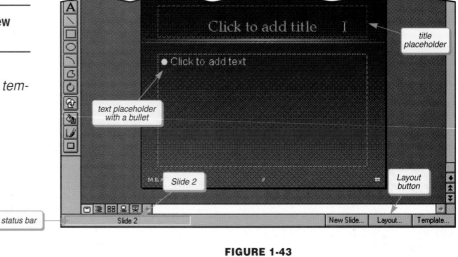

FIGURE 1-43

Because you selected the Bulleted List AutoLayout, PowerPoint displays Slide
2 with a title placeholder and a text placeholder with a bullet. You can change the
layout for a slide at any time during the creation of your presentation by clicking
the Layout button on the status bar and then selecting the AutoLayout of your
choice.

▶ CREATING THE REMAINING SLIDES IN THE PRESENTATION

 owerPoint assumes every new slide has a title. Therefore, any text you type after a new slide displays becomes the title object. The title for Slide 2 is Where to Start?. Perform the following step to enter this title.

TO TYPE THE TITLE FOR SLIDE 2 ▼

STEP 1 ▶

Type Where to Start?

The title, Where to Start?, displays in the title object (Figure 1-44).

FIGURE 1-44

Selecting the Text Placeholder

Before you can type text into the text placeholder, you must first select it. Perform the following step to select the text placeholder on Slide 2.

TO SELECT THE TEXT PLACEHOLDER ▼

STEP 1 ▶

Click on the bullet paragraph, located inside the text placeholder, labeled Click to add text.

The insertion point displays immediately after the bullet on Slide 2 (Figure 1-45).

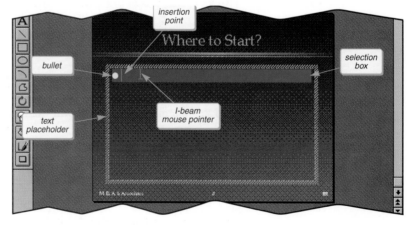

FIGURE 1-45

Typing a Bulleted List

Recall that a bulleted list is a list of paragraphs, each preceded by a bullet. Also recall that a paragraph is a segment of text ended by pressing the ENTER key. The next step is to enter the bulleted list. This bulleted list consists of the five entries shown in Figure 1-46. Perform the following steps to type a bulleted list.

TO TYPE A BULLETED LIST

Step 1: Type Newspaper and press the ENTER key.
Step 2: Type Trade publications and press the ENTER key.
Step 3: Type Employment agencies and press the ENTER key.
Step 4: Type Search firms and press the ENTER key.
Step 5: Type Word of mouth

Each time you press the ENTER key, PowerPoint places a bullet at the beginning of each new paragraph (Figure 1-46).

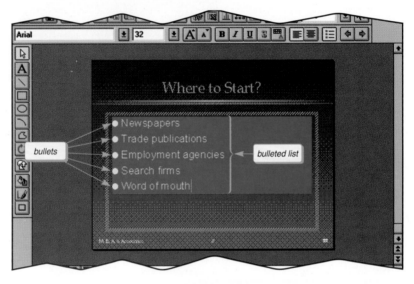

FIGURE 1-46

The ENTER key was not pressed after typing the last paragraph in Step 5. If the ENTER key is pressed, a new bullet displays after the last entry on this slide. To remove the extra bullet, press the BACKSPACE key.

TO CREATE SLIDE 3

Step 1: Add a new slide by choosing the New Slide button on the status bar.
Step 2: Select Bulleted List from the New Slide dialog box and choose the OK button.
Step 3: Type The Resume as the title for Slide 3.
Step 4: Select the text object by clicking anywhere inside the text placeholder.
Step 5: Type Job objectives and press the ENTER key.
Step 6: Type Qualifications and press the ENTER key.
Step 7: Type Education and press the ENTER key.
Step 8: Type Employment history and press the ENTER key.
Step 9: Type References

Slide 3 displays as shown in Figure 1-47.

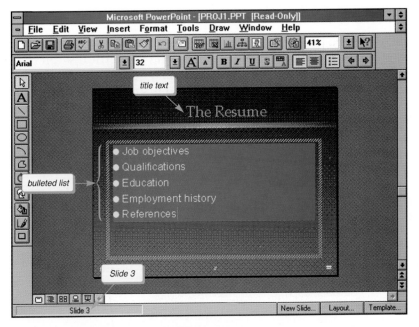

FIGURE 1-47

TO CREATE SLIDE 4

Step 1: Add a new slide by choosing the New Slide button on the status bar.

Step 2: Select Bulleted List from the New Slide dialog box and choose the OK button.

Step 3: Type Interview Preparation as the title for Slide 4.

Step 4: Select the text object by clicking anywhere inside the text placeholder.

Step 5: Type Research the company and press the ENTER key.

Step 6: Type Rehearse answers to likely questions and press the ENTER key.

Step 7: Type Prepare questions to ask prospective employer

The slide title and text object display, as shown in Figure 1-48.

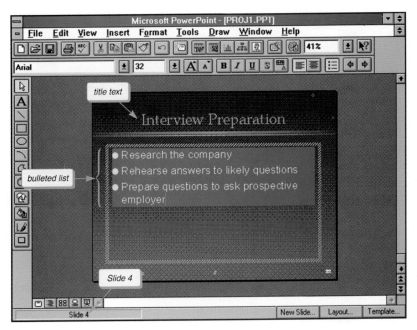

FIGURE 1-48

▶ MOVING TO ANOTHER SLIDE

When creating or editing your presentation, you will often want to display a slide other than the current one. Dragging the vertical scroll bar box up or down moves you through your presentation. The small box on the vertical scroll bar is called the **elevator** (▨) and is shown in Figure 1-49. When you drag the elevator, the **slide indicator box** (▐ Slide 4 ▌) shows you the number of the slide you are about to display. Once you see the number of the slide you wish to display in the slide indicator box, release the left mouse button. Perform the steps below to move through your presentation using the vertical scroll bar.

TO MOVE TO ANOTHER SLIDE ▼

STEP 1 ▶

Position the mouse pointer on the elevator. Press and hold the left mouse button.

Slide 4 (▐ Slide 4 ▌) displays in the slide indicator box (Figure 1-49).

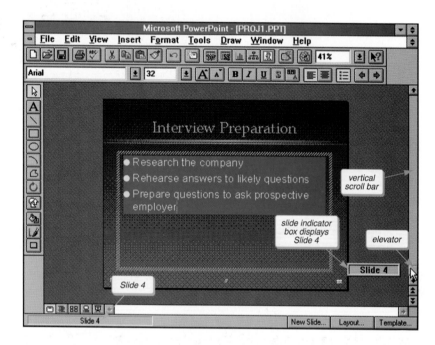

FIGURE 1-49

STEP 2 ▶

Drag the elevator up the vertical scroll bar until Slide 1 (▐ Slide 1 ▌) displays in the slide indicator box (Figure 1-50).

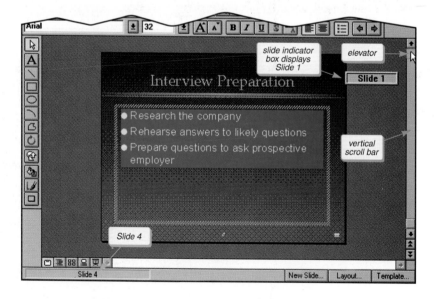

FIGURE 1-50

STEP 3 ▶

Release the left mouse button.

Slide 1 titled, Tips and Techniques for Finding the Right Job, displays in the PowerPoint window (Figure 1-51).

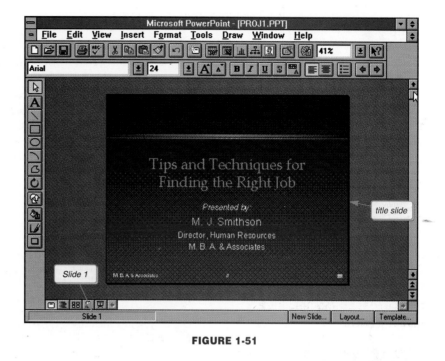

FIGURE 1-51

▶ VIEWING THE PRESENTATION USING SLIDE SHOW

he **Slide Show button** (🖳), located at the bottom left of the PowerPoint window, lets you display your presentation electronically using a computer. The computer acts like a slide projector, displaying each slide on a full screen. The full screen slide hides the toolbars, menus, and other PowerPoint window elements.

TO VIEW THE TITLE SLIDE USING SLIDE SHOW ▼

STEP 1 ▶

Position the mouse pointer on the Slide Show View button, located at the bottom left of the PowerPoint window (Figure 1-52).

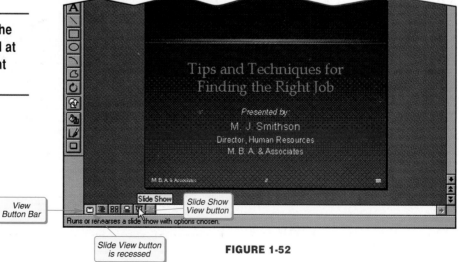

FIGURE 1-52

STEP 2 ▶

Click the left mouse button.

The title slide fills the screen (Figure 1-53). The date displaying on your screen will be different from the date displayed in Figure 1-53. The date stored as the system date displays at the bottom of the slide. The PowerPoint window is hidden.

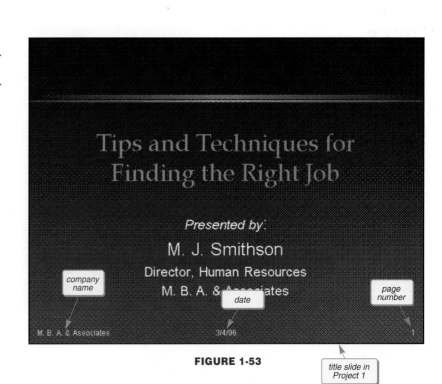

FIGURE 1-53

STEP 3 ▶

Click the left mouse button until the last slide of the presentation, Slide 4, displays (Figure 1-54).

Each slide in your presentation displays on the screen, one slide at a time. Each time you click the left mouse button, the next slide displays.

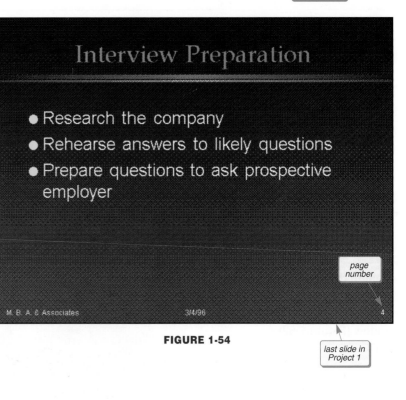

FIGURE 1-54

STEP 4 ▶

Click the left mouse button.

You have attempted to advance past the last slide in your presentation. PowerPoint exits Slide Show view after the last slide in your presentation and displays Slide 1, which was the current slide when you clicked the Slide Show View button (Figure 1-55).

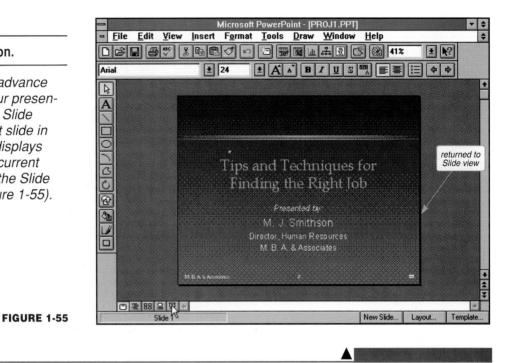

FIGURE 1-55

To use the keyboard in Slide Show view to advance through the entire presentation one slide at a time, press the PAGE DOWN key. To go back one slide at a time in Slide Show view, click the right mouse button or press the PAGE UP key. The ESC key allows you to exit from Slide Show view and return to the view you were in when you clicked the Slide Show View button.

Running slide show is an excellent way to practice a presentation prior to giving it. You can view your presentation using slide show from Slide view, Outline view, Slide Sorter view, or Notes Pages view.

▶ USING THE NEXT SLIDE BUTTON TO ADVANCE ONE SLIDE

W hen you want to advance one or two slides, it is quicker to click the Next Slide button instead of dragging the elevator on the vertical scroll bar. Perform the steps below to use the Next Slide button.

TO USE THE NEXT SLIDE BUTTON TO ADVANCE ONE SLIDE ▼

STEP 1 ▶

Position the mouse pointer on the Next Slide button (Figure 1-56).

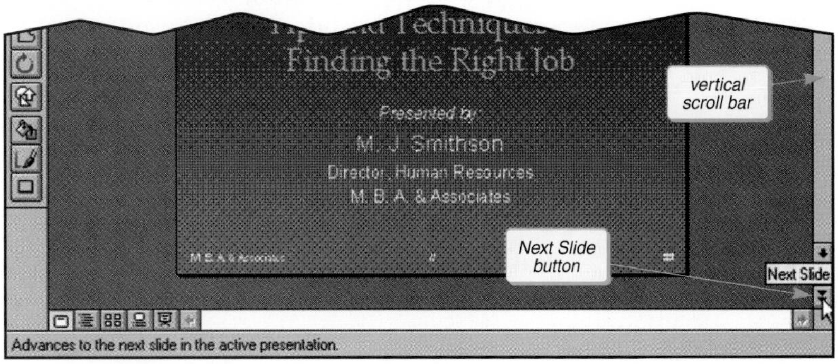

FIGURE 1-56

STEP 2 ▶

Choose the Next Slide button.

Slide 2 displays in the PowerPoint window (Figure 1-57).

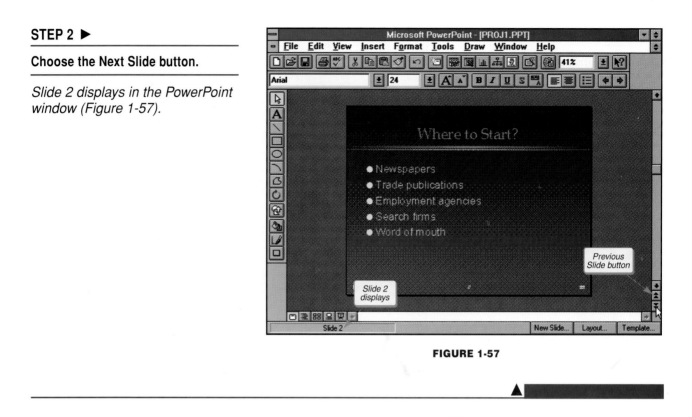

FIGURE 1-57

To return to the previous slide, choose the Previous Slide button. The Previous Slide button is located above the Next Slide button. Both the Next Slide button and the Previous Slide button advance/return the number of slides based upon the number of clicks. For example, if you double-click, you move two slides; if you triple-click, you move three slides. You may not advance beyond the last slide in your presentation or backup beyond the first slide in your presentation.

▶ CHANGING SLIDE MASTER COMPONENTS

The Slide Master contains the basic format used by all slides you create. The Slide Master has formatted placeholders for the slide title, text, and background items. These formatted placeholders are called the Master title and the Master text. The **Master title** controls the attributes and alignment of the slide title object. The **Master text** controls the main slide text attributes and alignment of the text objects.

Each template has a specially designed Slide Master. So, if you select a template but want to change a component of that template, you can override that component by changing the Slide Master. Any change to the Slide Master results in changing every slide in the presentation. For example, if you change the title text style to italic, every slide following the master changes to italicized title text.

Each view has its own master. You can access the master by pressing the SHIFT key while clicking the appropriate view button. For example, pressing the SHIFT key and clicking the Slide View button displays the Slide Master. To exit a master, click the view button to which you wish to return.

The key components most frequently changed on the Slide Master are listed in Table 1-3.

▶ **TABLE 1-3**

COMPONENT	DESCRIPTION
Font	Defines the appearance and shape of letters, numbers, and special characters.
Font size	Specifies the size of the characters on the screen. Character size is gauged by a measurement system called points. A single point is about 1/72 of an inch in height. Thus, a character with a point size of 18 is about 18/72 of an inch in height.
Text style	Text may have one or more styles at a time. Text styles include plain, italic, bold, shadowed, and underlined.
Text position	Position of text in a paragraph is left-aligned, right-aligned, centered, or justified. Justified text is proportionally spaced across the object.
Color scheme	A coordinated set of eight colors designed to complement each other. Color schemes consist of background color, line and text color, shadow color, title text color, object fill color, and three different accent colors.
Background items	Any object other than the title object or text object. Typical items include borders, graphics such as a company logo, page number, date, and time.
Page number	Inserts the special symbol used to print the slide number.
Date	Inserts the special symbol used to print the date the presentation was printed.
Time	Inserts the special symbol used to print the time the presentation was printed.

Changing Line Spacing on the Slide Master

To make the slide in the presentation easier to read, the spacing on the Slide Master is set to one line after the paragraph. When you choose the **Line Spacing command**, the Line Spacing dialog box displays. The Line Spacing dialog box allows you to adjust line spacing on the Slide Master within the paragraph, before the paragraph, and after the paragraph. Perform the following steps to change line spacing from zero lines after the paragraph to one-half of a line after the paragraph.

TO CHANGE LINE SPACING ON THE SLIDE MASTER ▼

STEP 1 ▶

Point to the Slide View button (◻) and press and hold the SHIFT key.

When you press and hold the SHIFT key, the Slide Master ToolTips box displays Slide Master (Figure 1-58).

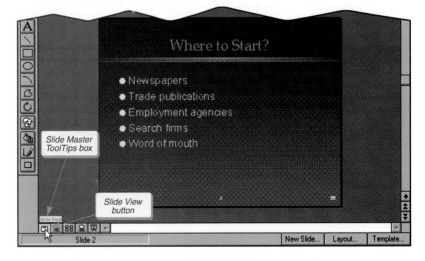

FIGURE 1-58

STEP 2 ▶

While holding down the SHIFT key, click the left mouse button, then release the SHIFT key.

The Slide Master displays (Figure 1-59).

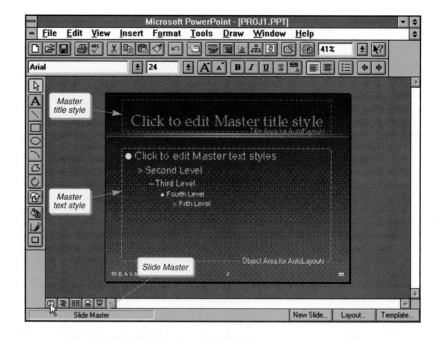

FIGURE 1-59

STEP 3 ▶

Click anywhere on the bullet paragraph, Click to edit Master text styles.

The insertion point displays at the point where you clicked (Figure 1-60). The text object area is selected.

FIGURE 1-60

STEP 4 ▶

Select the Format menu and point to the Line Spacing command (Figure 1-61).

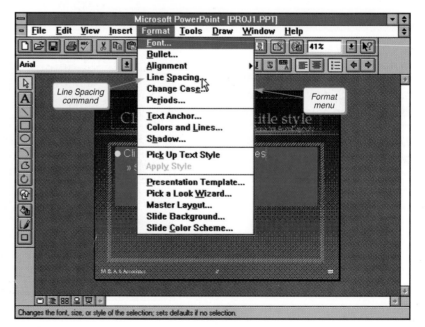

FIGURE 1-61

STEP 5 ▶

Choose the Line Spacing command
from the Format menu by clicking
the left mouse button.

*PowerPoint displays the Line
Spacing dialog box (Figure 1-62).*

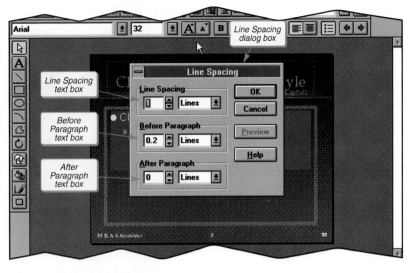

FIGURE 1-62

STEP 6 ▶

Position the mouse pointer on the
up arrow box next to the After
Paragraph text box.

*The After Paragraph text box dis-
plays the current setting, 0, for the
number of lines after a paragraph
(Figure 1-63).*

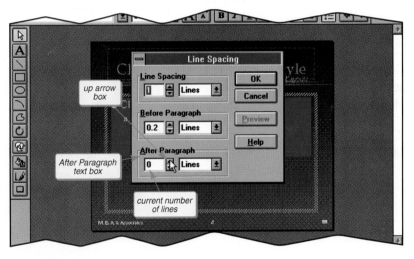

FIGURE 1-63

STEP 7 ▶

Click the up arrow box next to the
After Paragraph text box so 0.5
displays.

*The After Paragraph text box dis-
plays 0.5 (Figure 1-64).*

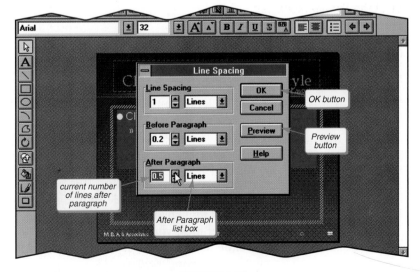

FIGURE 1-64

STEP 8 ▶

Choose the OK button in the Line Spacing dialog box.

The Slide Master text placeholder displays the new after paragraph line spacing (Figure 1-65). Depending on the video drivers installed, the spacing on your screen may appear slightly different from this figure.

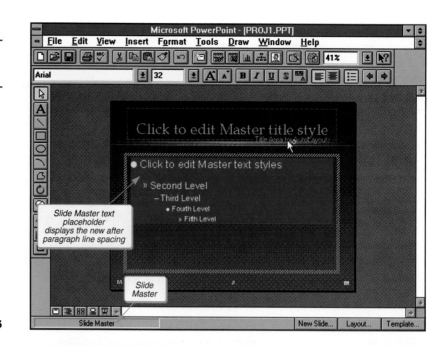

FIGURE 1-65

STEP 9 ▶

Choose the Slide View button, located at the bottom left of the PowerPoint window.

Slide 2 displays with the after paragraph line spacing set at 0.5 lines (Figure 1-66).

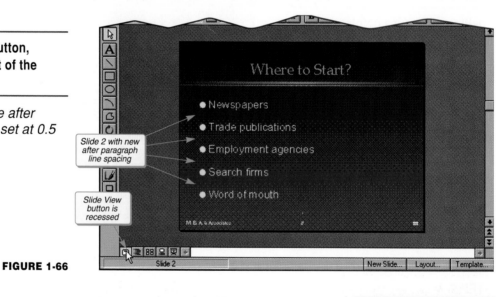

FIGURE 1-66

The after paragraph line spacing is controlled by setting the number of units after a paragraph. Units are either lines or points. Lines are the default unit. Points may be selected by clicking the arrow next to the After Paragraph line spacing drop-down list box (Figure 1-64 on page PP39). Recall from page PP20 that a single **point** is about 1/72 of an inch in height.

The placeholder at the top of the Slide Master (Figure 1-65) is for editing the Master title style. The large placeholder under the Master title placeholder is for editing the Master text styles. It is here you make changes to the various bullet levels. Changes could be made to line spacing, bullet font, text and line color, alignment, and text shadow. It is also the object area for AutoLayouts.

Sometimes, you need to change the location of text to improve the readability of a slide. Other times, you need to add blank space to a slide that appears to be cluttered or congested.

PRESENTATION TIP

Resist the temptation to regard blank space on a slide as wasted space. Blank space added for the purpose of directing the attention of the audience to specific text or graphics is called **white space**. White space is a powerful design tool. Used effectively, white space improves audience attention.

During a presentation, the audience is using several demanding, cognitive skills to interpret your information, such as:

▸ Retrieving relevant data from their long-term memory
▸ Watching the presenter for non-verbal cues (body language)
▸ Listening to and interpreting what the presenter says
▸ Comparing what is said verbally to what is said through the presenter's body language and then trying to identify any inconsistencies
▸ Formulating questions about unclear or confusing information
▸ Deciding what is important on each slide, based on the message of the text and the arrangement of the text
▸ Recognizing words and comprehending their meanings
▸ Analyzing the phrases on the slide
▸ Organizing the ideas presented in the text
▸ Incorporating the ideas with their prior knowledge and experience

▸ OVERRIDING THE SLIDE MASTER

Recall that a change to the Slide Master affects all slides in the presentation. When you changed the after paragraph line spacing in the previous section, you changed the way the sub-title displays on the title slide. In this section, you will return to the title slide and decrease the after paragraph line spacing for only the title slide. This change will override the format for the Slide Master and only change the title slide. The other slides in your presentation will retain the one line after paragraph setting, as determined in the previous section.

TO OVERRIDE THE SLIDE MASTER ▼

STEP 1 ▶

Click the Previous Slide button once.

Slide 1 displays (Figure 1-67). The actual amount of space displaying on the screen depends upon the video driver. Your screen may vary from the screen in this figure.

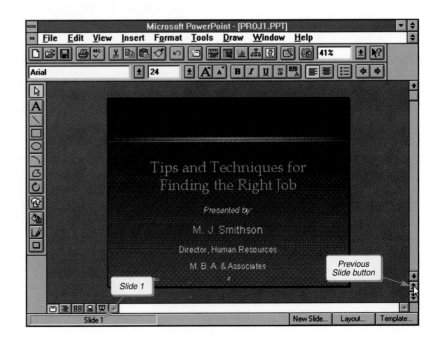

FIGURE 1-67

STEP 2 ▶

Select the sub-title text by dragging the mouse pointer from the letter P in Presented through the third letter s in Associates (Figure 1-68).

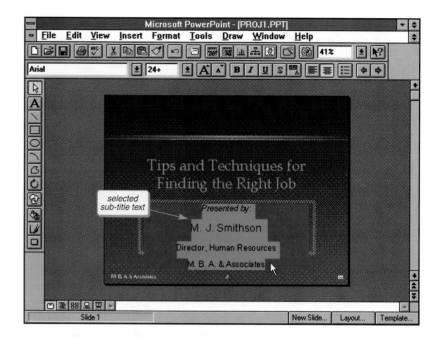

FIGURE 1-68

STEP 3 ▶

From the Format menu, choose the Line Spacing command, and click the down arrow next to the After Paragraph text box once so the After Paragraph text box displays 0 (Figure 1-69).

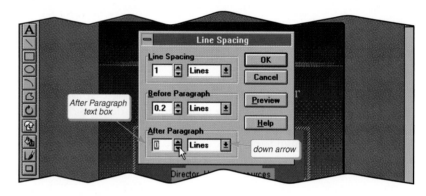

FIGURE 1-69

STEP 4 ▶

Choose the OK button in the Line Spacing dialog box.

The sub-title after paragraph line spacing returns to zero (Figure 1-70).

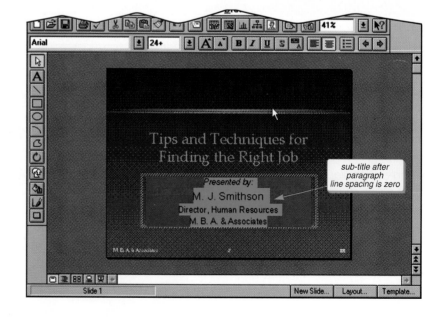

FIGURE 1-70

Changing the after paragraph line spacing to zero overrides the after paragraph line spacing format of the Slide Master. Only the title slide changed. The other three slides in your presentation still have one line after each paragraph, as formatted by the Slide Master.

▶ CHECKING SPELLING

PowerPoint checks your presentation for spelling errors using a standard dictionary contained in the Microsoft Office group. This dictionary is shared with the other Microsoft Office applications, such as Word and Excel. A **custom dictionary** is available if you want to add special words, such as proper names, cities, and acronyms. When checking a presentation for spelling errors, PowerPoint opens the standard dictionary and automatically opens the custom dictionary file, if one exists. If a word is not found in either dictionary, PowerPoint displays a dialog box. When a word appears in the dialog box, you have several options. Your options are explained in Table 1-4.

▶ **TABLE 1-4**

OPTION	DESCRIPTION
Manually correct the word	Retype the word with the proper spelling and choose Change. PowerPoint continues checking the rest of the presentation.
Ignore the misspelling	Choose Ignore when the word is spelled correctly but not found in the dictionaries. PowerPoint continues checking the rest of the presentation.
Ignore all occurrences of the misspelling	Choose Ignore All when the word is spelled correctly but not found in the dictionaries. PowerPoint continues checking the rest of the presentation.
Change to another spelling	Choose Change after selecting the proper spelling of the word from the list displayed in the Suggestions box. PowerPoint continues checking the rest of the presentation.
Change all occurrences of the misspelling to another spelling	Choose Change All after selecting the proper spelling of the word from the list displayed in the Suggestions box. PowerPoint continues checking the rest of the presentation.
Add a word to the custom dictionary	Choose Add. PowerPoint opens the custom dictionary, adds the word, and continues checking the rest of the presentation.
Suggest alternative spellings	Choose Suggest. PowerPoint lists suggested spellings. Select the correct word or type the proper spelling and then choose Change. PowerPoint continues checking the rest of the presentation.

PowerPoint begins to check spelling from the insertion point and continues to the end of the presentation. This allows you to begin the spell checking anywhere in the presentation without having to go to the first slide. Perform the following steps on the next page to use the PowerPoint spelling checker. In the following example, the name Smithson is not in the standard or custom dictionary, which causes the spelling checker to treat the name as a misspelled word. Depending on the accuracy of your typing, your presentation may have additional misspelled words.

TO CHECK THE SPELLING OF A PRESENTATION ▼

STEP 1 ▶

Position the mouse pointer on the Spelling button (📝) on the Standard toolbar (Figure 1-71).

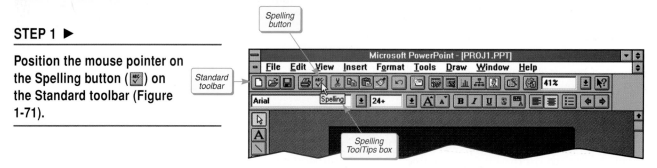

FIGURE 1-71

STEP 2 ▶

Choose the Spelling button.

The Spelling dialog box displays Smithson in the Not in Dictionary box (Figure 1-72). The name Smiths displays in both the Change To box and the Suggestions box.

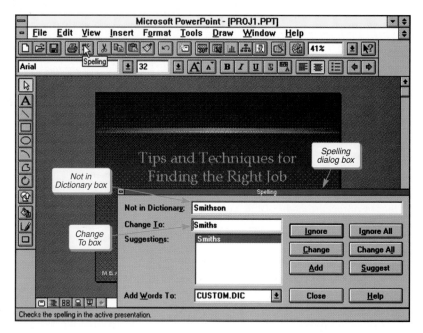

FIGURE 1-72

STEP 3 ▶

Position the mouse pointer on the Ignore All button (**Ignore All**) in the Spelling dialog box. (Figure 1-73).

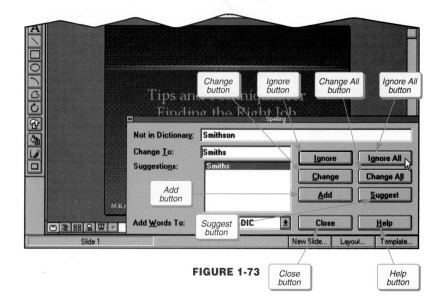

FIGURE 1-73

STEP 4 ▶

Choose the Ignore All button in the Spelling dialog box.

PowerPoint ignores all occurrences of the word Smithson and continues searching for additional misspelled words after Smithson until it returns to the slide where you began the spelling check. PowerPoint may stop on additional words depending on your typing accuracy. When PowerPoint has checked all slides for misspellings, it displays the Microsoft PowerPoint information box (Figure 1-74).

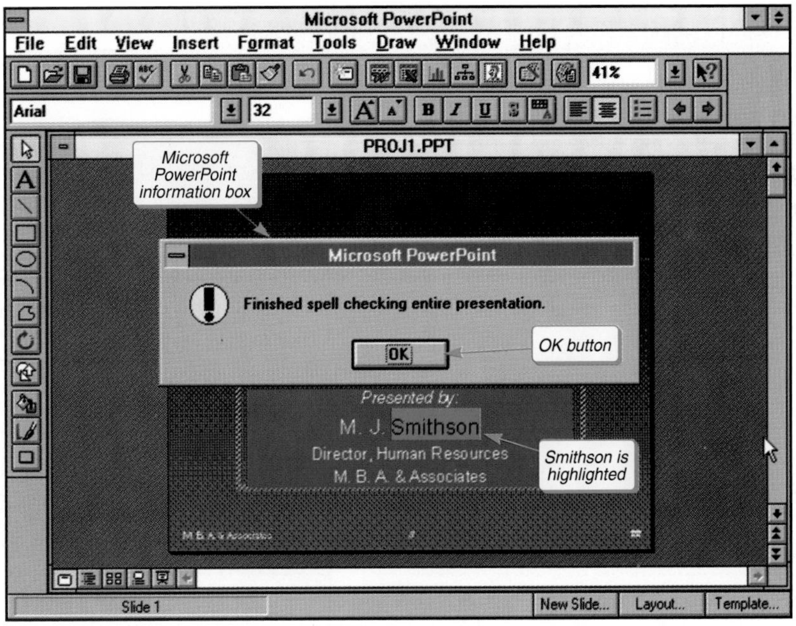

STEP 5

Choose the OK button in the Microsoft PowerPoint information box.

Slide 1 displays.

FIGURE 1-74

The PowerPoint dictionary contains commonly used English words. It does not contain proper names, abbreviations, technical terms, poetic contractions, foreign words, or antiquated terms. PowerPoint treats words not found in the dictionaries as misspellings. You may choose to ignore these misspellings or add them to the custom dictionary.

When PowerPoint encounters a word not found in either the standard dictionary or the custom dictionary, it highlights the word and places it in the Not in Dictionary box, located at the top of the Spelling dialog box. Suggestions display as long as the Always Suggest option is chosen in the Options dialog box. To display the Options dialog box, choose the **Options command** from the Tools menu.

If the spelling change suggested by the PowerPoint spelling checker is not your choice, you can select any of the words in the list of suggested words by choosing the desired word. The word you choose appears in the Change To box in the Spelling dialog box. If your choice is not in the list of suggested words, you may type your desired word directly into the Change To box. When you choose the Change button, the word in the Change To box replaces the misspelled word.

▶ VIEWING THE PRESENTATION IN SLIDE SORTER VIEW

T he presentation for Project 1 is complete. The next step is to review the presentation in Slide Sorter view. This allows you to look at several slides in one window. This is useful for proofreading your presentation. Perform the following steps on the next page to view the presentation in Slide Sorter view.

TO VIEW THE PRESENTATION IN SLIDE SORTER VIEW ▼

STEP 1 ▶

Point to the Slide Sorter View button ( ), as shown in Figure 1-75.

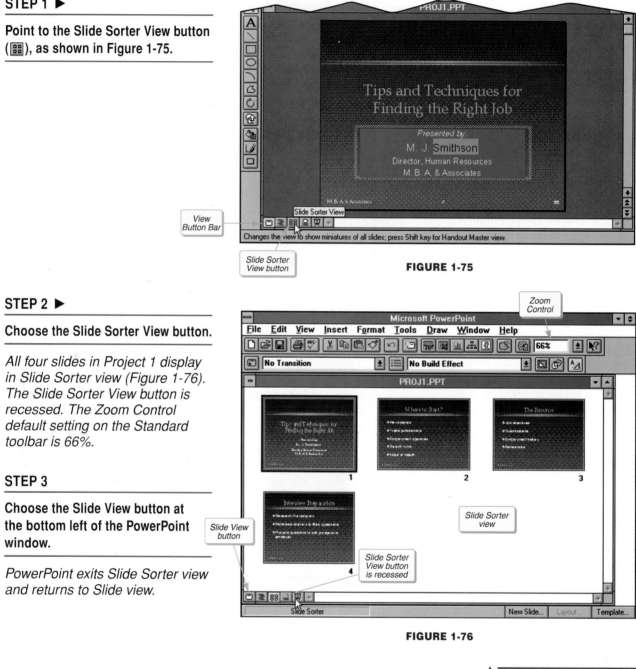

FIGURE 1-75

STEP 2 ▶

Choose the Slide Sorter View button.

All four slides in Project 1 display in Slide Sorter view (Figure 1-76). The Slide Sorter View button is recessed. The Zoom Control default setting on the Standard toolbar is 66%.

STEP 3

Choose the Slide View button at the bottom left of the PowerPoint window.

PowerPoint exits Slide Sorter view and returns to Slide view.

FIGURE 1-76

You can increase the size of the slide in Slide Sorter view by increasing the value in the Zoom Control box. When you increase the Zoom Control, you reduce the number of slides that display on one screen, but you increase the readability of each slide. Use the vertical scroll bar to view slides not visible in the PowerPoint window. Slide Sorter view has other features that will be introduced in later projects.

▶ SAVING AN EXISTING PRESENTATION WITH THE SAME FILENAME

S aving frequently can never be overemphasized. Prior to printing your presentation, you should save your work in the event you experience difficulties with the printer. You may occasionally encounter system problems that can only be resolved by restarting the computer. In this instance, you will need to start PowerPoint and open your presentation from the most recent copy of your presentation. As a precaution, always save your presentation before you print it. Perform the following steps to save the existing presentation.

TO SAVE AN EXISTING PRESENTATION WITH THE SAME FILENAME ▼

STEP 1 ▶

Insert your data disk into drive A. Position the mouse pointer on the Save button on the Standard toolbar (Figure 1-77).

STEP 2

Choose the Save button.

PowerPoint saves Project 1 to the disk in drive A, using the filename PROJ1.PPT as defined by the Save As dialog box earlier in this project.

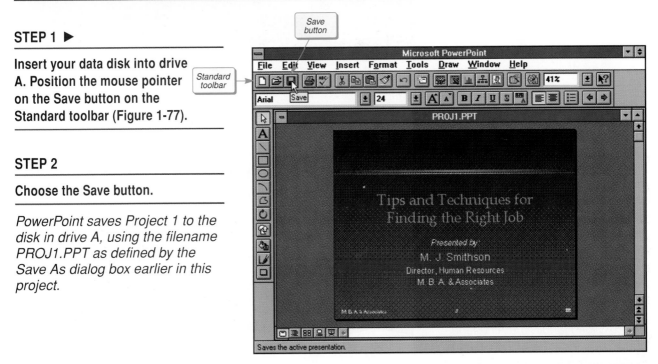

FIGURE 1-77

▶ PRINTING THE PRESENTATION

O nce you create a presentation and save it on disk, you need to print it. A printed version of the presentation is called a **hard copy**, or **printout**. The first printing of the presentation is called a **rough draft**. The rough draft allows you to proofread the presentation to check for errors and readability. After correcting errors, you will need to print the final copy of your presentation. If you made any changes to your presentation since your last save, be sure to save your presentation before you print it.

   Perform the following steps on the next page to print the rough draft of the presentation.

TO PRINT THE PRESENTATION ▼

STEP 1 ►

Ready the printer according to the printer instructions. Select the File menu and point to the Print command (Figure 1-78).

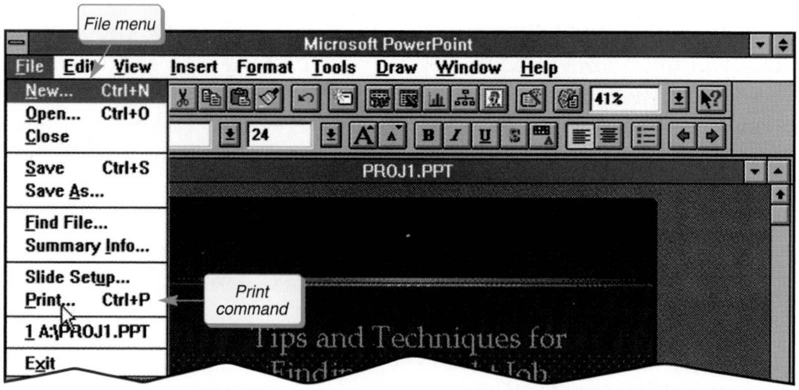

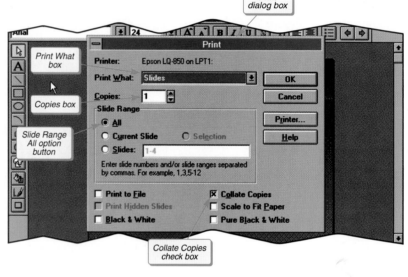

FIGURE 1-78

STEP 2 ►

Choose the Print command from the File menu by clicking the left mouse button. When PowerPoint displays the Print dialog box, point to the Scale to Fit Paper check box.

PowerPoint displays the Print dialog box (Figure 1-79). The PowerPoint default settings for the Print dialog box are Print What: displays Slides; Copies: displays 1 for printing one copy of the presentation; Slide Range: the All option button is selected and the Collate Copies check box is selected.

FIGURE 1-79

STEP 3 ►

Choose the Scale to Fit Paper and Pure Black & White check boxes by clicking them. Then, position the mouse pointer on the OK button.

The Scale to Fit Paper and Pure Black & White check boxes are selected (Figure 1-80). The Scale to Fit Paper option automatically resizes slides to fit the paper loaded in the printer. The Pure Black & White option turns all colors and fills to white and all text and lines to black. Pure Black & White is used for rough drafts.

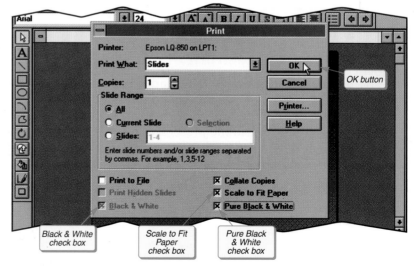

FIGURE 1-80

STEP 4 ▶

Choose the OK button.

The mouse pointer momentarily changes to an hourglass shape (⧗), and PowerPoint displays the Print Status dialog box (Figure 1-81). The presentation begins printing on the printer.

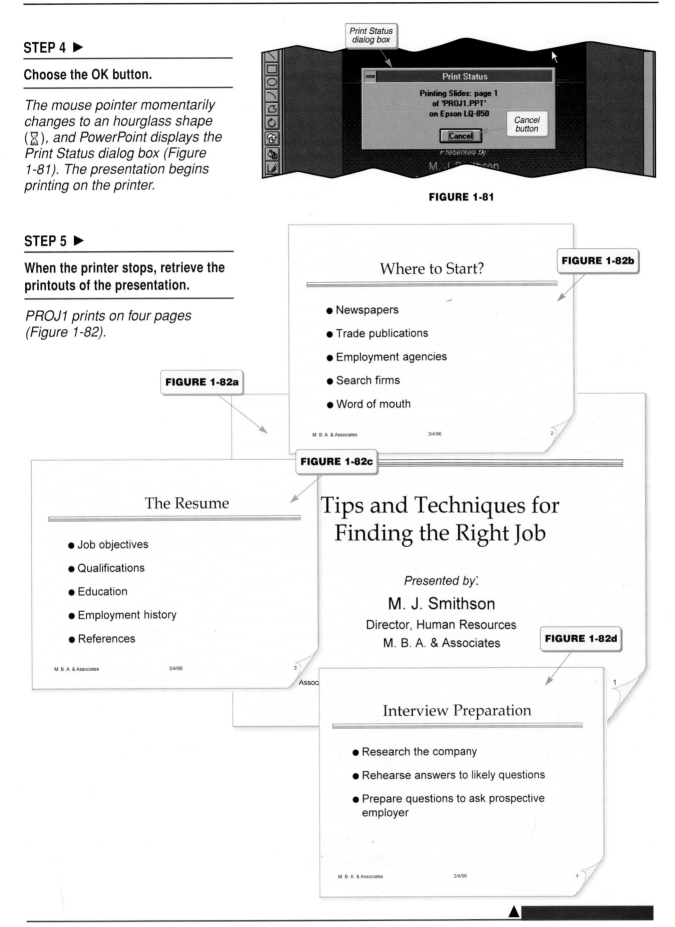

FIGURE 1-81

STEP 5 ▶

When the printer stops, retrieve the printouts of the presentation.

PROJ1 prints on four pages (Figure 1-82).

FIGURE 1-82a

FIGURE 1-82b

FIGURE 1-82c

FIGURE 1-82d

Pressing the Cancel button in the Print dialog box (Figure 1-80 on page PP48) ends the print request. Pressing the Cancel button in the Print Status dialog box (Figure 1-81 on the previous page) stops the printing process.

Selecting the Slide Range: All option button in the Print dialog box prints all the slides in the presentation (Figure 1-79 on page PP48). Selecting the Slide Range: Current Slide option button prints only the current slide. Selecting the Slide Range: Slides option button prints the range of slides you designate by entering the beginning and ending slide number in the text box. Choose the Current Slide option button or the Slides option button when you want to print a portion of your presentation.

Additionally, you may print your presentation by clicking the Print button on the Standard toolbar. PowerPoint immediately begins printing the presentation, using the settings last selected in the Print dialog box. The Print dialog box does not display. Use the Print button after selecting print options in the Print dialog box (Figure 1-80 on page PP48).

PRESENTATION TIP

One test every slide must pass is the **Floor Test**. You perform the Floor Test by placing the slide on the floor and trying to read it while you are standing. If the slide is readable, it passes the test. The slide fails the test if text is too small to read. Text too small to read during the Floor Test will be too small to read when displayed on the overhead projector. If the slide fails the Floor Test, you need to modify the slide to make text larger.

▶ EXITING POWERPOINT

The creation of the presentation is now complete. When you exit PowerPoint, PowerPoint prompts to save any changes made to the presentation since the last save, closes all PowerPoint windows, and then quits PowerPoint. Quitting PowerPoint returns control to the Program Manager. Perform the following steps to exit PowerPoint.

TO EXIT POWERPOINT ▼

STEP 1 ▶

Select the File menu and point to the Exit command (Figure 1-83).

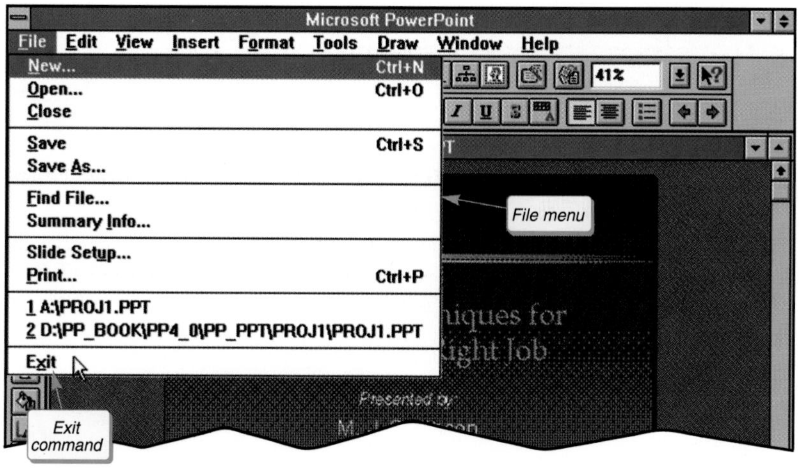

FIGURE 1-83

STEP 2 ▶

Choose the Exit command.

If you made changes to the pre-sentation, the Microsoft PowerPoint dialog box displays, asking Save changes to "PROJ1.PPT"? (Figure 1-84). Choose the Yes button (Yes) to save the changes to PROJ1.PPT before exiting PowerPoint. Choose the No button (No) to exit PowerPoint with-out saving the changes to PROJ1.PPT. Choose the Cancel button (Cancel) to terminate the Exit command and return to the presentation. If you did not make changes to your presentation since your last save, this dialog box does not display.

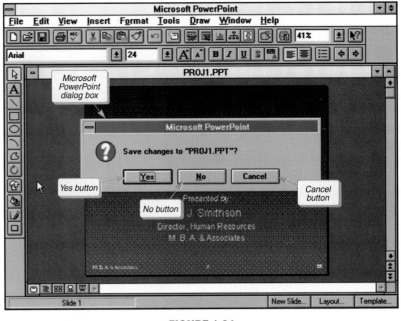

FIGURE 1-84

You can also exit PowerPoint by double-clicking the Control-menu box in the application title bar or by pressing ALT+F4.

▶ OPENING A PRESENTATION

E arlier, the presentation built in Project 1 was saved on disk using the file-name PROJ1.PPT. Once you create and save a presentation, you may have to retrieve it from disk to make changes. For example, you might want to replace the template or modify some text. After starting PowerPoint, perform the following steps to open PROJ1.PPT, using the PowerPoint dialog box.

Starting PowerPoint

Perform the following steps to start PowerPoint. Refer to Figures 1-3 through 1-5 on pages PP5 and PP6 to review these steps in detail.

TO START POWERPOINT

Step 1: Double-click the Microsoft PowerPoint program-item icon in the Micro-soft Office group window.
Step 2: Choose the OK button in the Tip of the Day dialog box.

The PowerPoint startup dialog box displays (see Figure 1-5 on page PP6).

TO OPEN A PRESENTATION ▼

STEP 1 ▶

Click the Open an Existing
Presentation option button, located
at the bottom of the PowerPoint
startup dialog box. Then, point to
the OK button.

The Open an Existing Presenta-
tion option button is selected in the
PowerPoint startup dialog box
(Figure 1-85).

FIGURE 1-85

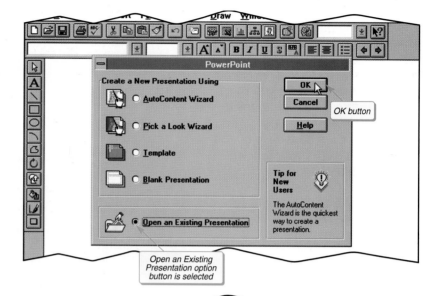

STEP 2 ▶

Choose the OK button in the
PowerPoint startup dialog box.

PowerPoint displays the Open dia-
log box (Figure 1-86).

FIGURE 1-86

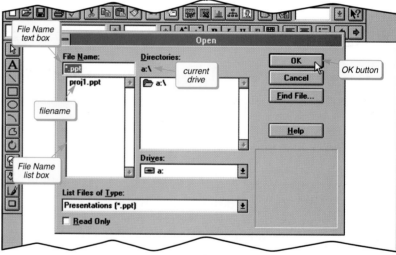

STEP 3 ▶

If drive A is not the current drive,
select drive A (refer to Figures 1-36
and 1-37 on page PP25 to review this
technique). Select proj1.ppt by
clicking its filename in the File Name
list box.

The first slide in your presentation
displays in the Open dialog box
(Figure 1-87).

FIGURE 1-87

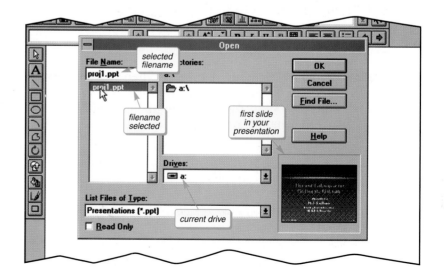

STEP 4 ▶

Choose the OK button in the Open dialog box.

PowerPoint loads the presentation with the filename PROJ1.PPT from drive A: into main memory and displays the first slide on the screen (Figure 1-88).

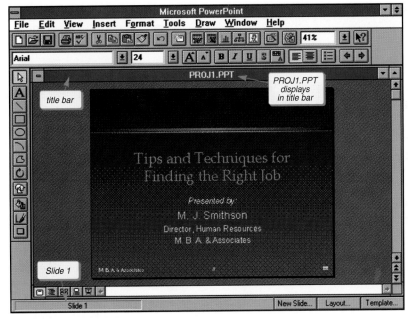

FIGURE 1-88

Project 1 is loaded into memory and Slide 1 displays on the screen. You may now correct errors or make additions to your presentation. The next section explains how to correct errors.

▶ CORRECTING ERRORS

A fter creating a presentation, you may find you must make changes. Changes may be required because a slide contains an error, because the scope of the presentation shifted, or because a slide failed the Floor Test. The next section explains the types of errors that commonly occur when creating a presentation.

Types of Corrections Made to Presentations

There are usually three types of corrections to text in a presentation: additions, deletions, or replacements.

▶ *Additions*   Additions are necessary when you omit text from a slide and need to add it later. You may need to insert text in the form of a sentence, a word, or a single character. For example, you might want to add the rest of the presenter's first name on your title slide in Project 1.

▶ *Deletions*   Deletions are required when text on a slide is incorrect or is no longer relevant to the presentation. For example, in Slide 4, you might want to remove the word likely from the bullet item Rehearse answers to likely questions.

▶ *Replacements*   Replacements are needed when you want to revise the text in your presentation. For example, you may want to exchange one word for another. On Slide 4, you might want to substitute the words prospective employer with the word interviewer.

Editing text in PowerPoint is basically the same as editing text in a word processing package. The following steps illustrate the most common changes made to a presentation.

Inserting Text into an Existing Slide

If you forget to type a word or phrase, you can insert the text by positioning the insertion point to the right of the location where you want the text inserted. PowerPoint inserts text to the left of the insertion point. The text to the right of the insertion point moves to the right and downward to accommodate the added text. Perform the following steps to add the rest of M. J. Smithson's first name, Michael.

TO INSERT TEXT

Step 1: Position the insertion point between the letter M and the period in the second line of the sub-title text on the title slide by clicking the left mouse button.
Step 2: Type `ichael`

The title slide now shows Michael J. Smithson's first name instead of his initials. The period will be removed in the next section.

Deleting Text

There are three methods to delete text. One is to use the **BACKSPACE** key to remove text just typed. The second is to position the insertion point to the left of the text you wish to delete and then press the **DELETE** key. The third method is to drag through the text to delete and press the DELETE key. (Use the third method when deleting large sections of text.)

TO DELETE TEXT

Step 1: Position the insertion point between the letter l in Michael and the period on Slide 1.
Step 2: Press the DELETE key.

The period is deleted from Slide 1, and the text shifts to the left one space.

TO REPLACE TEXT

Step 1: Click the Next Slide button three times so Slide 4 displays.
Step 2: Drag through the words prospective employer on the last paragraph of Slide 4.
Step 3: Type `interviewer`

PowerPoint replaces the words prospective employer with the word interviewer.

▶ POWERPOINT ONLINE HELP

A t anytime while using PowerPoint, you can select the Help menu to gain access to **online Help**. The PowerPoint Help menu (Figure 1-89 below) displays several commands. Table 1-5 explains the purpose of each command.

▶ **TABLE 1-5**

COMMAND	PURPOSE
Contents command	To access the Help Contents window.
Search for Help on	To navigate around Help.
Index	To find information about PowerPoint from an alphabetical list.
Quick Preview	To watch a demonstration of PowerPoint.
Tip of the Day	To display a tip explaining an efficient way to complete a task.
Cue Cards	To display an abbreviated instruction card that stays on the screen while you work.
Technical Support	To find out what to do when you have a technical question.
About Microsoft PowerPoint	To see release information and information about how PowerPoint is using your system.

Pressing F1 displays the PowerPoint Help Contents window.

You can print the information in the Help window by choosing the **Print Topic command** from the File menu in the Help window. You close a Help window by choosing Exit from the File menu in the Help window or by double-clicking the Control-box in the title bar in the Help window.

PowerPoint's online Help has features that make it powerful and easy to use. The best way to familiarize yourself with online Help is to use it. Begin with the **How to Use Help command** in the Help menu. To get to the How to Use Help command, choose the **Contents command** from the Help menu. The PowerPoint Help menu displays. Choose the How to Use Help command from the Help menu in the PowerPoint Help dialog box. Then, choose a topic, such as Help Basics.

Viewing Quick Preview

Quick Preview is a five-minute demonstration of the features in PowerPoint. Available through the Help menu, Quick Preview gives you a quick product overview. A demonstration of the main features shows you how PowerPoint works and the types of presentations you can create.

TO VIEW QUICK PREVIEW ▼

STEP 1 ▶

Select the Help menu and point to the Quick Preview command (Figure 1-89).

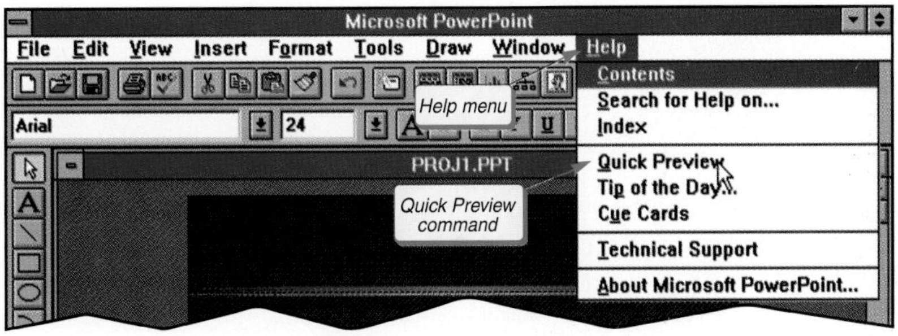

FIGURE 1-89

STEP 2 ▶

Choose the Quick Preview command.

The Quick Preview welcome window displays (Figure 1-90).

STEP 3

Choose the Click to Start (Click to Start) button.

Quick Preview begins.

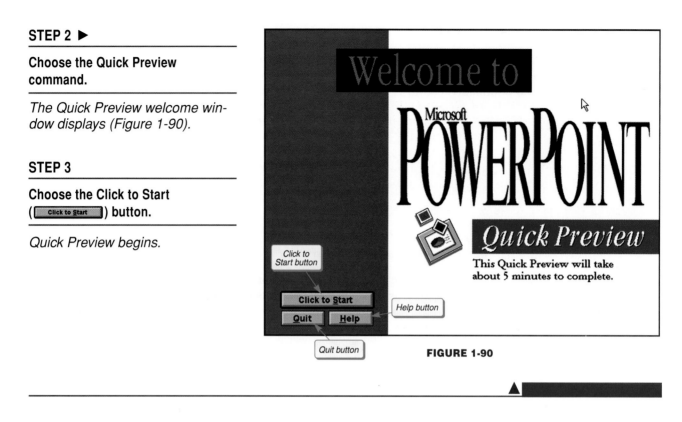

FIGURE 1-90

When Quick Preview begins, four buttons display at the lower left of the Quick Preview window. Choose the Back button (< Back) to go to the previous Quick Preview window. Choose the Quit button (Quit) to exit Quick Preview. Choose the Next button to go to the subsequent Quick Preview window. Choose the Help button for information about the buttons in Quick Preview.

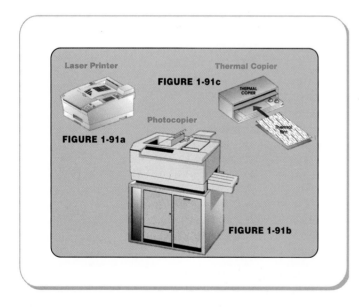

Making a Transparency

Making a transparency is accomplished using one of several devices. One device is a printer, attached to your computer, such as an ink jet printer or a laser printer (Figure 1-91a). Transparencies produced on a printer may be black and white or color, depending on the printer. Another device is a photocopier (Figure 1-91b). A third device is a thermal copier (Figure 1-91c). A thermal copier transfers a carbonaceous substance, such as toner from a photocopier, from a paper master to an acetate film. Because each of the three devices requires a special transparency film, check the user's manual for the film requirement of your specific device.

▶ Designing a Presentation

hen you design a presentation, use the following preparation steps as a guide:

1. Identify the purpose of the presentation. Is this presentation selling an idea or product? Is it reporting results of a study? Is the presentation educating your audience? Whatever the purpose, your goal is to capture the attention of the audience and to explain the data or concept in a manner that is quickly and easily understood. Presentation graphics help people *see* what they *hear*. People remember:

   - 10% of what they *read*
   - 20% of what they *hear*
   - 30% of what they *see*
   - 70% of what they *see* and *hear*

2. Identify the audience. How many people will attend the presentation? Is this an informal presentation to your peers or is this a formal presentation to management or a client? The characteristics of the audience determine which presentation media to use:

   - Overhead transparencies are best when you want audience interaction in a lighted room, for groups less than 40 people, or when other equipment is not available.

   - An electronic presentation using a projection device attached to a personal computer is good for any size audience, depending on the projection device: up to five people when using a laptop with a 14-inch or 17-inch monitor, 25 to 50 people when using an LCD panel or projector, or up to 100 people when using a large-screen video projector. Using an electronic presentation enables you to display embedded audio and video clips into the presentation without switching to another device, such as a video cassette recorder. Use an electronic presentation when you don't have time to make slides or overheads. Be certain that you have a pre-tested system and everything works like it should.

   - 35mm slides are best for a formal presentation to any size audience. 35mm slide presentations are highly recommended when audience size exceeds 50 people. 35mm slide presentations are best-suited for a non-interactive presentation because the room is dark. However, you may use 35mm slides for an interactive presentation in a semi-darkened room if you use slide colors that project in ambient light.

3. Identify the goals you expect to achieve. If you are selling a product, your presentation must focus on why this product is best for this audience. If you are reporting the results of a study, make sure you actually give the results of the study, not just the history of how you conducted the study.

4. Analyze the content. Keep to one concept per slide. Highlight the subject instead of presenting a page of text. Limit your slide to five to seven words per line and five to seven lines per slide. Don't clutter; use empty space effectively.

5. Establish a format and use it. Use one of the PowerPoint templates or create your own. Be consistent with color and text attributes. Remember to use bold and italics sparingly for emphasis and to use no more than two type fonts and styles.

Two acronyms pertain directly to presentation design:

— K.I.S. (Keep It Simple)
— C.C.C. (Clutter Creates Confusion)

▶ PROJECT SUMMARY

Project 1 introduced you to starting PowerPoint and creating a presentation. This project also illustrated how to create a bulleted list presentation. You learned about PowerPoint objects, attributes, and templates. You set the foundation of your presentation using the Pick a Look Wizard. It was here that you selected a template and information to display on every slide. Project 1 illustrated how to change the text style to italics and decrease font size on the title slide. After completing these tasks, you saved your presentation. After saving, you changed line spacing. Using the PowerPoint spelling checker, you learned how to spell check a presentation. You learned how to print a presentation, then how to exit PowerPoint, and open an existing PowerPoint presentation. You learned how to correct errors and use PowerPoint online Help. Finally, you learned preparation steps for designing a presentation.

▶ KEY TERMS AND INDEX

AutoContent wizard *(PP6)*
.ppt *(PP26)*
Apply button *(PP11)*
attribute buttons *(PP14)*
attributes *(PP12)*
Author box *(PP27)*
AutoContent Wizard *(PP6)*
AutoLayout object area *(PP15)*
background items *(PP37)*
BACKSPACE key *(PP54)*
bulleted list *(PP4)*
bullet *(PP4)*
clip art *(PP3)*
color scheme *(PP37)*
Comments box *(PP27)*
Contents command *(PP55)*
custom dictionary *(PP43)*
Customize command *(PP14)*
date *(PP37)*
Decrease Font Size button *(PP22)*
default setting *(PP12)*
DELETE key *(PP54)*
drawing *(PP3)*
Drawing toolbar *(PP14)*
elevator *(PP32)*
Exit command *(PP50)*
Find File command *(PP27)*
Floor Test *(PP50)*
font *(PP20, PP37)*
font size *(PP20, PP37)*

Font Size box *(PP22)*
Formatting toolbar *(PP14)*
graphing *(PP2)*
hard copy *(PP47)*
horizontal scroll bar *(PP15)*
How to Use Help command *(PP55)*
Increase Font Size button *(PP23)*
insertion point *(PP17)*
Italic button *(PP21)*
Keywords box *(PP27)*
Layout button *(PP13)*
Line Spacing command *(PP37)*
line wraps *(PP17)*
Master text *(PP36)*
Master title *(PP36)*
menu bar *(PP13)*
mouse pointer *(PP16)*
Next Slide button *(PP15)*
New Slide button *(PP13)*
Notes Pages view *(PP12)*
objects *(PP12)*
online Help *(PP55)*
Options command *(PP45)*
Outline view *(PP12)*
outlining *(PP2)*
page number *(PP37)*
paragraph *(PP17)*
Pick a Look Wizard *(PP6)*
placeholders *(PP15)*

point *(PP20, PP40)*
PowerPoint window *(PP12)*
presentation graphics program *(PP2)*
presentation management *(PP3)*
Previous Slide button *(PP15)*
Print command *(PP48)*
Print Topic command *(PP55)*
printout *(PP47)*
Quick Preview command *(PP55)*
Restore button *(PP16)*
rough draft *(PP47)*
selection box *(PP17)*
slide *(PP12)*
slide indicator box *(PP32)*
Slide Master *(PP7)*
Slide Show button *(PP33)*
Slide Show view *(PP12)*
Slide Sorter view *(PP12)*
Slide view *(PP12)*
Spelling button *(PP44)*
Standard toolbar *(PP14)*
status bar *(PP13)*
Subject box *(PP27)*
subscript *(PP20)*
superscript *(PP20)*
sub-title placeholder *(PP15)*
template *(PP6)*
Template button *(PP13)*
text attribute *(P19)*

QUICK REFERENCE

In PowerPoint, you can accomplish a task in a number of ways. The following table provides a quick reference to each task in this project with its available options. The commands listed in the Menu column can be executed using either the keyboard or mouse.

Task	Mouse	Menu	Keyboard Shortcuts
Context-Sensitive Help			Press F1 when dialog box displays
Display a Presentation on a Screen	Click Slide Show button on toolbar	From File menu, choose Slide Show	
Exit PowerPoint	Double-click Control-menu box in title bar	From File menu, choose Exit	Press ALT+F4
First Slide	Drag elevator to top of vertical scroll bar		Press CTRL+PAGE UP
Help	Click Help button on Standard toolbar	Select Help menu	Press F1
Italicize Text	Click Italic button on Formatting toolbar	From Text menu, choose Style, then choose Italic	Press CTRL+I
Last Slide	Drag elevator to bottom of vertical scroll bar		Press CTRL+PAGE DOWN
New Slide	Click New Slide button	From Slide menu, choose New Slide	Press CTRL+N
Next Slide	Click Next Slide button		Press PAGE DOWN
Open a Presentation	Click Open button on Standard toolbar	From File menu, choose Open	Press CTRL+O
Previous Slide	Click Previous Slide button		Press PAGE UP
Print a Presentation	Click Print button on Standard toolbar	From File menu, choose Print	Press CTRL+P
Save a Presentation	Click Save button on Standard toolbar	From File menu, choose Save	Press CTRL+S

S T U D E N T   A S S I G N M E N T S

STUDENT ASSIGNMENT 1
True/False

Instructions: Circle T if the statement is true or F if the statement is false.

T   F   1. PowerPoint is a complete presentation graphics program that allows you to produce professional-looking presentations.

T   F   2. The mouse pointer can become one of several different shapes, depending on the task you are performing in PowerPoint and the pointer's location on the screen.

T   F   3. The basic unit of a PowerPoint presentation is the document.

T   F   4. Toolbars consist of buttons that access commonly used PowerPoint tools.

T   F   5. The PowerPoint file extension is PPT.

T   F   6. PowerPoint allows you to create automatic bulleted lists, combine words and images, check spelling, find and replace text, and use multiple fonts and type sizes.

T   F   7. Selecting Pure Black & White from the Print dialog box turns all colors and fills to black and all text and lines to white.

T   F   8. The New Slide button allows you to select a template for your presentation.

T   F   9. The Drawing toolbar is a collection of tools for drawing, graphing, and adding text to a slide.

T   F   10. The Scale to Fit Paper option in the Print dialog box allows you to print more than one slide on one sheet of paper.

T   F   11. The Print button is located on the Formatting toolbar.

T   F   12. To start PowerPoint, type POWERPNT at the DOS prompt.

T   F   13. When you add a slide to an open presentation, PowerPoint prompts you to choose a template.

T   F   14. To view Quick Preview, choose the Quick Preview command from the View menu.

T   F   15. The current slide number displays on the status bar.

T   F   16. When you save a presentation, it disappears from the screen.

T   F   17. When selected text has been italicized, the Italic button appears recessed.

T   F   18. To save a document, click the Save button on the Formatting toolbar.

T   F   19. The Pick a Look Wizard asks you questions about the type of presentation media you are using for your presentation, such as color overheads or video screen.

T   F   20. PowerPoint provides five families of templates: VIDSCREN, B&WOVHD, CLROVHD, ONSCRNSL, and 35MSLIDE.

STUDENT ASSIGNMENT 2
Multiple Choice

Instructions: Circle the correct response.

1. When the mouse pointer is positioned on a menu, it has the shape of a(n) _____ .
   a. I-beam   b. hourglass   c. vertical bar   d. left-pointing block arrow

2. To save a presentation after it was saved once, use the _____ button.
   a. Save   b. Save As   c. Close   d. Exit

3. _____ displays miniature versions of a presentation.
   a. Slide view   b. Notes Pages view   c. Slide Sorter view   d. Outline view

4. Five of the major features of PowerPoint are _____ .
   a. spreadsheet, graphing, drawing, wizard, and outlining
   b. word processing, graphing, database, wizard, and outlining
   c. word processing, graphing, drawing, wizards, and outlining
   d. word processing, graphing, drawing, cut/paste, and outlining

5. To start Microsoft PowerPoint for Windows, _____ .
  a. point to the Microsoft PowerPoint program-item icon and click the left mouse button
  b. point to the Microsoft PowerPoint program-item icon and double-click the left mouse button
  c. point to File Manager and double-click the left mouse button
  d. point to the Open command on the File menu and click the left mouse button
6. Before you change the font size of a line of text, you must _____ .
  a. position the mouse pointer beside the first character in the line to be formatted
  b. highlight the first word in the line to be formatted
  c. underscore the line to be formatted
  d. highlight the line to be formatted
7. PowerPoint automatically adds the extension of _____ to a filename when you save a presentation.
  a. .DOC   b. .TXT   c. .PPT   d. .XLS
8. To erase a character to the left of the insertion point, press the _____ key.
  a. BACKSPACE   b. INSERT   c. DELETE   d. both a and c
9. When you exit PowerPoint, _____ .
  a. control is returned to Program Manager
  b. it is erased from disk
  c. it is removed from the screen
  d. both b and c
10. The template controls the placement and attributes of the _____ .
  a. body object
  b. title object
  c. title text
  d. all the above

STUDENT ASSIGNMENT 3
Understanding the PowerPoint Window

Instructions: In Figure SA1-3, arrows point to the major components of the PowerPoint window in Slide view. Identify the various parts of the window in the spaces provided.

FIGURE SA1-3

STUDENT ASSIGNMENT 4
Understanding the Standard Toolbar

Instructions: In Figure SA1-4, arrows point to several buttons on the PowerPoint window. In the spaces provided, list the name and a brief explanation of each button.

Button Name	Explanation
1. _____	_____
2. _____	_____
3. _____	_____
4. _____	_____
5. _____	_____
6. _____	_____
7. _____	_____
8. _____	_____
9. _____	_____

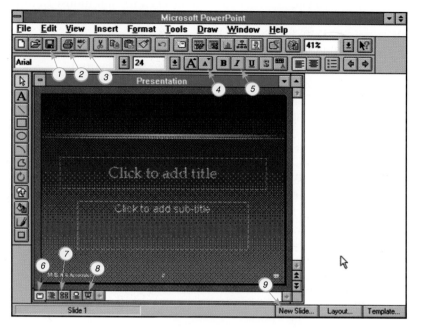

FIGURE SA1-4

STUDENT ASSIGNMENT 5
Understanding How to Change Line Spacing

Instructions: Fill in the number for each step listed below to indicate the proper sequence. These steps override the Slide Master and change the line spacing of each paragraph of the body text shown in Figure SA1-5 to 0.75 lines after each paragraph.

STEP ____: From the Format menu, choose the Line Spacing command.

STEP ____: Choose the OK button from the Line Spacing dialog box.

STEP ____: Click the down arrow next to the After Paragraph text box once so 0.75 displays.

STEP ____: Select the paragraphs to be changed by dragging the mouse pointer.

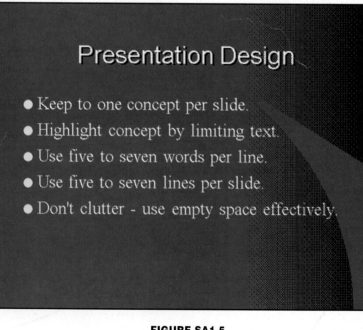

FIGURE SA1-5

STUDENT ASSIGNMENT 6
Understanding the Print Dialog Box

Instructions: Answer the following questions concerning the Print dialog box in Figure SA1-6. The numbers in the figure correspond to the numbers in the following questions.

1. What is the purpose of the Pure Black & White option?

_____

2. What is the purpose of the Scale to Fit Paper option?

_____

3. What is the purpose of the Slide Range All option?

_____

4. What is the purpose of the Copies box?

_____

5. What is the purpose of the Cancel button?

_____

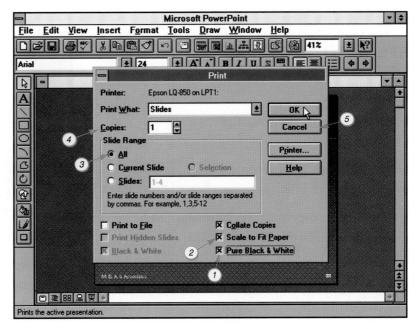

FIGURE SA1-6

COMPUTER LABORATORY EXERCISES

COMPUTER LABORATORY EXERCISE 1
Using the Quick Preview

Instructions: Perform the following tasks using a computer:

1. Start PowerPoint. From the Help menu on the menu bar, choose the Quick Preview command. Choose the Click to Start button. Read the contents of the screen. Choose the Next button. Continue until you reach the end of Quick Preview.
2. To close Quick Preview, choose the Quit button.

COMPUTER LABORATORY EXERCISE 2
Formatting a Slide

Instructions: Start PowerPoint. Open the presentation CLE1-2.PPT from the PPOINT subdirectory on the Student Diskette that accompanies this book.

(continued)

Perform the following tasks to change the slide so it looks like the one in Figure CLE1-2.

1. Highlight the bulleted paragraphs.
2. Select the Format menu from the menu bar and point to the Line Spacing command.
3. From the Format menu, choose the Line Spacing command by clicking the left mouse button.
4. Click the up arrow box next to the After Paragraph text box until 0.5 displays.
5. Choose the OK button from the Line Spacing dialog box.
6. Italicize the body object text.
7. Save the presentation on your data disk with the filemane CLE1-2A.
8. Print the presentation by selecting the File menu, choosing the Print button, and selecting Slides in the Print What box.
9. Choose the OK button in the Print dialog box.
10. From the File menu, choose the Exit command to exit PowerPoint.

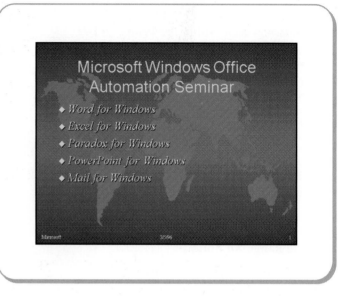

FIGURE CLE1-2

COMPUTER LABORATORY EXERCISE 3
Spell Checking a Presentation

Instructions: Start PowerPoint. Open the presentation CLE1-3.PPT from the PPOINT subdirectory on the Student Diskette that accompanies this book. CLE1-3.PPT is shown in Figures CLE1-3a and CLE1-3b.

Perform the following tasks:

1. Choose the Spelling button from the Standard toolbar.
2. Choose the Suggest button in the Spelling dialog box to display a list of suggested spellings for the incorrect word.
3. Change the incorrect word Useer by choosing the word User from the list of suggested spellings.
4. Ignore the spelling check message regarding the acronym OLE by choosing the Ignore button.
5. Ignore PowerPoint by choosing the Ignore button.

Microsoft Windows

♦ Graphical Useer Interface
  ↝ GUI
♦ Object Link and Embedding
  ↝ OLE
♦ Run Multiple Applications
♦ Transfer Information Between Applications
♦ What You See is What You Get!
  ↝ WYSIWYG

FIGURE CLE1-3a

6. Change the incorrect spacing in your presentation by positioning the insertion point between the letter r in your and the letter p in presentation and then pressing the SPACEBAR. Then, choose the Change button.
7. Save the presentation on your data disk with the filename CLE1-3A.
8. Print the slides for the corrected presentation.
9. From the File menu, choose the Exit command to exit PowerPoint.

FIGURE CLE1-3b

COMPUTER LABORATORY ASSIGNMENTS

COMPUTER LABORATORY ASSIGNMENT 1
Building a Presentation Using the Pick a Look Wizard

Purpose: To become familiar with building a presentation, applying a template, printing a presentation, and saving a presentation.

Problem: You are the director of benefits for Intergalactic Pipeline. Your primary responsibility is the company insurance plan. A new health insurance plan begins the first of next month. You are presenting the 1996 health insurance coverage to the employees next week.

Instructions: Perform the following tasks:

1. Using the Pick a Look Wizard, create an On-screen presentation with the Double Lines template. Add the company name, date, and page number, as shown in Figure CLA1-1.
2. Create a title slide for Intergalactic Pipeline using your name as the presenter.
3. Add a new slide using the Bulleted List AutoLayout.
4. Type the title and body text for the slide shown in Figure CLA1-1.
5. Adjust the paragraph line spacing to 0.5 lines after each paragraph.
6. Save the presentation on your data disk with the filename CLA1-1.
7. Print the presentation slides.
8. Exit PowerPoint.

FIGURE CLA1-1

COMPUTER LABORATORY ASSIGNMENT 2
Building a Presentation Using the Pick a Look Wizard
and Changing Paragraph Line Spacing

Purpose: To become familiar with building a presentation, applying a template, changing paragraph line spacing, printing a presentation, and saving a presentation.

Problem: You are the assistant manager of Maximum Savings and Loan. Your area of responsibility is the loan department. Maximum Savings and Loan is starting its annual home improvement loan campaign. You have been asked to develop a presentation on consumer credit for the home improvement loan campaign.

Instructions: Perform the following tasks:

1. Using the Pick a Look Wizard, choose the Blue Diagonal template and add company name, date, and page number, as shown in Figure CLA1-2.
2. Create a title slide using your name as the presenter.
3. Create a bulleted list for the slide shown in Figure CLA1-2.
4. Adjust the paragraph line spacing to one line after each paragraph.
5. Save the presentation on your data disk with the filename CLA1-2.
6. Print the presentation slides choosing the Print command from the File menu.
6. Exit PowerPoint.

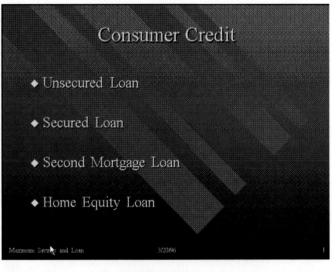

FIGURE CLA1-2

COMPUTER LABORATORY ASSIGNMENT 3
Building a Presentation Using a Template, Changing
Paragraph Line Spacing, and Spell Checking

Purpose: To become familiar with designing and building a presentation, applying a template using the Pick a Look Wizard, changing paragraph line spacing, spell checking a presentation, printing a presentation, and saving a presentation.

Problem: You are the assistant director of admissions at Western State University. You have been asked by the chancellor to give a presentation on Western State University. Create a title slide and the bulleted list of the issues you plan to discuss (Figure CLA1-3). Create at least three more slides to complete the presentation. The paragraphs on the next page are excerpts from the Western State University catalog. Use the underlined passages to complete your presentation.

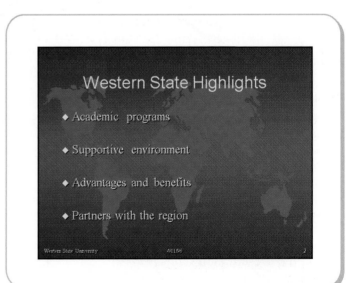

FIGURE CLA1-3

Western State University is <u>a comprehensive university dedicated to serving the professional, cultural, and general educational needs of the citizens of Western Arizona</u>. The university provides <u>programs that meet the professional, cultural, and general educational needs of the citizens and communities</u>. Its <u>academic programs</u> lead <u>to post baccalaureate and technical proficiency certificates</u> and <u>associate, baccalaureate, and master's degrees</u>. Drawing upon the university's considerable computer resources, the faculty attempts to provide students with both technical skills and awareness of the social and ethical implications of new technology.

Western State University's <u>outreach activities include interactions with local school systems, governments, human services agencies, businesses, and industries—interactions ranging from continuing education and special training to professional assistance from faculty, staff, and students.</u>

Western State University is a community committed to people as its most important resource. The institution strives to foster cultural diversity and to provide a supportive environment where students, staff, and faculty can grow and thrive, through:

- <u>a hospitable atmosphere for a student body of diverse career goals and ethnic backgrounds, old and young, of both sexes and all races</u>
- <u>a faculty and staff reflecting cultural diversity</u>
- <u>academic consideration of cultural differences</u>
- public programs featuring diverse speakers, performers, and programs
- <u>affirmative action hiring and student recruiting</u>
- outreach to public schools with minority students representing the broad range of citizens of the region

Western State University encourages all who are qualified or who are qualifiable to attend by:

- <u>placing a primary emphasis on educational activities</u>
- <u>offering pre-college course work</u>
- <u>offering reasonable in-state tuition rates, with state support paying for two-thirds of the cost of education</u>
- <u>offering financial aid</u>
- <u>providing strong student support services</u>
- scheduling classes to facilitate the teaching/learning process
- <u>offering flexible courses, scheduling, and sites</u>
- emphasizing lifelong learning

Western State University is <u>a partner with the region it serves both by helping citizens and institutions of the region and by garnering support from them to maintain the university's strength.</u>

Instructions: Perform the following tasks:

1. Create an On-screen presentation using the Pick a Look Wizard to add the World template. Add company name, date, and page number.
2. Create a title slide with your name as the presenter.
3. Create the bulleted list shown in Figure CLA1-3.
4. Create at least three additional slides for your presentation.
5. Adjust the after paragraph line spacing to create an appealing presentation.
6. Save the presentation on your disk with the filename CLA1-3.
7. Check the spelling of your presentation.
8. Save the presentation again.
9. Print the presentation slides.
10. Exit PowerPoint.

firm

COMPUTER LABORATORY ASSIGNMENT 4
Designing a Slide

Purpose: To provide practice in planning, designing, and creating a presentation.

Problem: You are the director of financial aid at Western State University. You have been asked by the chancellor to give a five-slide presentation on financial aid available at Western State University. The information you will need is provided below.

To help students meet the cost of their education, Western State University provides financial assistance. The purpose of the Office of Financial Aid is to help students meet educational costs beyond those which they and their families are able to contribute.

There are three types of financial aid for college students available from federal, state, and university programs:

1. Grants or scholarships, which do not have to be repaid.
2. Loans, which must be repaid.
3. College work-study programs, where the student earns money.

To apply for financial aid, a student must:

> ▸ Apply for admission to Western State University as a degree-seeking student. Financial aid through the university is not available for non degree-seeking students.
> ▸ Apply for financial aid by submitting a Financial Aid Form (FAF) through the College Scholarship Service. This form is available through high school guidance offices and the Western State University Office of Financial Aid.

For Arizona residents only: Designate the State Student Assistance Commission of Arizona as recipient of the analysis in order to apply for the State Higher Education Award and Lilly Endowment Educational Award.

The analysis of the information provided on the form allows the university to evaluate student need for aid. If the student is eligible, the university will put together a "package" of aid to help meet the student's educational expense. Students receive an Award Notification from the Office of Financial Aid and must return the Financial Aid Acceptance Form to indicate whether they accept the types of funds awarded.

Once a student registers for classes, a bill is generated and mailed to the student. The student must then report to the Bursar's Office to have the financial aid applied to tuition and fees.

If the financial aid amount is greater than tuition and fees, the student will receive a check for the difference.

Important Dates

January 1 - March 1: File the Financial Aid Form (FAF) with the College Scholarship Service for priority consideration. Students filing after March 1 may apply only for a Pell Grant by completing the Financial Aid Form or an application for Federal Student Aid. Students filing late will be considered for campus aid as they complete their files, depending on qualifications and available funds.

June: Award Notifications will be sent out to all applicants with complete files.

Instructions: Design and create a presentation consisting of five slides. Your presentation must include a title slide with your name as the presenter. Select a template that enhances your presentation. Print the date at the bottom of each slide. Adjust after paragraph line spacing, as necessary, to make your slides appealing. Be sure to check the spelling of your presentation before printing it. Save your presentation using the filename CLA1-4. Exit PowerPoint.

MICROSOFT POWERPOINT 4 FOR WINDOWS

PROJECT TWO

▼

CREATING A PRESENTATION IN OUTLINE VIEW

OBJECTIVES You will have mastered the material in this project when you can:

▸ Create a presentation in Outline view
▸ Describe the PowerPoint window in Outline view
▸ Demote text
▸ Promote text
▸ Paste clip art into a presentation from the ClipArt Gallery

▸ Add an AutoShapes object
▸ Add text to an object
▸ Change text color
▸ Color fill an object
▸ Change slide order
▸ Print a presentation outline

▸ INTRODUCTION

I n both the academic and business environments, you will be asked to make presentations. Most business presentations are some form of a sales presentation: selling your proposal or product to a client, convincing management to approve a new project, or persuading the board of directors to accept the fiscal budget. In all probability, sometime during your professional life, you will make a sales presentation, usually with very short notice. As an alternative to creating your presentation in Slide view, as you did in Project 1, PowerPoint provides an outlining feature to help you organize your thoughts. When the outline is complete, it becomes the foundation for your presentation.

Outlining in PowerPoint is performed in Outline view. However, unlike Slide view, where you type your text directly on the slide, Outline view allows you to type your text as if you were typing an outline on a sheet of paper. First, you would type a title for the outline, which would be the subject matter of the presentation and which would later become the title slide. Then, you would type the remainder of the outline, indenting appropriately to establish a structure or hierarchy. Once the outline is complete, you may then make your presentation more persuasive by adding graphics. This project uses outlining to create the presentation and graphics to visually support the text.

▶ Project Two — San Baarbo Vacations

P roject 2 uses PowerPoint to create the four slides shown in Figures 2-1a through 2-1d. San Baarbo Vacations is a travel agency making presentations to local organizations to promote their two new vacation packages to San Juan, Puerto Rico. The purpose of the presentation is to entice members of the audience to buy one or both of the San Juan vacation packages. To persuade the audience, San Baarbo Vacations chose a template with a travel theme and included graphics to enhance the bulleted text.

Slide Preparation Steps

The following slide preparation steps summarize how to create the slides shown in Figures 2-1a through 2-1d. If you are creating these slides on a personal computer, read these steps without doing them.

1. Start the PowerPoint program.
2. Apply template travels.ppt using the Pick a Look Wizard.
3. Create the presentation in Outline view.

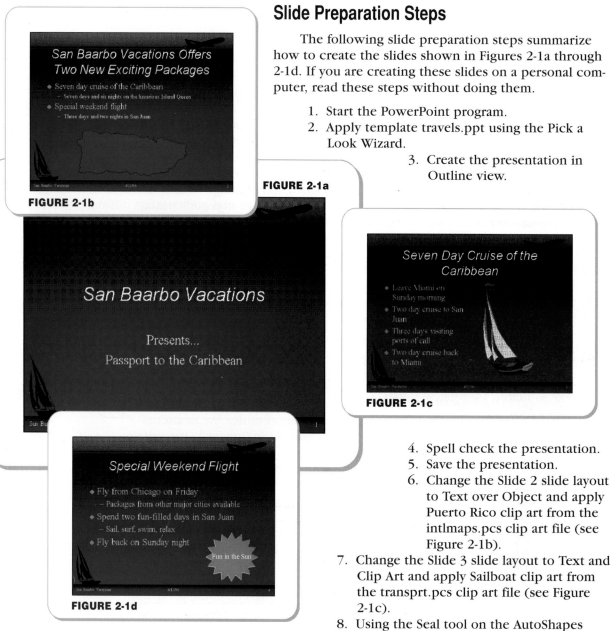

FIGURE 2-1b

FIGURE 2-1a

FIGURE 2-1c

FIGURE 2-1d

4. Spell check the presentation.
5. Save the presentation.
6. Change the Slide 2 slide layout to Text over Object and apply Puerto Rico clip art from the intlmaps.pcs clip art file (see Figure 2-1b).
7. Change the Slide 3 slide layout to Text and Clip Art and apply Sailboat clip art from the transprt.pcs clip art file (see Figure 2-1c).
8. Using the Seal tool on the AutoShapes toolbar, apply the seal object to Slide 4. Add yellow text to the seal object. Color fill the seal object red (see Figure 2-1d).
9. Change slide order in Outline view and in Slide Sorter view.
10. Copy and paste Slide 2 in Slide Sorter view.
11. Use the Undo button to reverse the pasting of Slide 2.

12. Save the presentation.
13. Print the presentation outline and slides.
14. Quit PowerPoint.

▶ STARTING POWERPOINT

T o start PowerPoint, the Windows Program Manager must display on the screen and the Microsoft Office group window must be open. Double-click the Microsoft PowerPoint program-item icon in the Microsoft Office group window. Then, choose the OK button in the Tip of the Day dialog box.

▶ USING ADDITIONAL FEATURES OF THE PICK A LOOK WIZARD

I n Project 1, you created a presentation by first developing the "look" of the presentation by selecting options in the Pick a Look Wizard. You selected a template and then embellished the presentation by adding the company name, the date, and the page number to the bottom of each slide. Similarly, in Project 2, you will add a template, but this time you will select the template from the template directory. Clicking the **More button** in the Pick a Look Wizard — Step 3 of 9 dialog box allows you to select a template from one of three subdirectories in the template directory. You will again add the company name, date, and a page number to the bottom of each slide. You will also add the company name, date, and a page number to each outline page. However, on the outline pages, the company name displays in the **header**, or top of the page, and the date and page number display in the **footer**, or bottom of the page.

The following steps explain how to select a template choosing the More button in the Pick a Look Wizard — Step 3 of 9 dialog box and how to add a company name, a date, and a page number to the outline pages.

Starting the Pick a Look Wizard

Recall from Project 1 that the Pick a Look Wizard is a quick way to establish the overall format of your presentation. Perform the following steps to start the Pick a Look Wizard.

TO START THE PICK A LOOK WIZARD

Step 1: Click the Pick a Look Wizard option button in the PowerPoint dialog box.

Step 2: Choose the OK button in the PowerPoint dialog box.

Step 3: Choose the Next button in the Pick a Look Wizard — Step 1 of 9 dialog box.

Step 4: Choose the Next button in the Pick a Look Wizard — Step 2 of 9 dialog box. When the Pick a Look Wizard — Step 3 of 9 dialog box displays, point to the More button.

The Pick a Look Wizard — Step 3 of 9 dialog box displays (Figure 2-2 on the next page).

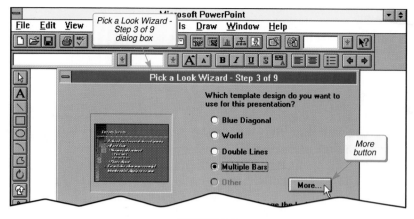

FIGURE 2-2

The next section explains how to select a template from the Presentation Template dialog box.

Selecting a Template from the Presentation Template Dialog Box

Recall from Project 1 that the Pick a Look Wizard — Step 3 of 9 dialog box displays option buttons for four templates: Blue Diagonal, World, Double Lines, and Multiple Bars. These templates are suitable for many presentations, but sometimes you want a template that adds intensity to your presentation. PowerPoint has more than 100 artist-created templates in its three template subdirectories: bwovrhd, clrovrhd, and sldshow. The bwovrhd subdirectory contains templates created for black-and-white overhead transparencies. Actually, the templates in the bwovrhd subdirectory use shades of black and gray. The clrovrhd subdirectory contains templates for color overhead transparencies. The templates designed for color overhead transparencies use shades of black and gray and include some color. The sldshow subdirectory contains templates for on-screen slide shows. The templates designed for on-screen slide shows use the most color with background color ranging from shades of gray to bright red. The best way to decide on a template is to browse through the template subdirectories until you find one that suits your presentation.

PRESENTATION TIP

The template conveys a silent message just by the use of color. Color serves many functions:

▶ Heightens the realism of the image by displaying its actual colors

▶ Points out differences and similarities

▶ Creates an emotional response

Knowing how people perceive color helps you emphasize your message. Color sets a mood for the presentation. People respond to color. The psychological basis for which some colors are "cool" (blue, green, and violet) and other colors are "hot" (red and orange) is the manner in which the human eye focuses. Warmer colors seem to reach toward the audience while cooler colors seem to pull away from the audience. The design principle to remember is light, bright colors seem to jump out from a dark background and are easiest to see. White or yellow text, used with a dark gray drop shadow, on a dark blue, green, purple, or black background is ideal.

TO SELECT A TEMPLATE FROM THE PRESENTATION TEMPLATE DIALOG BOX ▼

STEP 1 ►

Choose the More button in the Pick a Look Wizard – Step 3 of 9 dialog box. When the Presentation Template dialog box displays, point to the File Name scroll bar elevator in the File Name list box.

The Presentation Template dialog box displays (Figure 2-3). The File Name list box contains a list of templates available in the sldshow template subdirectory.

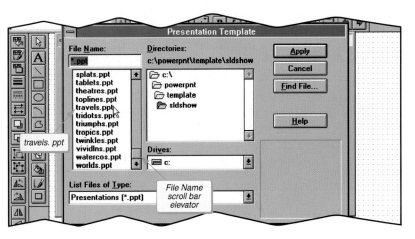

FIGURE 2-3

STEP 2 ►

Drag the File Name scroll bar elevator down to the bottom of the scroll bar. Then, point to travels.ppt in the File Name list box (Figure 2-4).

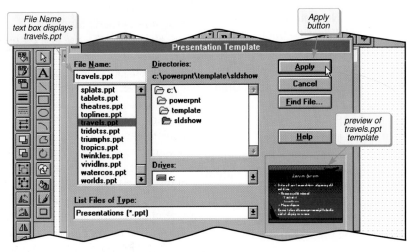

FIGURE 2-4

STEP 3 ►

Select the travels.ppt template. Then, point to the Apply button in the Presentation Template dialog box.

A preview of the travels.ppt template displays in the preview box (Figure 2-5). The filename, travels.ppt, is highlighted and displays in the File Name text box.

FIGURE 2-5

STEP 4 ▶

Choose the Apply button. When the Pick a Look Wizard – Step 3 of 9 dialog box displays, point to the Next button.

The Pick a Look Wizard – Step 3 of 9 dialog box displays (Figure 2-6). The travels.ppt template displays in the preview box. Notice the Other option button is selected.

STEP 5 ▶

Choose the Next button. When the Pick a Look Wizard – Step 4 of 9 dialog box displays, remove the x in the Speaker's Notes check box and the x in the Audience Handout Pages check box by pointing to each box and clicking the left mouse button. Then, point to the Next button.

The Pick a Look Wizard – Step 4 of 9 dialog box displays (Figure 2-7). The Full-Page Slides and Outline Pages check boxes are selected.

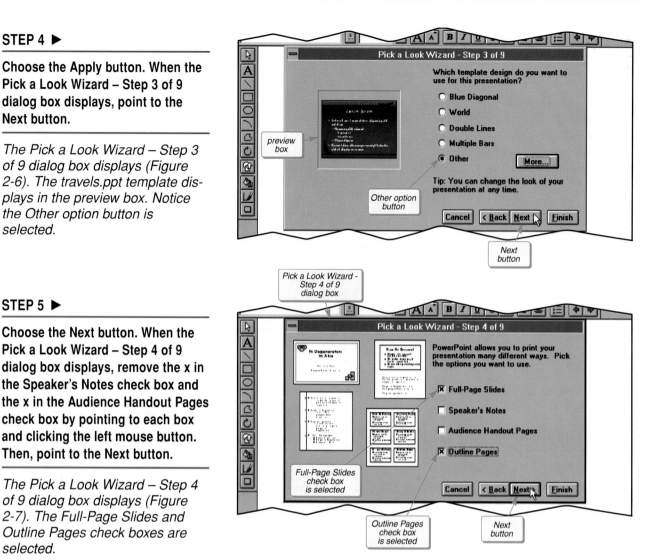

FIGURE 2-7

STEP 6 ▶

Choose the Next button. When the Pick a Look Wizard – Slide Options dialog box displays, select the check boxes for Name, company, or other text; Date; and Page Number. Drag the mouse pointer through the existing text in the Name, company, or other text box and type San Baarbo Vacations for the company name. Then, point to the Next button.

San Baarbo Vacations displays in the text box and all three check boxes are selected in the Pick a Look Wizard – Slide Options dialog box (Figure 2-8).

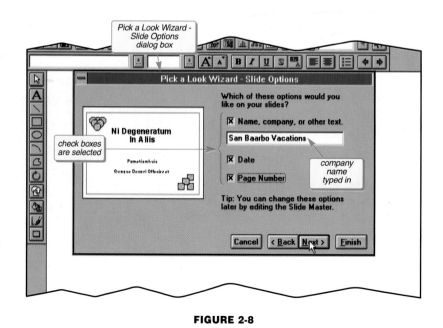

FIGURE 2-8

STEP 7 ▶

Choose the Next button.

The Pick a Look Wizard – Outline Options dialog box displays (Figure 2-9). San Baarbo Vacations displays in the text box because you typed it in the Pick a Look Wizard – Slide Options dialog box. PowerPoint automatically selects the Page Number check box.

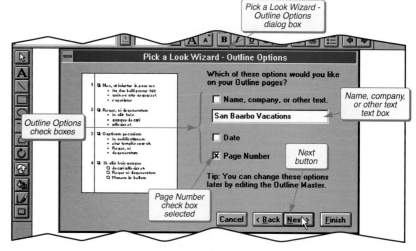

FIGURE 2-9

STEP 8 ▶

Select the check box for Name, company, or other text and the check box for Date. Then, point to the Next button.

All three check boxes are selected in the Pick a Look Wizard – Outline Options dialog box (Figure 2-10).

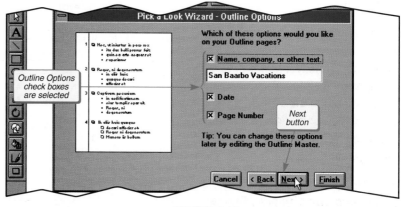

FIGURE 2-10

STEP 9 ▶

Choose the Next button. When the Pick a Look Wizard – Step 9 of 9 dialog box displays, choose the Finish button.

Slide 1 displays the title slide with the travels.ppt template and the placeholders for the title and sub-title (Figure 2-11).

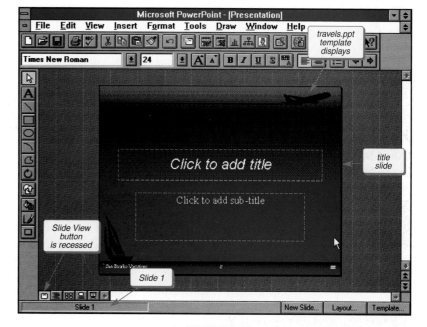

FIGURE 2-11

Maximizing the PowerPoint Window

The PowerPoint window is not always maximized when you start PowerPoint. Recall from Project 1 that maximizing the PowerPoint window makes it easier to see the contents of the window. If your window is not already maximized, click the Maximize button on the title bar. For a detailed explanation of how to maximize the PowerPoint window, see page PP16.

▶ USING OUTLINE VIEW

Outline view provides a quick and easy way to create a presentation. Outlining allows you to organize your thoughts in a structured format. An outline uses indentation to establish a hierarchy, which denotes levels of importance to the main topic. An **outline** is a summary of thoughts, presented as headings and subheadings, often used as a preliminary draft when creating a presentation. In Outline view, title text displays at the left side of the window along with a slide icon and a slide number. Indented under the title text is the body text. Graphic objects, such as pictures, graphs, or tables, do not display in Outline view. When a slide contains a graphic object, the slide icon next to the slide title displays with a small graphic on it. The slide icon is blank when a slide does not contain graphics. The attributes for text in Outline view are the same as in Slide view except for color and paragraph style.

PowerPoint limits the number of outline levels to six. PowerPoint refers to outline levels as heading levels. The outline begins with a title on **heading level one**. The title is the main topic of a slide. Text supporting the main topic begins on **heading level two** and indents under heading level one. **Heading level three** indents under heading level two and contains text to support heading level two. **Heading level four**, **heading level five**, and **heading level six** indent under heading level three, heading level four, and heading level five, respectively. Use heading levels four, five, and six as required for presentations requiring vast amounts of detail, such as scientific or engineering presentations. Business and sales presentations usually focus on summary information and use heading level one, heading level two, and heading level three.

PRESENTATION TIP

A topic needing more than six heading levels has too much detail and may overwhelm the audience. Decompose large topics into two or more subtopics. Then, create a new slide for each group of subtopics.

The audience ultimately determines the level of detail you place on one slide. Before you create your presentation, determine who is likely to attend. Design your presentation around the amount of detail the audience wants to see. Remember, you want to keep their attention. One sure way to lose their attention is to bore them with details when a summary will suffice. Additionally, try to pace your information over several slides. The purpose of a slide is to identify ideas or concepts. This differs from a page of printed text that tells the whole story on one page. Don't expect your audience to read a slide filled with text. As the presenter, it is your responsibility to introduce the topic and then explain the details.

You may create and edit your presentation title and text in Outline view. Outline view also makes it easy to sequence slides and to relocate title and text from one slide to another.

PowerPoint can make slides from an outline created in Microsoft Word or another word processor if you save it as an RTF file or as plain text. The file extension **RTF** stands for **R**ich **T**ext **F**ormat.

TO USE OUTLINE VIEW ▼

STEP 1 ▶

Point to the Outline View button (▤) at the lower left of the PowerPoint screen (Figure 2-12).

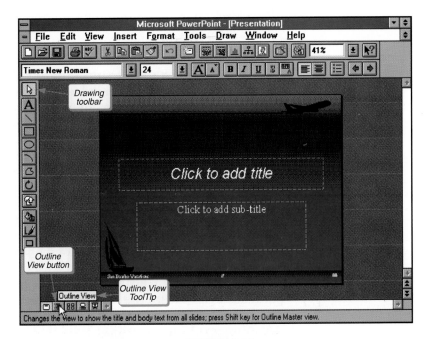

FIGURE 2-12

STEP 2 ▶

Click the Outline View button.

PowerPoint displays the Outline View window (Figure 2-13).

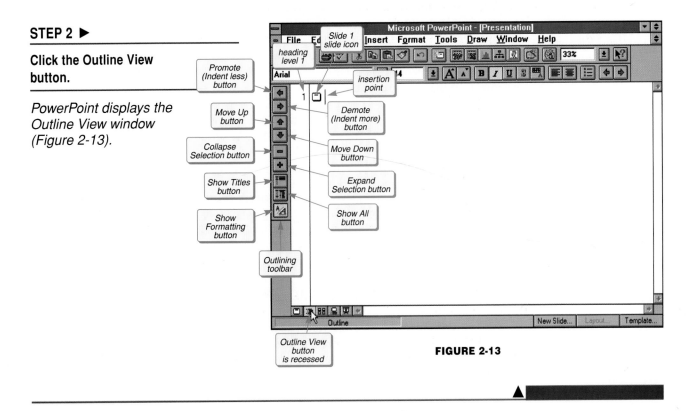

FIGURE 2-13

▶ THE POWERPOINT SCREEN IN OUTLINE VIEW

The PowerPoint screen in Outline view differs from the screen in Slide view in that the Outlining toolbar displays and the Drawing toolbar does not display. (See Figures 2-12 and 2-13 on the previous page to compare the differences.) The Outlining toolbar contains the following tools:

PROMOTE BUTTON   The **Promote (Indent less) button** (◀) moves the selected paragraph up one level in the outline hierarchy each time you click the button. Promoting a paragraph outdents or moves it to the left until you reach heading level one.

DEMOTE BUTTON   The **Demote (Indent more) button** (▶) moves the selected paragraph down one level in the outline hierarchy each time you click the button. Demoting a paragraph indents or moves it to the right. You can only demote down to the sixth heading level.

MOVE UP BUTTON   The **Move Up button** (▲) moves selected text up one paragraph at a time while maintaining its hierarchical outline level and text style. The selected text changes position with the paragraph located above it.

MOVE DOWN BUTTON   The **Move Down button** (▼) moves selected text down one paragraph at a time while maintaining its hierarchical outline level and text style. The selected text changes position with the paragraph located below it.

COLLAPSE SELECTION BUTTON   The **Collapse Selection button** (−) hides all heading levels except the slide title of the selected slide. The button is useful when you want to collapse one slide in your outline.

EXPAND SELECTION BUTTON   The **Expand Selection button** (+) displays all heading levels for the selected slide. The button is useful when you want to expand one slide in your outline.

SHOW TITLES BUTTON   The **Show Titles button** (▤) collapses all heading levels to show only the slide titles. This button is useful when you are looking at the organization of your presentation and do not care to see all the details.

SHOW ALL BUTTON   The **Show All button** (▤) expands all heading levels to display the slide title and text for all slides in the presentation.

SHOW FORMATTING BUTTON   The **Show Formatting button** (⅍) is a toggle that displays or hides the text attributes in Outline view. This button is useful when you want to work with plain text as opposed to working with bolded, italicized, or underlined text. When printing your outline, plain text often speeds up the printing process.

▶ CREATING A PRESENTATION IN OUTLINE VIEW

In Outline view, you can view title and body text, add and delete slides, rearrange slides or slide text by dragging and dropping, promote and demote text, save the presentation, print the outline or slides, copy and paste slides or text to and from other presentations, apply a template, and import an outline.

Developing a presentation in Outline view is quick because you type the text for all slides at one time. Once you type the outline, the presentation is fundamentally complete. If you choose, you can then go to Slide view to enhance your presentation with graphics.

Creating a Title Slide in Outline View

Recall from Project 1 that the title slide introduces the presentation to the audience. Additionally, Project 2 uses the title slide to capture the attention of the audience. The travels template enhances the presentation title by displaying an airplane at the top of the slide and a sailboat at the bottom of the slide. Perform the following steps to create a title slide in Outline view.

TO CREATE A TITLE SLIDE IN OUTLINE VIEW ▼

STEP 1 ▶

Type San Baarbo Vacations **and press the ENTER key.**

San Baarbo Vacations displays as the title for Slide 1 and is called heading level 1. A slide icon displays to the left of each slide title. In Outline view, the Zoom Control default setting is 33% of actual slide size. Pressing the ENTER key moves you to the next line and maintains the same heading level. Therefore, the insertion point is in position for typing the title for Slide 2 (Figure 2-14).

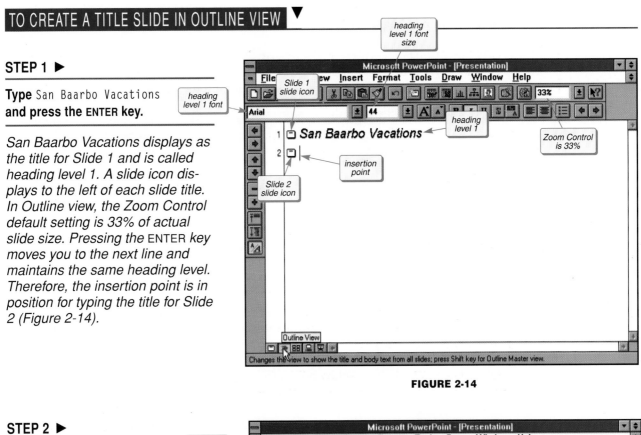

FIGURE 2-14

STEP 2 ▶

Point to the Demote (Indent more) button on the Outlining toolbar (Figure 2-15).

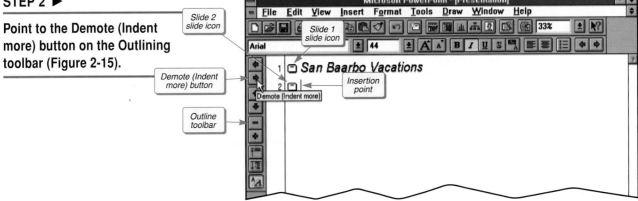

FIGURE 2-15

STEP 3 ▶

Click the Demote (Indent more) button.

The Slide 2 slide icon no longer displays (Figure 2-16). The insertion point is indented to the right and is now in position for typing the sub-title text. By default, heading level two is a sub-title on the title slide.

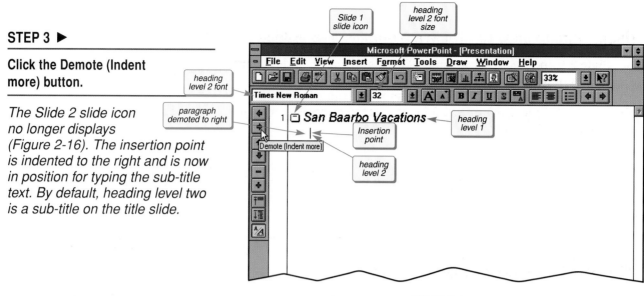

FIGURE 2-16

STEP 4 ▶

Type Presents... **and press the ENTER key. Then, type** Passport to the Caribbean

Slide 1 title text is heading level one and the sub-title text is heading level two (Figure 2-17).

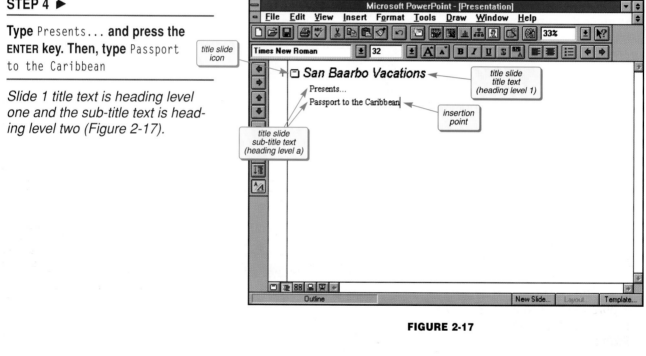

FIGURE 2-17

The title slide for Project 2 is complete. The following section explains how to add bulleted list slides in Outline view.

▶ ADDING BULLETED LIST SLIDES IN OUTLINE VIEW

R ecall that when you add a new slide, PowerPoint defaults to the Bulleted List slide layout. This is true in Outline view as well. Begin by typing your list of topics and then demoting each topic to the appropriate heading level. Each time you demote a paragraph, PowerPoint adds a bullet to the left of each heading level. Each heading level has a different bullet font.

Using Outline View to Create a Multiple Level Bulleted List Slide

Slide 2 is the first informational slide for Project 2. Slide 2 introduces the main topic: two new vacation packages offered by San Baarbo Vacations. Each vacation package displays as heading level two, and its supportive paragraph displays as heading level three. Perform the following steps to create a multiple level bulleted list slide in Outline view.

TO USE OUTLINE VIEW TO CREATE A MULTIPLE LEVEL BULLETED LIST SLIDE ▼

STEP 1 ►

Point to the Insert New Slide button (⬚) on the Standard toolbar (Figure 2-18).

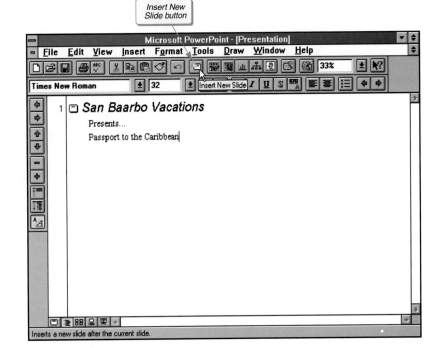

FIGURE 2-18

STEP 2 ►

Click the Insert New Slide button.

The Slide 2 slide icon displays (Figure 2-19). The insertion point is in position to type the title for Slide 2.

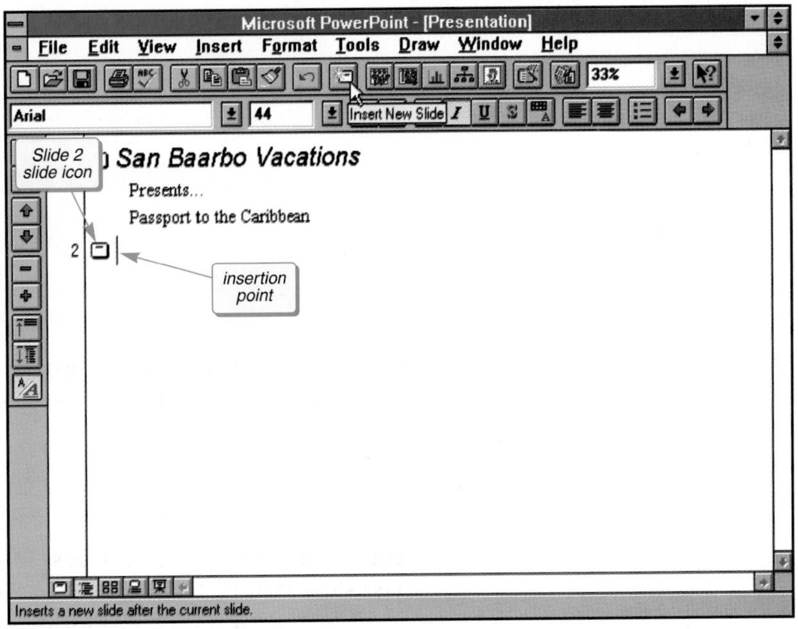

FIGURE 2-19

STEP 3 ▶

Type the title for Slide 2 San Baarbo Vacations Offers Two New Exciting Packages **and press the ENTER key. Then, click the Demote (Indent more) button on the Outlining toolbar to demote to heading level two.**

The title for Slide 2 displays and the insertion point is in position to type the first bulleted paragraph (Figure 2-20). A diamond-shaped bullet displays to the left of the insertion point.

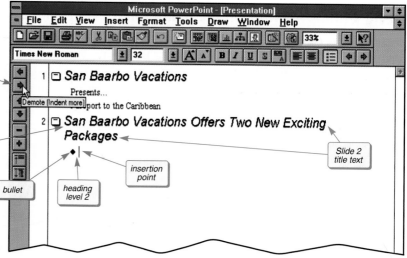

FIGURE 2-20

STEP 4 ▶

Type the first bulleted paragraph Seven day cruise of the Caribbean **and press the ENTER key. Then, click the Demote (Indent more) button on the Outlining toolbar to demote down to heading level three.**

Slide 2 displays three heading levels: the title on heading level one, the bulleted paragraph on heading level two, and the insertion point on heading level three (Figure 2-21). The bullet for heading level two is a diamond. The bullet for heading level three is a dash.

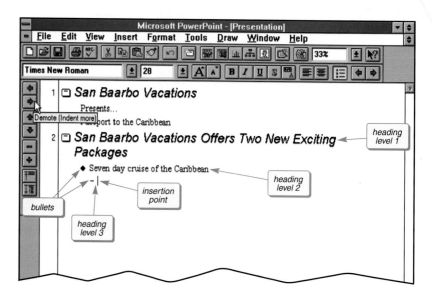

FIGURE 2-21

STEP 5 ▶

Type Seven days and six nights on the luxurious Island Queen **and press the ENTER key. Then, point to the Promote (Indent less) button on the Outlining toolbar.**

Pressing the ENTER key begins a new paragraph at the same heading level as the previous paragraph (Figure 2-22).

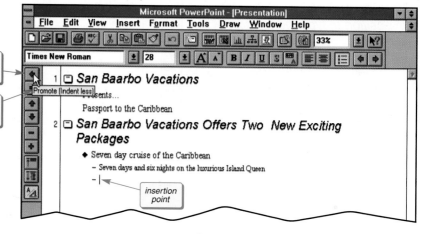

FIGURE 2-22

STEP 6 ▶

Click the Promote (Indent less) button to promote up to heading level two.

Clicking the Promote (Indent less) button moves the insertion point left and promotes the paragraph to heading level two (Figure 2-23).

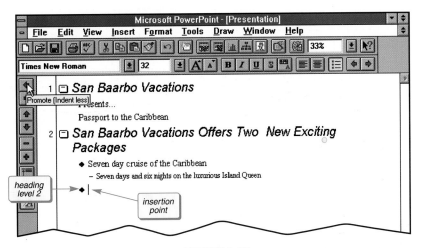

FIGURE 2-23

STEP 7 ▶

Type Special weekend flight **and press the ENTER key. Then, click the Demote (Indent more) button on the Outlining toolbar to demote down to heading level three (Figure 2-24).**

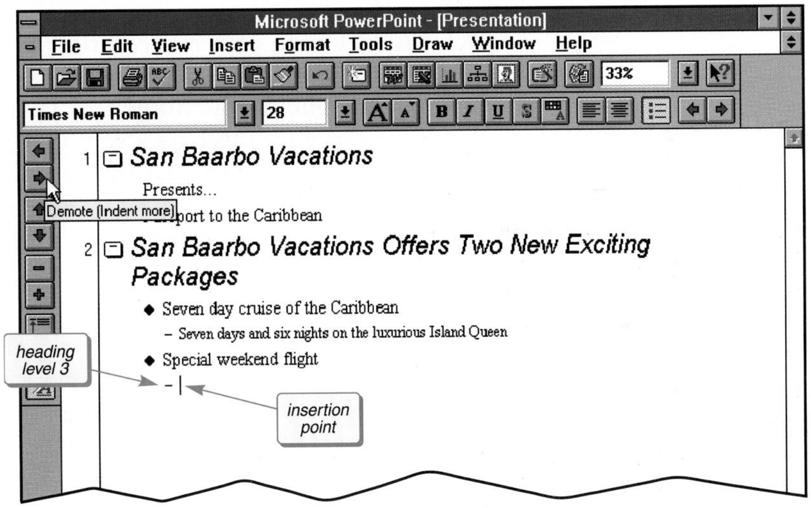

FIGURE 2-24

STEP 8 ▶

Type Three days and two nights in San Juan

Slide 2 is a multiple-level bulleted list. The title is heading level one. The major bulleted items are in heading level two. The minor bulleted items are in heading level three. The insertion point is positioned after the letter n in Juan (Figure 2-25).

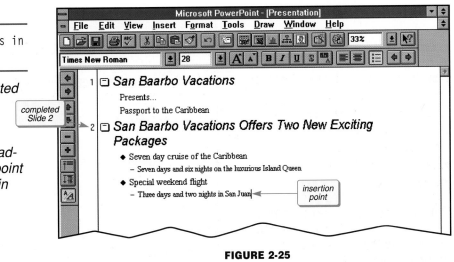

FIGURE 2-25

If your preference is to use the keyboard instead of the mouse when typing an outline, press the TAB key or the ALT+SHIFT+RIGHT ARROW keys to demote text and press the SHIFT+TAB keys or the ALT+SHIFT+LEFT ARROW keys to promote text.

When adding a new slide, click the Insert New Slide button on the Standard toolbar or the New Slide button on the status bar. If you are using the keyboard to add a new slide, press the CTRL+M keys. Still another way to add a new slide is to promote a new paragraph to heading level one. You do this by pressing the ENTER key after typing the last line of text on the current slide and then clicking the Promote (Indent less) button until the insertion point is at heading level one. A slide icon displays when you reach heading level one.

Finishing the Outline for Project 2

Now that you have the basics for creating slides in Outline view, follow the steps below to complete the outline for Project 2.

Creating the First Subordinate Slide

When developing your presentation, begin with a main topic and follow with subsequent slides to support the main topic. Placing all your information on one slide would overwhelm your audience. Therefore, decompose your presentation into several slides with three to seven bullets per slide. Perform the following steps to create the first slide that supports the main topic in Slide 2.

TO CREATE THE FIRST SUBORDINATE SLIDE

Step 1: Click the Insert New Slide button on the Standard toolbar to add a new slide.

Step 2: Type Seven Day Cruise of the Caribbean and press the ENTER key.

Step 3: Click the Demote (Indent more) button on the Outlining toolbar to demote to heading level two.

Step 4: Type Leave Miami on Sunday morning and press the ENTER key.

Step 5: Type Two day cruise to San Juan and press the ENTER key.

Step 6: Type Three days visiting ports of call and press the ENTER key.

Step 7: Type Two day cruise back to Miami

The screen displays, as shown in Figure 2-26.

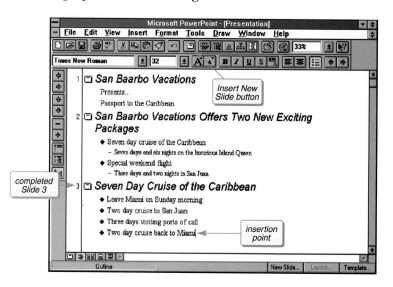

FIGURE 2-26

Creating the Second Subordinate Slide

The next step is to create the slide that supports the second bulleted item on Slide 2, Special Weekend Flight. Perform the following steps to create this subordinate slide.

TO CREATE THE SECOND SUBORDINATE SLIDE

Step 1: Click the Insert New Slide button on the Standard toolbar to add a new slide.

Step 2: Type Special Weekend Flight and press the ENTER key.

Step 3: Click the Demote (Indent more) button on the Outlining toolbar to demote to heading level two.

Step 4: Type Fly from Chicago on Friday and press the ENTER key.

Step 5: Click the Demote (Indent more) button on the Outlining toolbar to demote to heading level three.

Step 6: Type Packages from other major cities available and press the ENTER key.

Step 7: Click the Promote (Indent less) button on the Outlining toolbar to promote to heading level two.

Step 8: Type Spend two fun-filled days in San Juan and press the ENTER key.

Step 9: Click the Demote (Indent more) button on the Outlining toolbar to demote to heading level three.

Step 10: Type Sail, surf, swim, relax and press the ENTER key.

Step 11: Click the Promote (Indent less) button on the Outlining toolbar to promote to heading level two.

Step 12: Type Fly back on Sunday night

The screen displays, as shown in Figure 2-27.

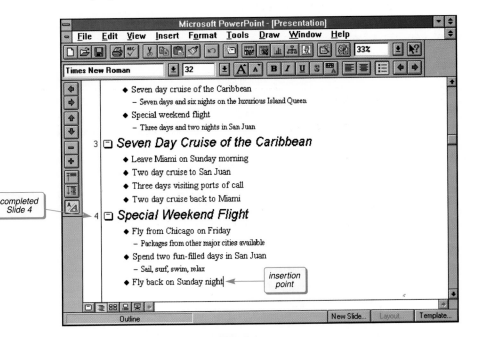

FIGURE 2-27

Saving the Presentation

Remember that it is wise to frequently save your presentation on disk. Because the outline is now complete, you should save your presentation now. For a detailed example of the steps summarized below, refer to pages PP24 through PP26 in Project 1.

TO SAVE A PRESENTATION

Step 1: Click the Save button on the Standard toolbar.
Step 2: Type proj2 in the File Name box. Do not press the ENTER key.
Step 3: Click the Drives drop-down box arrow and select the drive name a:.
Step 4: Choose the OK button from the Save As dialog box.
Step 5: Revise the information contained in the Summary Info dialog box and choose the OK button.

The presentation is saved to drive A: under the name PROJ2.PPT.

► CHANGING TO SLIDE VIEW

The outline for the San Baarbo Vacation presentation is complete. Outline view displays only text for each slide. Changing to Slide view allows you to display your slides as they appear in your presentation. After creating your presentation in Outline view, use Slide view to change to a slide layout more appropriate for your presentation. For example, you might want to change to a slide layout designed for displaying text and graphics. You must be in Slide view when you add objects to a slide. Perform the following steps to switch to Slide view.

TO CHANGE TO SLIDE VIEW ▼

STEP 1 ►

Point to the Slide 4 slide icon (▢).

The mouse pointer changes to a four-headed arrow (✛) when positioned over the slide icon in Outline view (Figure 2-28).

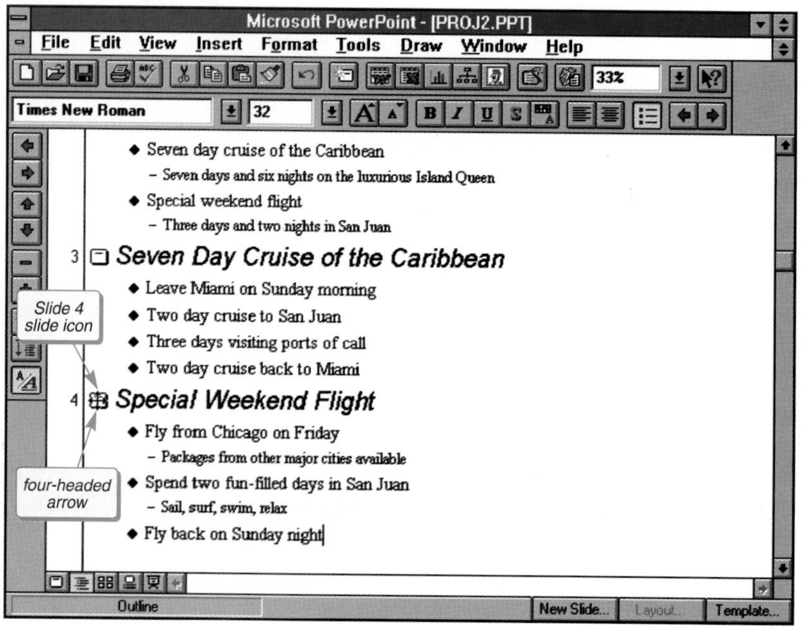

FIGURE 2-28

STEP 2 ▶

Double-click the slide icon for Slide 4.

Slide 4 displays in Slide view (Figure 2-29).

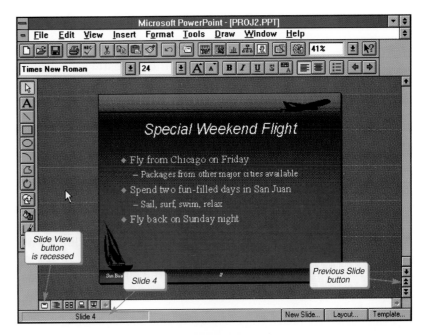

FIGURE 2-29

STEP 3 ▶

Click the Previous Slide button on the vertical scroll bar twice to display Slide 2.

Slide 2 displays in Slide view (Figure 2-30).

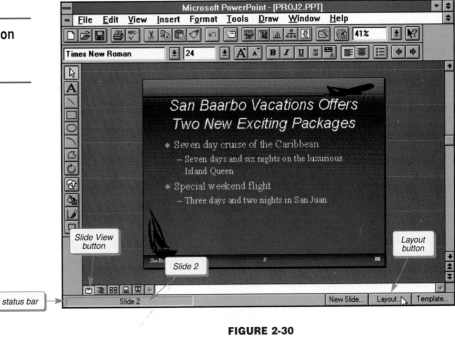

FIGURE 2-30

Recall that you could change to Slide view by clicking the Slide View button located at the lower left of the PowerPoint screen.

▶ ADDING CLIP ART TO A SLIDE

Clip art is a quick way to add professional-looking artwork to your presentation without creating the art yourself. There are over 1,000 graphic images in the PowerPoint **ClipArt Gallery**. PowerPoint combines topic-related clip art images into categories. PowerPoint stores these categories in the ClipArt Gallery. You include clip art in your presentation by selecting a clip art image from the ClipArt Gallery. Additionally, the ClipArt Gallery is shared among all Microsoft Office applications.

Table 2-1 gives you an idea of the organization of the ClipArt Gallery that accompanies PowerPoint. The table contains five of the filenames from the ClipArt Gallery and a description of the clip art contained in each file. You will be using clip art from the Transportation category and the Maps — International category. However, if PowerPoint was installed on your computer as a "typical" installation, these two categories will be missing. Contact your instructor if you are missing either clip art category when you perform the following steps. A full installation is required before all the clip art images are available for use.

▶ **TABLE 2-1**

CLIP ART CATEGORY	FILENAME	ART DESCRIPTION
Academic	ACADEMIC.PCS	46 slides, e.g., Professor, Girl Student, Boy Student.
Backgrounds	BACKGRND.PCS	58 scenic slides, e.g., Citiscape with Horizon, Mountain View, Road to Horizon.
Currency	CURRENCY.PCS	146 slides, e.g., Generic Stack of Coins, Generic Stack of Bills 1, Stack of Money.
Maps — International	INTLMAPS.PCS	180 maps, e.g., Africa, North America, Central America.
People	PEOPLE.PCS	111 artist drawings, e.g., Woman with Briefcase, Man with Briefcase, Man at Desk.
Sports & Leisure	SPORTS.PCS	41 sports symbols, e.g. Football & Goal Post, Golfer.

▶ ADDING CLIP ART OBJECTS TO YOUR PRESENTATION

The next step in creating your presentation is to add clip art to the slides. Recall that clip art is one type of object that may be added to a slide. PowerPoint makes it easy to add objects to a slide by providing several slide layouts with placeholders specifically designed for clip art and other objects (text, charts, tables, and graphs).

Changing Slide Layout

Recall from Project 1 that when you add a new slide, PowerPoint displays the AutoLayouts dialog box from which you choose one of the slide layouts. After creating a slide, you may change its layout by clicking the **Layout button** on the status bar. The Slide Layout dialog box then displays. Like the AutoLayout dialog box, the Slide Layout dialog box allows you to choose one of the twenty-one different slide layouts. As you create a presentation or as you edit an existing presentation, you may want to change the layout of a slide. With PowerPoint, you won't lose any text or graphics when you change to a new layout.

Using slide layouts eliminates the need to resize objects because PowerPoint automatically sizes the object to fit the placeholder. To keep your presentation interesting, PowerPoint includes several slide layouts to combine text with nontext objects such as clip art. The placement of the text, in relationship to the nontext object, depends on the slide layout. The nontext object placeholder may be to the right of the text, left of the text, above the text, or below the text. Additionally, some slide layouts are constructed with two nontext object placeholders. Refer to Project 1 for a list of the available slide layouts (Figure 1-40 on PP27). Perform the following steps to change the slide layout from a bulleted list to text over an object.

TO CHANGE SLIDE LAYOUT ▼

STEP 1

Point to the Layout button on the status bar (Figure 2-30 on page PP87).

STEP 2 ▶

Click the Layout button on the status bar and then point to the elevator on the Slide Layout vertical scroll bar.

The Slide Layout dialog box displays nine of the 21 available slide layouts (Figure 2-31). Bulleted List is selected because it is the current slide layout. Its name displays at the lower right of the Slide Layout dialog box.

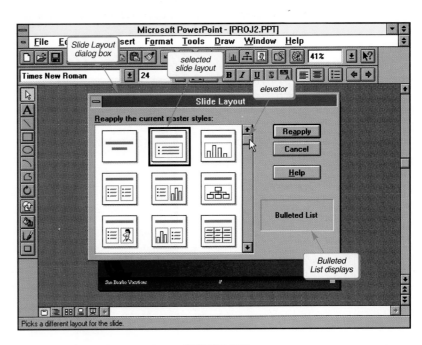

FIGURE 2-31

STEP 3 ▶

Drag the elevator to the bottom of the vertical scroll bar in the Slide Layout dialog box. Then, select the Text over Object slide layout (▦).

The Text over Object slide layout is selected (Figure 2-32). When you click a layout, its name displays in the text box at the lower right of the Slide Layout dialog box.

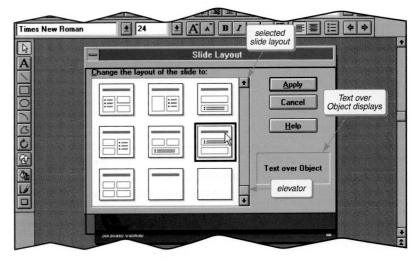

FIGURE 2-32

STEP 4 ▶

Point to the Apply button in the Slide Layout dialog box (Figure 2-33).

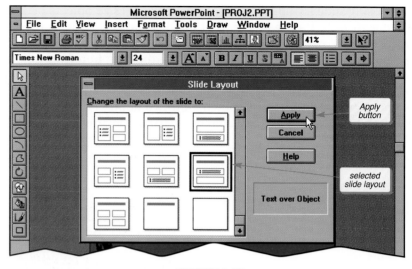

FIGURE 2-33

STEP 5 ▶

Choose the Apply button.

Slide 2 displays with an object placeholder at the bottom of the slide (Figure 2-34).

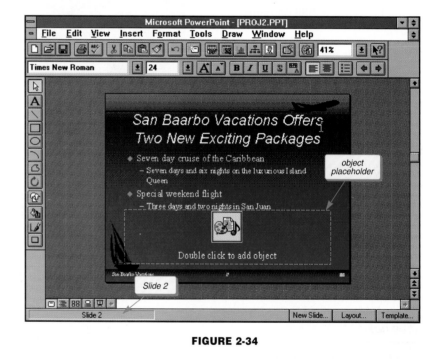

FIGURE 2-34

The object placeholder at the bottom of Slide 2 will hold a clip art image. The next section explains how to add clip art to your presentation.

Adding Clip Art

In a presentation, clip art serves a purpose — it conveys a message. It should not be used decoratively. Clip art should contribute to the understandability of the slide. Before adding clip art to a presentation, ask yourself: "Does the clip art convey or support the slide topic?" If the answer is no, do not put the clip art on the slide.

Perform the following steps to add the clip art map of Puerto Rico to Slide 2.

TO ADD CLIP ART ▼

STEP 1 ►

Point to the object placeholder at the bottom of Slide 2 (Figure 2-35).

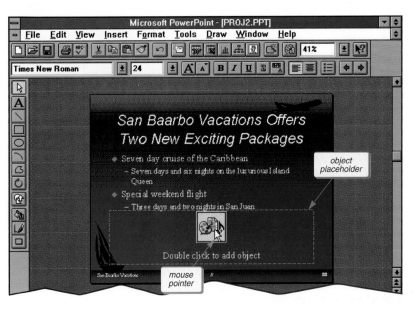

FIGURE 2-35

STEP 2 ►

Double-click the object placeholder. When the Insert Object dialog box displays, point to Microsoft ClipArt Gallery in the Object Type list box.

PowerPoint displays the Insert Object dialog box (Figure 2-36). The list of object types on your computer may look different from the one in the figure. The objects listed depend on the type of installation. If Microsoft ClipArt Gallery does not display, contact your instructor.

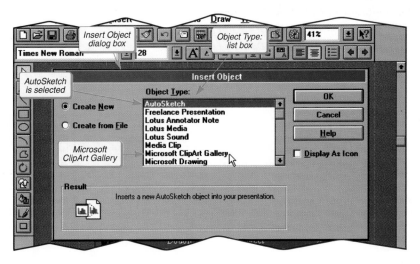

FIGURE 2-36

STEP 3 ►

Select Microsoft ClipArt Gallery. Then, point to the OK button.

Microsoft ClipArt Gallery is selected (Figure 2-37).

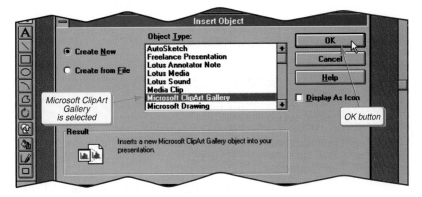

FIGURE 2-37

STEP 4 ▶

Choose the OK button. When the Microsoft ClipArt Gallery – Picture in PROJ2.PPT dialog box displays, point to the elevator in the Choose a category to view below list box.

The Microsoft ClipArt Gallery – Picture in PROJ2.PPT dialog box displays with a gallery of images (Figure 2-38). The selected image is a professor in the Academic category. Your selected image may be different, depending on the clip art installed on your computer. If this is the first time clip art has been accessed after an installation, the Microsoft ClipArt Gallery dialog box displays with a message asking if you would like to add clip art from PowerPoint now? Click the Yes button. PowerPoint will then display the Microsoft ClipArt Gallery – Picture in PROJ2.PPT dialog box.

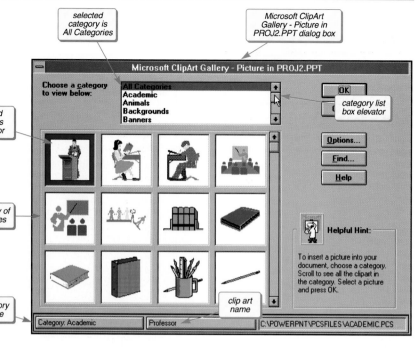

FIGURE 2-38

STEP 5 ▶

Drag the elevator until Maps – International displays. Then, point to the Maps – International clip art category (Figure 2-39).

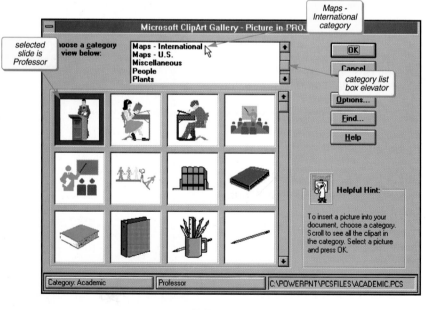

FIGURE 2-39

STEP 6 ▶

Select Maps – International and then point to the elevator in the gallery of images list box.

The selected category is Maps – International. The first image, Africa, is selected (Figure 2-40).

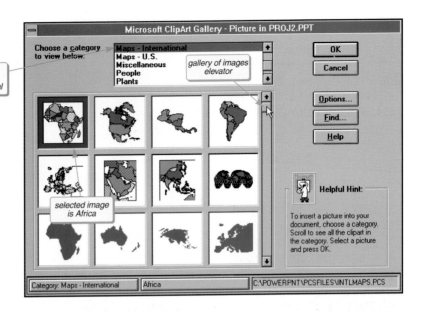

FIGURE 2-40

STEP 7 ▶

Drag the elevator down the vertical scroll bar until the map of Puerto Rico displays. Then, point to the map of Puerto Rico (Figure 2-41).

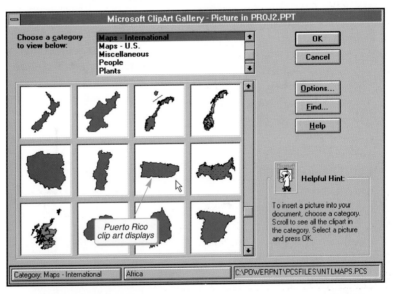

FIGURE 2-41

STEP 8 ▶

Select the map of Puerto Rico and then point to the OK button (Figure 2-42).

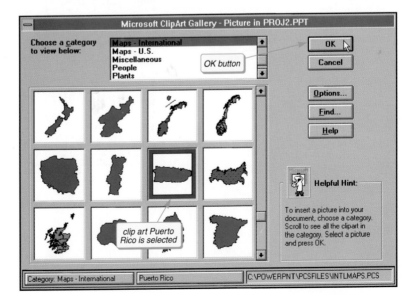

FIGURE 2-42

STEP 9 ▶

Choose the OK button.

Slide 2 displays with the map of Puerto Rico inserted in the object placeholder (Figure 2-43).

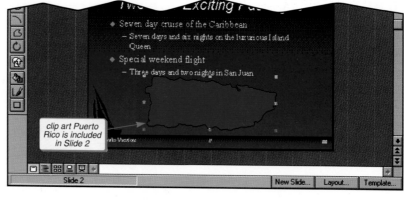

clip art Puerto Rico is included in Slide 2

FIGURE 2-43

PRESENTATION TIP

Use clip art in your presentation whenever appropriate to add power to the text. Through the use of clip art, misconceptions are reduced. If the presentation consists of words alone, the audience creates its own mental picture. The mental picture the audience creates may be different from the concept you are trying to convey. The audience will understand the concept better when clip art is included in the presentation.

▷ **TABLE 2-2**

FORMAT	FILE EXTENSION
AutoCAD Format 2-D	.dxf
AutoCAD Plot File	.adi
Compuserve GIF	.gif
Computer Graphics Metafile	.cgm
CorelDRAW!	.cdr
DrawPerfect	.wpg
Encapsulated PostScript	.eps
Hewlett-Packard Graphic Language	.hgl
Hewlett-Packard Plotter Print File	.plt
Kodak Photo CD	.pcd
Lotus 1-2-3 Graphics	.pic
Macintosh PICT	.pct
Micrografx Designer/Draw	.drw
PC Paintbrush	.pcx
Tagged Image Format	.tif
Targa	.tga
Windows Bitmaps	.dib, .bmp
Windows Device Independent Bitmap	.dib
Windows Metafile	.wmf

Besides the 1,000 graphic images in the PowerPoint ClipArt Gallery, there are additional sources for clip art, such as retailers specializing in computer software and bulletin board systems. A **bulletin board system** is a computer system that allows users to communicate with each other and share files. Additionally, you can include pictures into your presentation. These may include scanned photographs and line art, and artwork from compact disks. To insert a picture into a presentation, the picture must be saved in a format that PowerPoint can recognize. Table 2-2 identifies the formats PowerPoint recognizes.

Changing Text Size

Recall from Project 1 that you change text size by first selecting the text and then clicking the Font Size button until the font size you want displays. Perform the following steps to change text size.

TO CHANGE TEXT SIZE

Step 1: Select Seven days and six nights on the luxurious Island Queen by triple-clicking the paragraph.

Step 2: Click the Decrease Font Size button one time.

Step 3: Select Three days and two nights in San Juan by triple-clicking the paragraph.

Step 4: Click the Decrease Font Size button one time.

The decrease in font size on Slide 2 adds white space between the text and the clip art object (Figure 2-44).

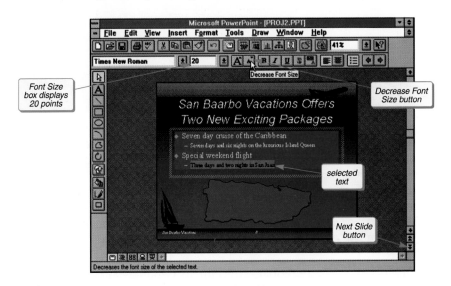

FIGURE 2-44

Changing Slide Layout for Slide 3

Recall that using a slide layout eliminates the need to resize objects because PowerPoint automatically sizes the object to fit the object placeholder. Slide 3 uses the Text & Clip Art slide layout (see Figure 2-45). Perform the following steps to change slide layout.

TO CHANGE SLIDE LAYOUT FOR SLIDE 3 ▼

STEP 1 ▶

Click the Next Slide button on the vertical scroll bar. Click the Layout button on the status bar. When the Slide Layout dialog box displays, select the Text & Clip Art slide layout (Figure 2-45).

FIGURE 2-45

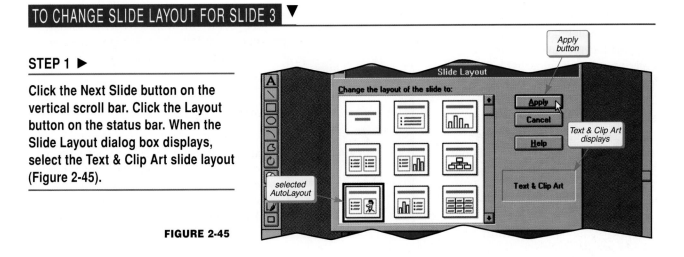

STEP 2 ▶

Choose the Apply button.

Slide 3 displays with a clip art placeholder at the right side of the slide (Figure 2-46).

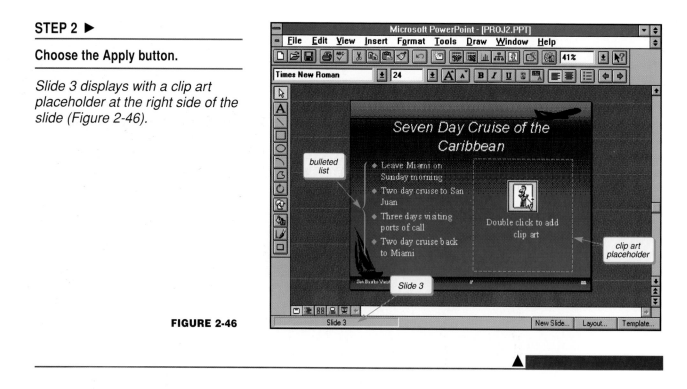

FIGURE 2-46

The next section explains how to add clip art to Slide 3.

Adding Clip Art to Slide 3

Slide 3 contains clip art of a sailboat. This clip art is called Sailboat and is located in the Transportation category. Perform the following steps to add clip art to Slide 3.

TO ADD CLIP ART TO SLIDE 3 ▼

STEP 1 ▶

Double-click the clip art placeholder at the right side of Slide 3. When the Microsoft ClipArt Gallery – Picture in PROJ2.PPT dialog box displays, drag the elevator in the Choose a category to view below list box until Transportation displays. Select the Transportation category. Drag the elevator down the vertical scroll bar in the gallery of images until the sailboat displays. Select the sailboat (Figure 2-47). Then, point to the OK button.

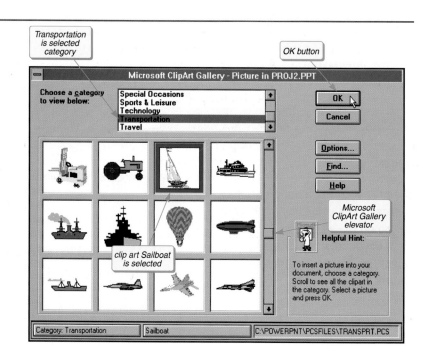

FIGURE 2-47

STEP 2 ▶

Choose the OK button.

Slide 3 displays with the sailboat inserted in the clip art placeholder (Figure 2-48).

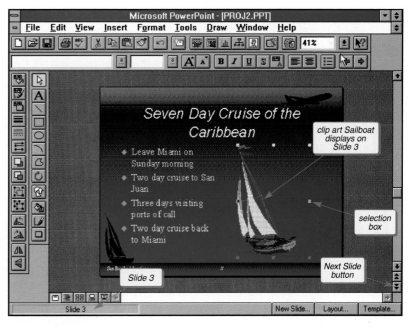

FIGURE 2-48

▶ USING THE AUTOSHAPES TOOLBAR

Y ou can use the PowerPoint drawing features to produce professional images and artwork for your presentation. In addition to the Drawing toolbar identified in Project 1, PowerPoint has two toolbars for adding graphics and visual support to your presentation: the AutoShapes and Drawing+ (pronounced as drawing plus) toolbars. The **AutoShapes toolbar** contains tools for drawing commonly used shapes, such as diamonds, stars, and triangles. The **Drawing+ toolbar** contains tools for modifying your graphics. For example, you could change the fill color of an object by selecting the Fill Color button (🔳) on the Drawing+ toolbar. **Fill color** is the interior color of an object.

You access the AutoShapes toolbar by clicking the AutoShapes button (🔳) on the Drawing toolbar. The AutoShapes toolbar displays twenty-four shapes. You draw a shape by clicking the button on the AutoShapes toolbar that represents the shape you wish to draw and positioning the cross-hair pointer (🔳) on the slide. Then, drag the shape until it takes on the proportions you want. Pressing and holding the SHIFT key when dragging the shape creates regular shapes. A **regular shape** is perfectly proportioned and can be inscribed within a square, such as a circle or a square. Holding the CTRL key when dragging the shape draws the shape outward from the center of the shape.

Accessing the AutoShapes Toolbar

To add a shape to your presentation, you must first access the AutoShapes toolbar. Perform the steps on the next page to access the AutoShapes toolbar.

TO ACCESS THE AUTOSHAPES TOOLBAR ▼

STEP 1 ▶

Click the Next Slide button on the vertical scroll bar and then point to the AutoShapes button on the Drawing toolbar.

Slide 4 displays (Figure 2-49).

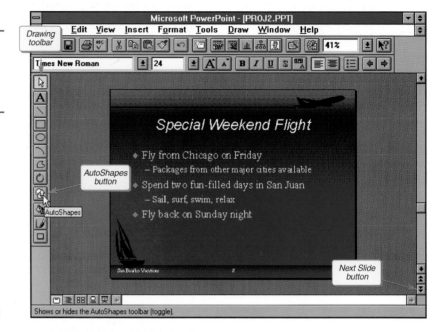

FIGURE 2-49

STEP 2 ▶

Click the AutoShapes button.

The AutoShapes toolbar displays in the PowerPoint window (Figure 2-50). The AutoShapes toolbar displays at the location it was positioned at during the last PowerPoint session.

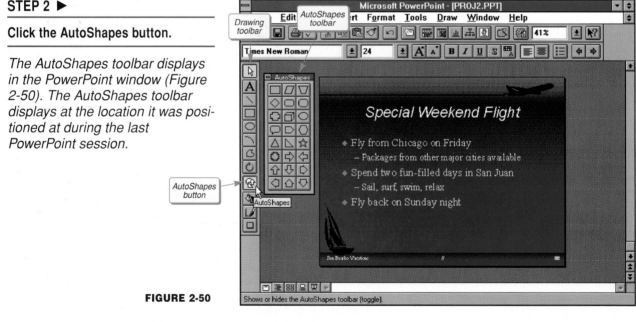

FIGURE 2-50

If the AutoShapes toolbar displays on top of your slide, you may want to move it out of your way. Move the AutoShapes toolbar by holding down the left mouse button on an open space on the toolbar (not a button) and then dragging the toolbar to another location on the PowerPoint window. When you drag the toolbar near the outer edges of the PowerPoint window, an outline of the AutoShapes toolbar displays. This outline indicates how the toolbar will display when you drop it in the new location.

Now that you have displayed the AutoShapes toolbar, you are ready to add the seal object to Slide 4. The seal object resembles a sunburst and is added to Slide 4 to persuade the audience to buy a vacation package by depicting the warm glow of the sun. Perform the following steps to add the seal object to Slide 4 using the Seal Tool button () from the AutoShapes toolbar.

TO ADD THE SEAL OBJECT TO SLIDE 4 ▼

STEP 1 ►

Click the Seal Tool on the AutoShapes toolbar (Figure 2-51).

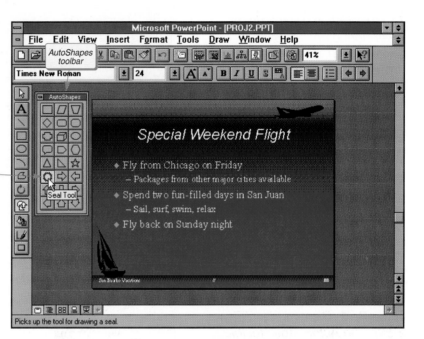

FIGURE 2-51

STEP 2 ►

Position the cross-hair pointer below the letter S in San Juan and to the right of the word relax in the paragraph Sail, surf, swim, relax (Figure 2-52).

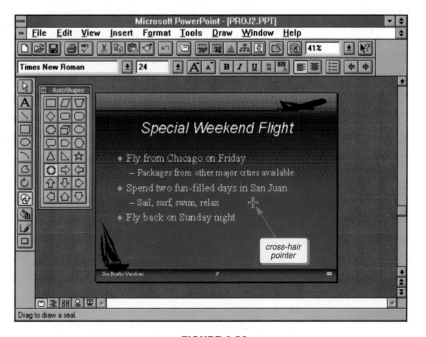

FIGURE 2-52

STEP 3 ▶

Press the left mouse button and drag diagonally down and to the right until the cross-hair pointer almost touches the horizon in the travels template. Drop the seal object by releasing the left mouse button.

The seal object displays in the lower right corner of Slide 4 (Figure 2-53). When you release the left mouse button, the cross-hair pointer becomes a two-headed arrow. Eight resize handles display around the seal object. Dragging a resize handle controls the size of the shape.

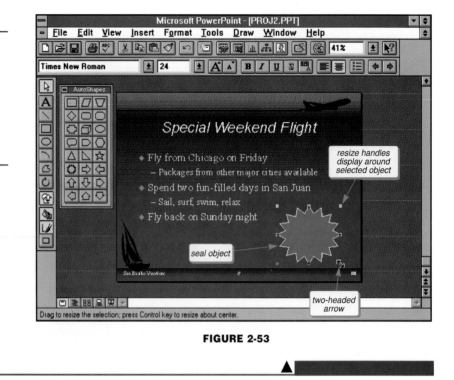

FIGURE 2-53

The two-headed pointer shows the direction in which you can resize the object. When you drag the resize handle, the two-headed arrow changes to a cross-hair pointer.

▶ ADDING TEXT TO AN OBJECT

Shapes drawn with the AutoShapes tools are objects. You can add text to any closed object drawn with the AutoShapes tools, such as rectangles, circles, and triangles. After drawing an object, just start typing. PowerPoint automatically centers your text in the object. As long as you add text immediately after drawing the object, you don't need to select it again, because it is already selected.

Adding text to an object is done for two reasons. Sometimes you add text for the purpose of labeling an object. For example, if you used PowerPoint to draw a floor plan, you could label each object simply by selecting it and typing its name. Other times, you place text inside the object to add drama to the presentation, as in Slide 4. Perform the following steps to add text to the seal object on Slide 4.

TO ADD TEXT TO AN OBJECT ▼

STEP 1

If the seal object is not selected, select it by clicking it.

STEP 2 ▶

Type Fun in the Sun

The text is centered in the seal object, as shown in Figure 2-54. A selection box displays when text is typed.

FIGURE 2-54

▲

Now that you have added text to the seal object, you will change the color of the text to yellow. The next section explains how to change text color.

▶ CHANGING TEXT COLOR

U sing color in a presentation can have dramatic effects. Recall that people perceive colors as warm or cool. For instance, red and yellow convey a feeling of warmth, while blue and white project a feeling of coolness. Additionally, warm colors seem to reach toward the audience while cool colors seem to pull away from the audience. Changing the color of the text changes the way the audience feels about the subject matter. Because this is a sales presentation and you are trying to create an emotional response, you want the audience to crave a warm, sunny vacation. In the following steps, you will use the Text Color button (▦) to change the color of the text within the seal object from a cool white to a warm yellow.

TO CHANGE TEXT COLOR ▼

STEP 1 ▶

Select the text in the seal object by triple-clicking it or dragging the I-beam pointer through it (Figure 2-55).

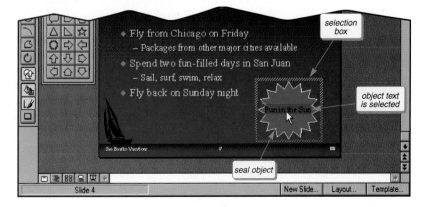

FIGURE 2-55

STEP 2 ▶

Point to the Text Color button on the
Formatting toolbar (Figure
2-56).

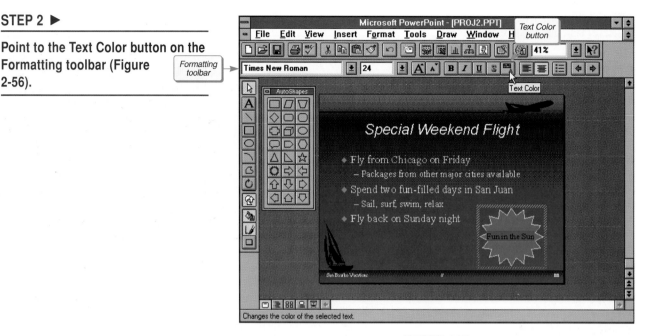

FIGURE 2-56

STEP 3 ▶

Click the Text Color button. When
the Text Color drop-down list box
displays, point to the Other Color
command.

*The Text Color drop-down list box
displays (Figure 2-57). White is the
current text color and is designated by the heavy black line surrounding the color sample.*

FIGURE 2-57

STEP 4 ▶

Click the Other Color command.
When the Other Color dialog box
displays, point to the yellow color
sample in the Color Palette area.
Yellow is in row 1, column 5.

*The Other Color dialog box dis-
plays the Color Palette (Figure
2-58). The current text color, white,
displays in the preview box in the
Other Color dialog box.*

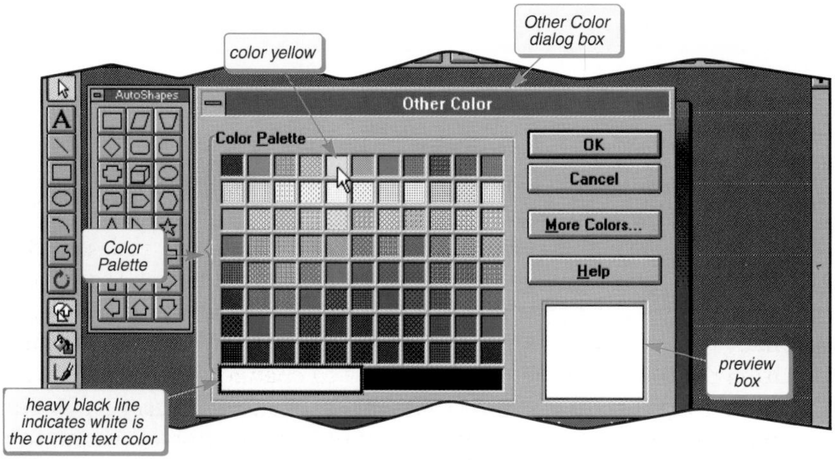

FIGURE 2-58

STEP 5 ▶

Click the yellow color sample and then point to the OK button.

The yellow color sample is selected and yellow displays in the preview box in the Other Color dialog box (Figure 2-59).

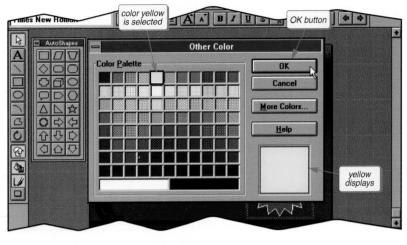

FIGURE 2-59

STEP 6 ▶

Choose the OK button.

The text in the seal object is yellow but does not display as such because the text is still highlighted (Figure 2-60).

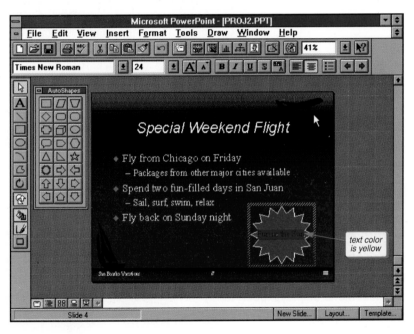

FIGURE 2-60

▶ CHANGING THE FILL COLOR OF THE SEAL OBJECT

When Slide 4 is complete, the seal object will be red. Recall from Project 1 that you want light colors on a dark background or dark colors on a light background. Because the text in the seal object is yellow, you will want to change the fill color of the seal. Additionally, you want to sell the audience a vacation to sunny San Juan. A quick way to change the fill color is to click the Fill Color button on the Drawing+ toolbar. But first, you must display the Drawing+ toolbar. The next section explains how to use the shortcut menu to display and manipulate the Drawing+ toolbar.

Shortcut Menus

In PowerPoint, the use of shortcut menus is limited. A **shortcut menu** is a menu containing frequently used PowerPoint commands. To display a toolbar shortcut menu, point to one of the toolbars and press the right mouse button. To display an editing or formatting shortcut menu, point to an object on a slide and press the right mouse button. This section discusses using the shortcut menu to work with the toolbars.

Occasionally, you may want to override a color that was determined by the default attributes of the template. You accomplish this using the Fill command. The Fill command is found on the Drawing+ toolbar as a button called Fill Color. You can quickly display the Drawing+ toolbar by using a shortcut menu. When pointing to any toolbar, press the right mouse button. The shortcut menu displays the names of the available PowerPoint toolbars. A check mark in front of the toolbar name indicates it is selected to display in the PowerPoint window. You select the toolbar by clicking on the toolbar name. The check mark displays in front of the toolbar name. You also deselect the toolbar by clicking on the toolbar name. However, when you deselect the toolbar, the check mark no longer displays in front of the name.

Two additional commands display in the shortcut menu: Toolbars and Customize. The Toolbars command displays the Toolbars dialog box, where you can select the toolbars to display on the PowerPoint window. The Customize command displays the Customize Toolbars dialog box, where you can add or delete buttons on a toolbar.

Perform the following steps to display the Drawing+ toolbar using a shortcut menu. If the Drawing+ toolbar is already displaying on your PowerPoint window (as shown in Figure 2-62), read the next two steps and proceed to the next section: Changing the Fill Color of the Seal Object.

TO DISPLAY THE DRAWING+ TOOLBAR ▼

STEP 1 ▶

Point to one of the toolbars and click the right mouse button. When the shortcut menu displays, point to Drawing+.

The shortcut menu displays (Figure 2-61). The shortcut menu displays at the location of the mouse pointer when you clicked the right mouse button. Therefore, your screen may look different from the one in Figure 2-61. A check mark displays in front of the toolbars currently selected to display on the PowerPoint window. The Drawing+ toolbar does not presently have a check mark. (If there is a check mark in front of the Drawing+ toolbar, press the ESC key to exit from the shortcut menu and proceed to Step 3.)

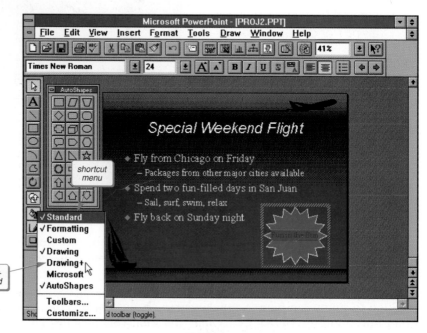

FIGURE 2-61

STEP 2 ▶

Click Drawing+ in the shortcut menu. Then, point to the Control-menu box on the AutoShapes toolbar.

The Drawing+ toolbar displays (Figure 2-62). (You will close the AutoShapes toolbar because it is no longer needed for this project and to reduce clutter on the PowerPoint window.)

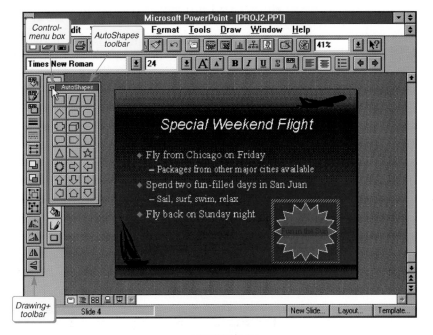

FIGURE 2-62

STEP 3 ▶

Double-click the Control-menu box to close the AutoShapes toolbar.

The AutoShapes toolbar no longer displays in the PowerPoint window (Figure 2-63). In addition to the Standard and Formatting toolbars, the Drawing+ and Drawing tool-bars display in the PowerPoint window. The location of your tool-bars is not important because you can drag them to a different loca-tion in the PowerPoint window.

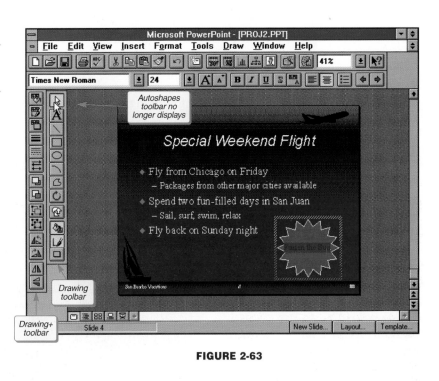

FIGURE 2-63

Instead of closing the AutoShapes toolbar, you could drag it to a new location. If, for example, you drag it to the top of the PowerPoint window, it would display horizontally like the Standard toolbar or the Formatting toolbar.

Changing the Fill Color of the Seal Object

Now that the Drawing+ toolbar displays in the PowerPoint window, you are ready to change the color of the seal object. You click the Fill Color button on the Drawing+ toolbar to display a drop-down box containing eight color samples and five commands. The eight color samples are the eight colors used in the color scheme for the current template. The five commands in the Fill Color drop-down box are described in Table 2-3.

▸ **TABLE 2-3**

COMMAND	DESCRIPTION
No Fill	Object is not filled, it is transparent.
Background	Fill color displays background color of the slide. Background color is determined by the template.
Shaded	Shaded creates a three-dimensional effect. There are six styles of shades: vertical, horizontal, diagonal right, diagonal left, from corner, from center.
Pattern	Displays Pattern Fill dialog box with 36 pattern styles. Two colors combine to create a pattern. Color can be assigned to the background and to the foreground of the pattern.
Other Color	Displays Color Palette of 90 color samples.

Fill color can be one solid color, two-color patterns, or shaded colors. A color-filled object is **opaque**, meaning that any objects behind the color-filled object would not display. An object with no fill is **transparent**, meaning that objects behind it would display.

Perform the following steps to change the fill color of the seal object to red.

TO CHANGE THE FILL COLOR OF THE SEAL OBJECT ▼

STEP 1 ▶

If the seal object is not selected, select it by clicking it. Then, point to the Fill Color button on the Drawing+ toolbar (Figure 2-64).

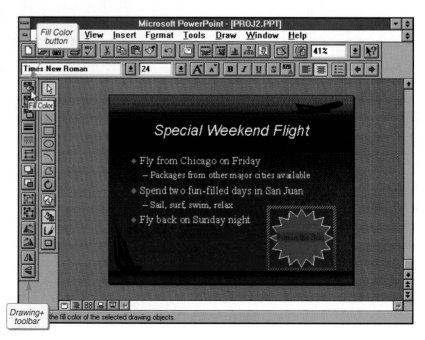

FIGURE 2-64

STEP 2 ▶

Click the Fill Color button. When the Fill Color drop-down box displays, point to the Other Color command.

The Fill Color drop-down box displays color samples and five commands (Figure 2-65). The current fill color is a two-color mix of purple and red, designated by the black border around the color sample. The color samples change each time you select a new color.

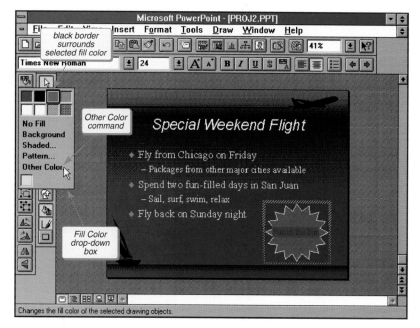

FIGURE 2-65

STEP 3 ▶

Click the Other Color command. When the Other Color dialog box displays, point to the red color sample in the Color Palette. Red is in row 1, column 2.

The Color Palette displays 90 color samples (Figure 2-66). The current fill color displays in the preview box in the Other Color dialog box.

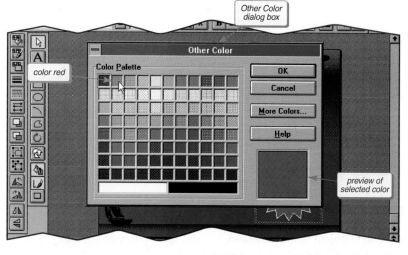

FIGURE 2-66

STEP 4 ▶

Click the red color sample and then point to the OK button.

The preview box displays the selected fill color (Figure 2-67). A black border surrounds the red color sample, which indicates it is the selected fill color.

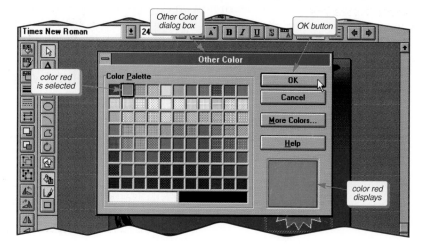

FIGURE 2-67

STEP 5 ▶

Choose the OK button. When Slide 4
displays, click outside the seal
object to deselect it.

*The seal object fill color is red and
the text is yellow (Figure 2-68).*

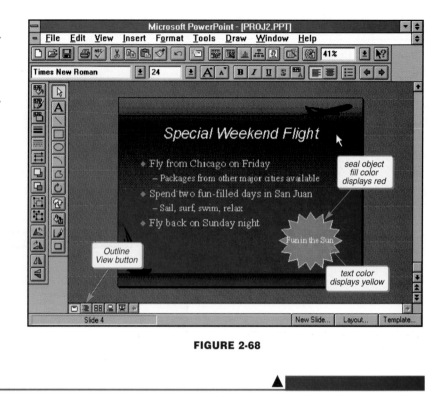

FIGURE 2-68

As an alternative to selecting a color sample and choosing the OK button,
double-click the color sample. PowerPoint returns to the slide and displays the
new fill color in the object.

Project 2 is complete and you should save the presentation again by clicking
the Save button on the Standard toolbar.

▶ EDITING THE PRESENTATION

N ow that Project 2 is complete, you will want to review it for content and
presentation flow. If you find that your slides need to be in a different
sequence, you can easily change the slide order by dragging the slide to
its new position. You can change slide order in either Outline view or Slide Sorter
view. The next sections explain several editing features of PowerPoint. First, you
will learn how to change slide order in Outline view and then in Slide Sorter view.
You will also learn how to copy a slide and paste it into the presentation. Finally,
you will learn how to use the Undo button to reverse the last edit action.

Changing Slide Order in Outline View

In Outline view, you move the slide to its new location by dragging the slide
icon until the placement indicator displays. In Outline view, the placement indicator is a horizontal line that identifies the new position of the slide. Perform the following steps to change slide order in Outline view.

TO CHANGE SLIDE ORDER IN OUTLINE VIEW ▼

STEP 1 ▶

Click the Outline View button located at the bottom of the PowerPoint screen. When Outline view displays, position the mouse pointer over the slide icon for Slide 4.

The outline for Project 2 displays (Figure 2-69). Slide 4 is high-lighted because it was the current slide in Slide view. Slides contain-ing graphics display with graphic symbols in the slide icon. The pointer becomes a four-headed arrow when positioned over the slide icon.

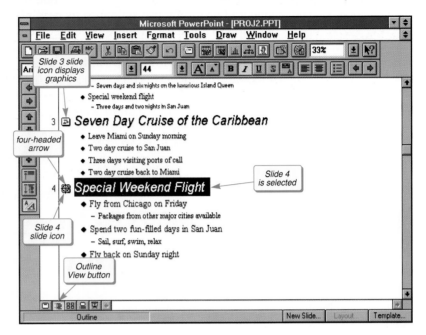

FIGURE 2-69

STEP 2 ▶

Press the left mouse button and drag the slide icon until the horizontal placement indicator displays below the paragraph, Three days and two nights in San Juan and above the paragraph Seven Day Cruise of the Caribbean. Then, drop Slide 4 above the Slide 3 slide icon by releasing the left mouse button.

Slide 4 and Slide 3 exchange posi-tions in the presentation outline (Figure 2-70). PowerPoint auto-matically renumbers the slides.

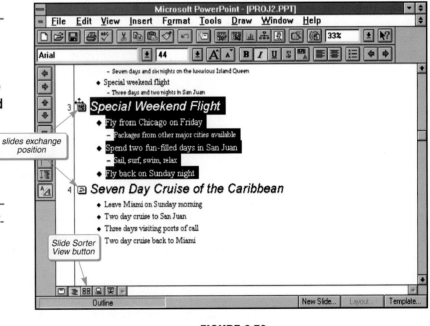

FIGURE 2-70

As you dragged the slide icon, a horizontal placement indicator displayed as soon as you moved off the slide. The placement indicator is useful for identifying the exact location to drop the slide when changing slide order in Outline view.

Changing Slide Order in Slide Sorter View

As previously stated, changing slide order in Slide Sorter view is simply dragging and dropping the slide into its new position. When you drag a slide to a new location in Slide Sorter view, the placement indicator displays to indicate where the slide will be positioned. In Slide Sorter view the **placement indicator** is a vertical dotted line with arrows at the top and bottom. The mouse pointer displays as a miniature slide icon (⬚) as soon as you drag the slide. You move the slide to its new location by dragging the miniature slide icon pointer until the placement indicator displays at the location where you want to insert the slide. Because you cannot drop the slide on top of another slide in Slide Sorter view, the placement indicator appears to jump in front of a slide or after a slide as the miniature slide icon pointer moves around the window. Perform the steps below to change slide order in Slide Sorter view.

TO CHANGE SLIDE ORDER IN SLIDE SORTER VIEW ▼

STEP 1 ▶

Click the Slide Sorter View button located at the bottom of the PowerPoint screen and point to Slide 3.

Project 2 displays in Slide Sorter view (Figure 2-71). Slide 3 is highlighted because it was the current slide in Outline view. PowerPoint assigns a number to each slide.

FIGURE 2-71

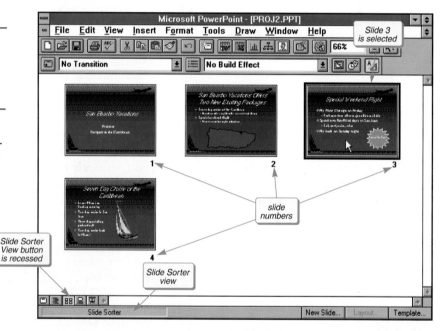

STEP 2 ▶

Press the left mouse button and drag Slide 3 down until the placement indicator displays after Slide 4 (Figure 2-72).

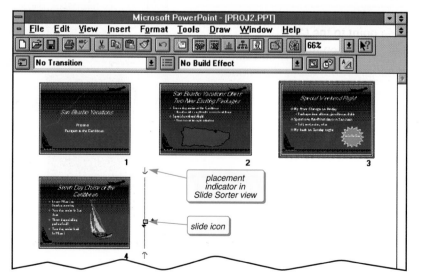

FIGURE 2-72

STEP 3 ▶

Release the left mouse button to drop Slide 3 after Slide 4.

Slide 4 and Slide 3 exchange positions (Figure 2-73). PowerPoint automatically renumbers the slides.

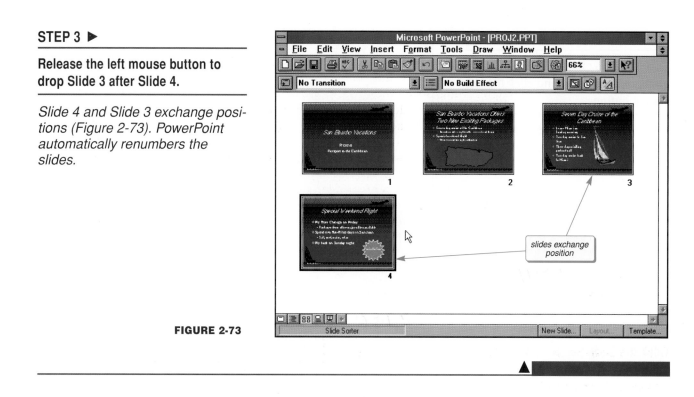

FIGURE 2-73

Copying a Slide

Occasionally you will want to copy a slide and then make changes to it. PowerPoint has a Copy command that allows you to quickly duplicate a slide or any object on a slide. After you make a copy, you will paste it someplace in your presentation. The next section explains how to copy and paste a slide in Slide Sorter view.

TO COPY AND PASTE A SLIDE IN SLIDE SORTER VIEW ▼

STEP 1 ▶

Click Slide 2 to select it and then point to the Copy button ( ) on the Standard toolbar (Figure 2-74).

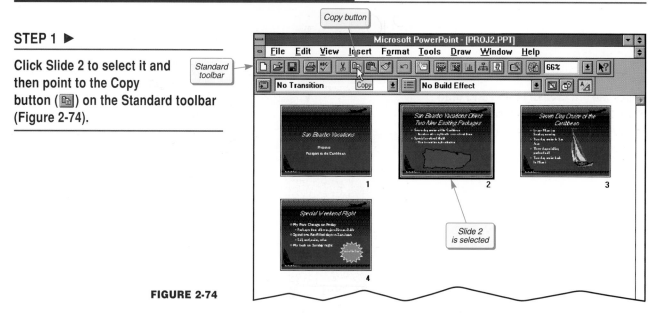

FIGURE 2-74

STEP 2 ▶

Click the Copy button and then point to the left of Slide 4 and click the left mouse button.

The insertion point displays in front of Slide 4 (Figure 2-75).

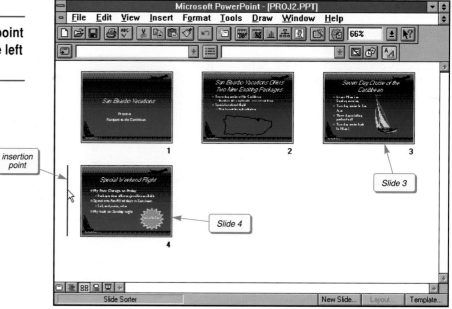

FIGURE 2-75

STEP 3 ▶

Point to the Paste button (📋) on the Standard toolbar (Figure 2-76).

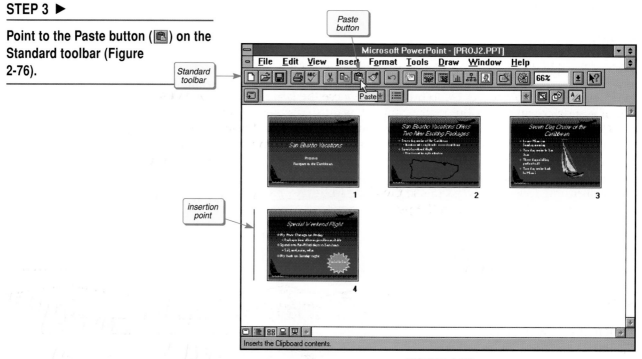

FIGURE 2-76

STEP 4 ►

Click the Paste button.

A copy of Slide 2 displays as Slide 4 and the former Slide 4 displays as Slide 5 (Figure 2-77).

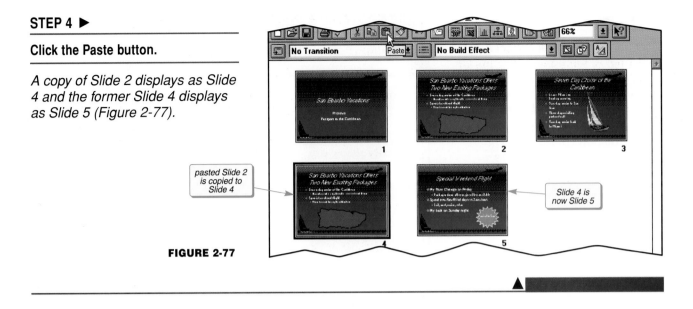

pasted Slide 2 is copied to Slide 4

Slide 4 is now Slide 5

FIGURE 2-77

An alternative to clicking the Copy and Paste buttons is to use the edit shortcut menu. To access the edit shortcut menu, point to the slide you wish to copy and click the right mouse button. When the edit shortcut menu displays, choose the Copy command. To paste a slide into the presentation, point to the location at which you wish to insert. Then, click the right mouse button and choose the Paste command.

Using the Undo Button to Reverse the Last Edit

PowerPoint provides an Undo button to reverse the last edit task. For example, if you delete an object but realize you still want to display it, you could click the Undo button and the object would again display. However, PowerPoint only stores the last edit in a buffer. A **buffer** is an area used to temporarily store data. As soon as you perform another edit task, the new task replaces the previous task stored in the Undo buffer.

Peform the following steps to use the Undo button to reverse the pasting of the copy of Slide 2 performed in the previous step.

TO USE THE UNDO BUTTON TO REVERSE THE LAST EDIT ▼

STEP 1 ►

Point to the Undo button on the Standard toolbar (Figure 2-78).

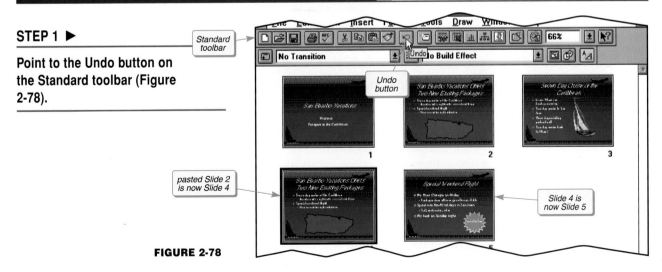

Standard toolbar

Undo button

pasted Slide 2 is now Slide 4

Slide 4 is now Slide 5

FIGURE 2-78

STEP 2 ▶

Click the Undo button.

The copy of Slide 2 pasted between Slide 3 and Slide 4 is gone (Figure 2-79). The insertion point displays where the slide previously displayed. PowerPoint automatically renumbers the slides.

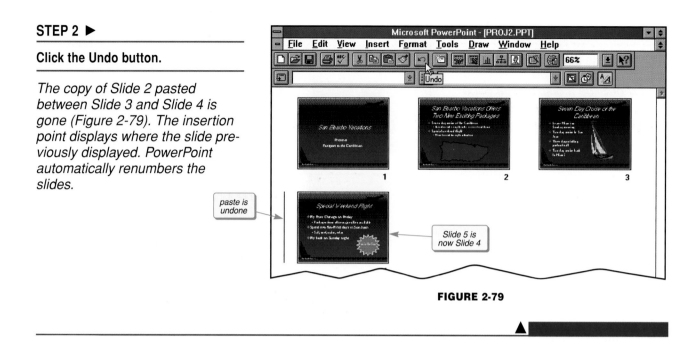

FIGURE 2-79

An added bonus to the Undo button is that because clicking the Undo button reverses or undoes your last action, you can return the presentation to the state it was in prior to clicking the Undo button the first time, by clicking the Undo button again.

The previous section on editing your presentation will save you time and effort when developing large presentations. Besides using the buttons on the toolbars, you can use a shortcut menu to cut, copy, or paste objects or slides. To use the shortcut menu, select the object or slide and then click the right mouse button. The shortcut menu displays. If you prefer to use PowerPoint menus, select the object on the slide, select the Edit menu from the menu bar, and then choose the edit command you want to use.

Checking Spelling and Saving Again

The presentation is now complete and should be checked for spelling errors. Check for spelling errors by clicking the Spelling button on the Standard toolbar.

If you made any changes to your presentation since your last save, you should save it again as PROJ2 using the Save button on the Standard toolbar.

▶ PRINTING THE PRESENTATION OUTLINE

During development of a lengthy presentation, it is often easier to review your outline in print rather than on-screen. Printing your outline is also useful for handouts or to review your subject matter prior to full development of your presentation.

Recall that the Print dialog box displays print options. When you wish to print your outline, specify Outline view in the Print What list box located in the Print dialog box. The outline prints **as last viewed** in Outline view. This means that you must select the Zoom Control to display the text the way in which you wish to print. Therefore, if you are uncertain of the Zoom Control setting, you should return to Outline view prior to printing your outline to review it. You may select the Print command from the File menu while in any view except Slide Show view. Perform the following steps to print your outline.

TO PRINT THE PRESENTATION OUTLINE ▼

STEP 1 ▶

Ready the printer according to the printer instructions. Select the File menu and choose the Print command. When the Print dialog box displays, point to the arrow on the Print What drop-down list box.

PowerPoint displays the Print dialog box (Figure 2-80).

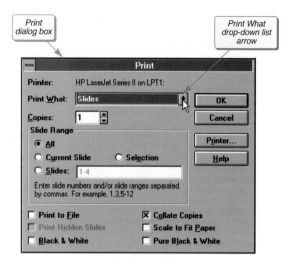

FIGURE 2-80

STEP 2 ▶

Click the left mouse button and point to Outline View.

A list of print options displays (Figure 2-81).

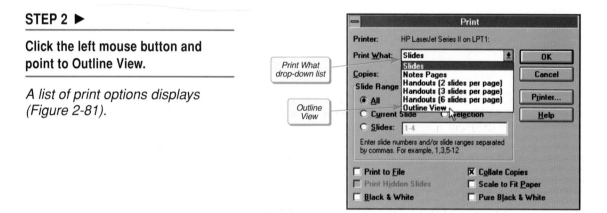

FIGURE 2-81

STEP 3 ▶

Select Outline View and point to the OK button (Figure 2-82).

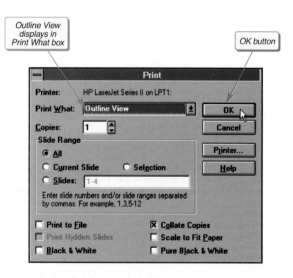

FIGURE 2-82

STEP 4 ▶

Choose the OK button.

The mouse pointer momentarily displays as an hourglass and PowerPoint displays the Print Status dialog box (Figure 2-83). The presentation outline begins printing on the printer.

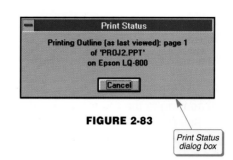

FIGURE 2-83

Print Status dialog box

STEP 5 ▶

When the printer stops, retrieve the printout (Figure 2-84).

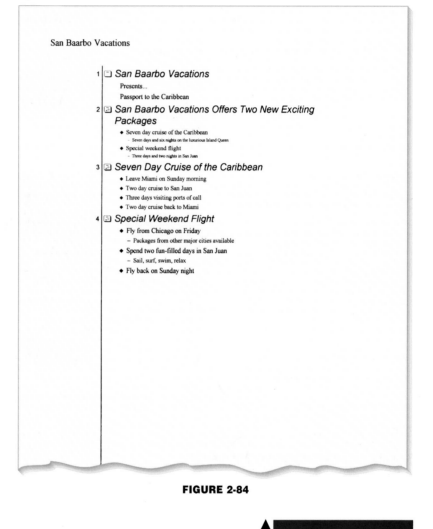

FIGURE 2-84

▶ PRINTING PRESENTATION SLIDES

Once you create a presentation, you may either print it or display it on your computer. After correcting errors, you will want to print the final copy of your presentation. If you made any changes to your presentation since your last save, be sure to save your presentation before you print.

Perform the following steps to print the presentation slides.

TO PRINT PRESENTATION SLIDES

Step 1: Ready the printer according to the printer instructions.
Step 2: From the File menu, choose the Print command.
Step 3: Click the Print What drop-down list box arrow and select Slides.
Step 4: Choose the Pure Black & White check box if printing on a noncolor printer.
Step 5: Choose the OK button in the Print dialog box.
Step 6: When the printer stops, retrieve the printout.

Your printout should look like the slides in Figures 2-85a through 2-85d.

The Print What drop-down list contains choices for printing two, three, or six slide images per page. These are labeled as Handouts [2 slides per page], Handouts [3 slides per page], and Handouts [6 slides per page]. Handouts are useful for reviewing a presentation because several slides are printed on one page. Many businesses distribute handouts before a presentation so the attendees have a hardcopy for reference.

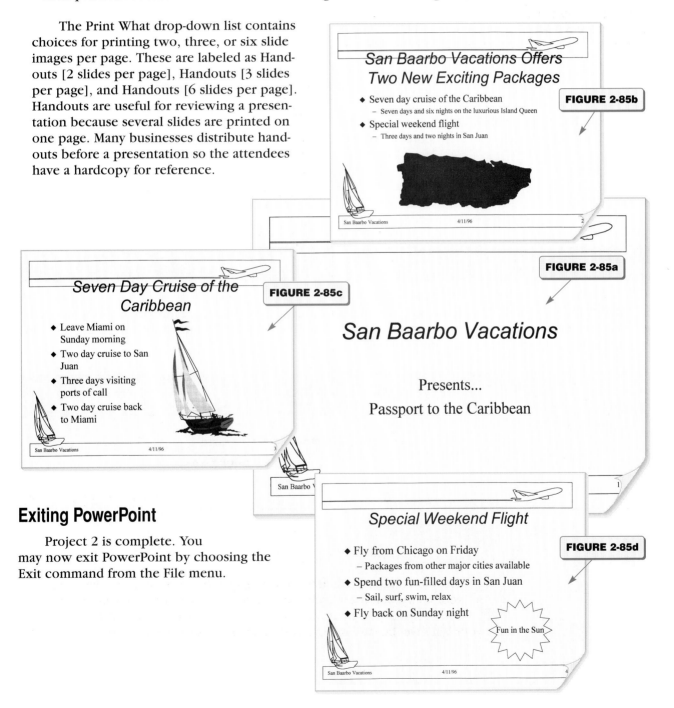

Exiting PowerPoint

Project 2 is complete. You may now exit PowerPoint by choosing the Exit command from the File menu.

▶ PROJECT SUMMARY

Project 2 introduced you to Outline view and clip art. You created a slide presentation in Outline view, where you entered all your text in the form of an outline. You arranged the text using the Promote (Indent less) and Demote (Indent more) buttons. Once your outline was complete, you changed slide layouts and added clip art. You added the seal object from the AutoShapes toolbar and then added text. You modified the text in the seal object by changing its color. You also learned how to change the fill color of an object. You edited a presentation by rearranging slide order, copying and pasting, and reversing the last edit by using the Undo button. Finally, you learned how to print your outline.

▶ KEY TERMS AND INDEX

as last viewed *(PP114)*
AutoShapes toolbar *(PP97)*
buffer *(PP113)*
bulletin board system *(PP94)*
clip art *(PP88)*
ClipArt Gallery *(PP88)*
Collapse Selection button *(PP78)*
Demote (Indent more) button *(PP78)*
Drawing+ toolbar *(PP97)*
Expand Selection button *(PP78)*
fill color *(PP97)*
footer *(PP71)*

header *(PP71)*
heading level five *(PP76)*
heading level four *(PP76)*
heading level one *(PP76)*
heading level six *(PP76)*
heading level three *(PP76)*
heading level two *(PP76)*
Layout button *(PP88)*
More button *(PP71)*
Move Down button *(PP78)*
Move Up button *(PP78)*
opaque *(PP106)*
outline *(PP76)*

Outline view *(PP76)*
placement indicator *(PP110)*
Promote (Indent less) button *(PP78)*
regular shape *(PP97)*
RTF *(PP77)*
shortcut menu *(PP104)*
Show All button *(PP78)*
Show Formatting button *(PP78)*
Show Titles button *(PP78)*
transparent *(PP106)*

QUICK REFERENCE

In PowerPoint, you can accomplish a task in a number of ways. The following table provides a quick reference to each task in this project with its available options. The commands listed in the Menu column can be executed using either the keyboard or mouse.

Task	Mouse	Menu	Keyboard Shortcuts
Change Fill Color	Click Fill Color button and click color sample	From Format menu, choose Colors and Lines, choose Fill, then choose color sample in Color drop-down list box	
Change Template	Click Template button	From Format menu, choose Presentation Template, then choose template file	
Change Layout	Click Layout button	From Format menu, choose Slide Layout, then choose a slide layout	
Change Text Color	Click Text Color button and click color sample	From Format menu, choose Font, then choose color sample in Text Color drop-down list box	

Task	Mouse	Menu	Keyboard Shortcuts
Demote a Paragraph	Click Demote (Indent more) button or select text and drag four-headed pointer right to new heading level		Press TAB or ALT+SHIFT+RIGHT ARROW
Insert a New Slide	Click Insert New Slide button on Standard toolbar or New Slide on status bar	From Insert menu, choose New Slide	Press CTRL+M
Move a Paragraph Down	Click Move Down button		Press ALT+SHIFT+DOWN ARROW
Move a Paragraph Up	Click Move Up button		Press ALT+SHIFT+UP ARROW
Promote a Paragraph	Click Promote (Indent less) button or select text and drag four-headed pointer left to new heading level		Press SHIFT+TAB or ALT+SHIFT+LEFT ARROW
Show All Text and Headings	Click Show All button		Press ALT+SHIFT+A
Show Heading Level 1	Click Show Titles button		Press ALT+SHIFT+1

S T U D E N T   A S S I G N M E N T S

STUDENT ASSIGNMENT 1
True/False

Instructions: Circle T if the statement is true or F if the statement is false.

T   F   1. An outline is a summary of thoughts, presented as headings and subheadings, often used as a preliminary draft when creating a presentation.

T   F   2. The Fill Color button is used to change the text color of an object.

T   F   3. The placement indicator displays when you drag a slide to a new location.

T   F   4. In Outline view, the subtitle on the title slide displays as heading level one.

T   F   5. The Promote (Indent less) button moves the selected paragraph up one level in the outline hierarchy each time you click the button.

T   F   6. Clip art is a quick way to add professional-looking artwork to your presentation without creating the art yourself.

T   F   7. The insertion point displays when you drag a slide to a new location.

T   F   8. Selecting a template may only be done in the Pick A Look Wizard — Step 3 of 9 dialog box.

T   F   9. PowerPoint automatically sizes the object to fit the placeholder.

T   F   10. Zoom Control in Outline view will affect the size of text when printing the outline.

T   F   11. A bulletin board system is a computer system that allows users to communicate with each other and share files.

T   F   12. Outline view provides a quick, easy way to create a presentation.

(continued)

STUDENT ASSIGNMENT 1 (continued)

T F   13. The file extension RTF stands for Real Text Format.

T F   14. The Slide Show button on the Standard toolbar lets you print your presentation electronically using your computer.

T F   15. PowerPoint limits the number of outline levels to three.

T F   16. The Color Palette displays 90 color samples.

T F   17. To display an editing or formatting shortcut menu, point to an object on a slide and click the left mouse button.

T F   18. A check mark in front of a toolbar name in a shortcut menu indicates it is selected to display on the PowerPoint window.

T F   19. PowerPoint has an AutoShapes toolbar to help you add graphics and visual support to your presentation.

T F   20. The AutoShapes toolbar contains twenty-four shapes.

STUDENT ASSIGNMENT 2
Multiple Choice

Instructions: Circle the correct response.

1. Sources of clip art include _____ .
   a. Microsoft ClipArt Gallery
   b. bulletin board systems
   c. computer software retailers
   d. all of the above

2. To display a toolbar shortcut menu, point to one of the toolbars and _____ .
   a. press the left mouse button
   b. press the F1 key
   c. press the right mouse button
   d. both a and c

3. PowerPoint has more than 100 artist-created templates in its three template subdirectories: _____ .
   a. powerpnt, template, and samples
   b. xlators, pcsifiles, and sldshow
   c. bwovrhd, clrovrhd, and sldshow
   d. none of the above

4. _____ provides a quick, easy way to create a presentation.
   a. Slide Sorter view
   b. Notes Pages view
   c. Slide Show view
   d. Outline view

5. To add a new slide to a presentation in Outline view, _____ .
   a. click the New Slide button on the status bar
   b. click the Promote (Indent less) button until the insertion point reaches heading level one
   c. press CTRL+M
   d. all of the above

6. The outline begins with a title on _____ .
   a. Outline level zero
   b. Outline level two
   c. Outline level one
   d. none of the above

7. In Outline view, move a slide by dragging the _____ to its new position.
   a. paragraph
   b. slide icon
   c. bullet
   d. none of the above
8. PowerPoint provides a(n) _____ button to reverse the last edit task.
   a. Paste   b.   Undo   c.   Edit   d.   Copy
9. The presentation outline may be printed by selecting the Print command from the File menu when in

   _____ .
   a. Notes Pages view
   b. Slide view
   c. Slide Sorter view
   d. all of the above
10. The _____ button moves selected text up one paragraph at a time while maintaining its hierarchical outline level and text style.
   a. Move Up
   b. Promote (Indent less)
   c. Move Down
   d. Demote (Indent more)

STUDENT ASSIGNMENT 3
Understanding the Outlining View Window

Instructions: Arrows in Figure SA2-3 point to the major components of a PowerPoint Outline view window. Identify the various parts of the window in the spaces provided.

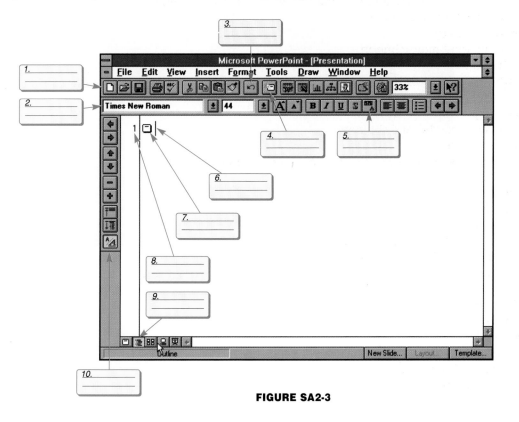

FIGURE SA2-3

STUDENT ASSIGNMENT 4
Understanding the Outlining Toolbar

Instructions: In Figure SA2-4, arrows point to several of the buttons on the Outlining toolbar. In the spaces provided, briefly explain the purpose of each button.

STUDENT ASSIGNMENT 5
Understanding How to Change Slide Layout

Instructions: Assume you are in Outline view. Write numbers in front of the steps below to indicate the sequence of steps necessary to change the slide layout from Bulleted List to the slide layout shown in Figure SA2-5.

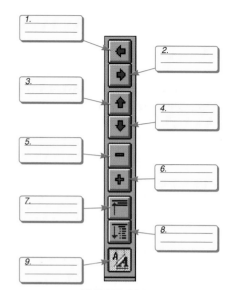

FIGURE SA2-4

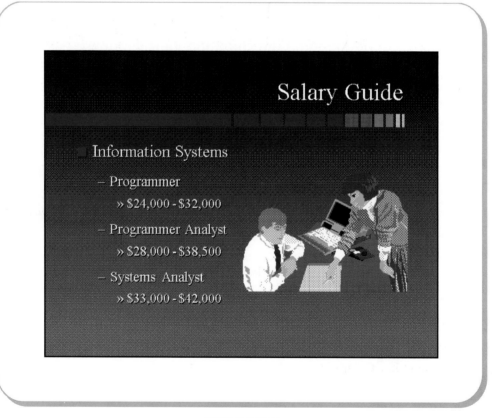

FIGURE SA2-5

STEP _____ :   Click the Text & Clip Art slide layout in the Slide Layout dialog box.

STEP _____ :   Click the slide icon of the slide that is changing layouts.

STEP _____ :   Click the Layout button.

STEP _____ :   Choose the Apply button in the Slide Layout dialog box.

STEP _____ :   Click the Slide View button.

STUDENT ASSIGNMENT 6
Changing Text Color Within an Object

Instructions: Write numbers in front of the steps below to indicate the sequence of steps necessary to change the text color to black, as shown in Figure SA2-6.

FIGURE SA2-6

STEP _____ :   Click the Text Color button on the Formatting toolbar.

STEP _____ :   Select the text that is being changed.

STEP _____ :   Click the black color sample in the Other Color dialog box.

STEP _____ :   Choose the OK button in the Other Color dialog box.

STEP _____ :   Click the Other Color command.

COMPUTER LABORATORY EXERCISE 1
Using an Outline to Create a Slide

Instructions: Start PowerPoint. Open the presentation CLE2-1.PPT from the PPOINT4 subdirectory on the Student Diskette that accompanies this book. Perform the following tasks to change the slide so it looks like the one in Figure CLE2-1.

FIGURE CLE2-1

1. Change to Slide view by clicking the Slide View button.
2. Click the Layout button and apply the Text & Clip Art slide layout.
3. Double-click on the clip art placeholder located on the slide.
4. Choose the Sports & Leisure category in the Microsoft ClipArt Gallery Picture in CLE2-1.PPT dialog box.
5. Select Football & Goal Post in the Microsoft ClipArt Gallery — Picture in CLE2-1.PPT dialog box and then choose the OK button.
6. Save the presentation on your data disk with the filename CLE2-1A using the Save As command from the File menu.
7. Print the presentation outline by selecting the File menu, choosing the Print command, selecting Outline View from the Print What drop-down list box, and then choosing the OK button in the Print dialog box.
8. Print the presentation slide by selecting the File menu, choosing the Print command, selecting Slides from the Print What drop-down list box, clicking the Pure Black & White check box, and then choosing the OK button in the Print dialog box.
9. Select the File menu and choose the Close command to close the presentation.

COMPUTER LABORATORY EXERCISE 2
Changing Slide Order

Instructions: Start PowerPoint. Open the presentation CLE2-2.PPT from the PPOINT4 subdirectory on the Student Diskette that accompanies this book.

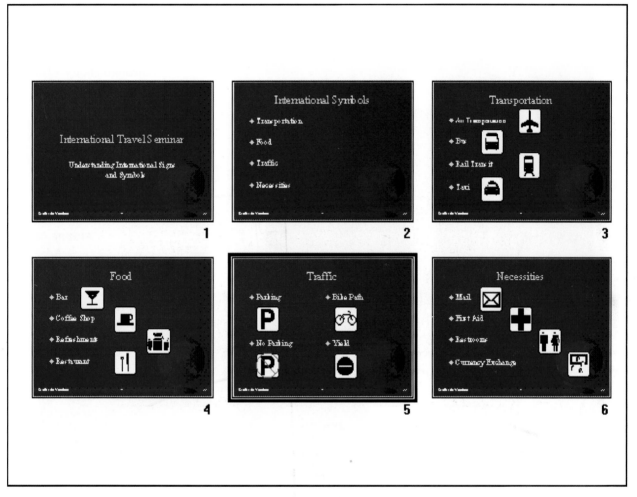

FIGURE CLE2-2

Perform the following tasks to change the slides so they look like the ones in Figure CLE2-2:

1. Change view to Slide Sorter view by clicking the Slide Sorter button.
2. Drag the title slide, Slide 5 (International Travel Seminar) and drop it in front of Slide 1 (International Symbols).
3. Drag the new Slide 5 (Food) and drop it in front of Slide 4 (Necessities).
4. Drag Slide 6 (Traffic) and drop it in front of Slide 5 (Necessities).
5. Save the presentation on your data disk with the filename CLE2-2A using the Save As command from the File Menu.
6. Print the presentation slide images by selecting the File menu, choosing the Print command, selecting Handouts (6 slides per page) from the Print What drop-down list box, clicking the Pure Black & White check box, and then choosing the OK button in the Print dialog box.
7. Choose the Close command from the File menu to close the presentation.

COMPUTER LABORATORY EXERCISE 3
Modifying a Presentation

Instructions: Start PowerPoint. Open the presentation CLE2-3.PPT from the PPOINT4 subdirectory on the Student Diskette that accompanies this book. Perform the following tasks to modify the presentation so it looks like the slides in Figure CLE2-3a and Figure CLE2-3b.

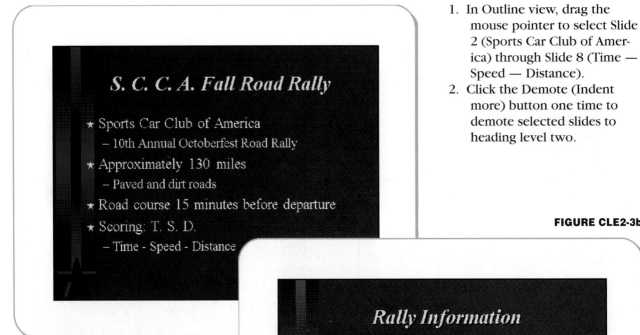

FIGURE CLE2-3a

FIGURE CLE2-3b

1. In Outline view, drag the mouse pointer to select Slide 2 (Sports Car Club of America) through Slide 8 (Time — Speed — Distance).
2. Click the Demote (Indent more) button one time to demote selected slides to heading level two.
3. Click on the paragraph, 10th Annual Octoberfest Road Rally, and click the Demote (Indent more) button one time to demote to heading level three.
4. Click on the paragraph, Paved and dirt roads, and then click the Demote (Indent more) button one time to demote to heading level three.
5. Click on the paragraph, Time — Speed — Distance, and then click the Demote (Indent more) button one time to demote to heading level three.
6. Drag the mouse pointer to select Slide 3 (Portsmith High School parking lot) through Slide 9 (Awards ceremony at end of rally) and click the Demote (Indent more) button one time to demote to heading level two.
7. Click on the paragraph, Inspections, and click the Demote (Indent more) button one time to demote to heading level three.
8. Click on the paragraph, 1 minute intervals between cars, and click the Demote (Indent more) button one time to demote to heading level three.
9. Click the Template button on the status bar.

10. Apply template dropstrs.ppt located in the c:\powerpnt\template\sldshow subdirectory.
11. Save the presentation on your data disk with the filename CLE2-3A using the Save As command from the File menu.
12. Print the presentation outline by selecting the File menu, choosing the Print command, selecting Outline View from the Print What drop-down list box, and then choosing the OK button in the Print dialog box.
13. Print the presentation slides by selecting the File menu, choosing the Print command, selecting Handouts (2 slides per page) from the Print What drop-down list box, clicking the Pure Black & White check box, and then choosing the OK button in the Print dialog box.
14. Choose the Close command from the File menu to close the presentation.

C O M P U T E R   L A B O R A T O R Y   A S S I G N M E N T S

COMPUTER LABORATORY ASSIGNMENT 1
Building a Presentation Using an Outline

Purpose: To become familiar with building a presentation using Outline view, applying a template, saving a presentation, and printing a presentation in Slide view and Outline view.

Problem: You are a marketing executive for the Fly High Golf Ball Company. Fly High is sponsoring the 1996 Midwest Open Golf Benefit. The Midwest Open Golf Benefit raises money for Dreams Come True, a foundation that grants the wishes of terminally ill children. Your responsibility is to create a presentation to promote the Midwest Open Golf Benefit.

Instructions: Perform the following tasks:

1. Start the PowerPoint program. When the New Presentation dialog box displays, click Blank Presentation and then choose the OK button.
2. When the New Slide dialog box displays, click the Bulleted List slide layout and then choose the OK button.
3. Change view to Outline view.
4. Use the outline shown in Figure CLA2-1a to create the presentation in Figure CLA2-1b, and Figure CLA2-1c on the next page.

I. Fly High Presents the 1996 Midwest Open
  A. October 12th - 15th
  B. Play the fabulous Willowdale Country Club
  C. $200,000 in prizes
  D. All proceeds donated to Dreams Come True
II. Willowdale Country Club
  A. Winner of the 1995 Pro Choice Award
  B. Designed by Amie Nicklaus
  C. Tree-lined fairways
  D. Famous 15th hole
    1. 125 yards
    2. Par 3
    3. 200 foot vertical drop
III. Prizes
  A. First place $100,000
  B. Second place $50,000
  C. Third place $25,000
  D. Fourth place $15,000
  E. Fifth place $10,000
IV. Dreams Come True
  A. Fulfills wishes of terminally ill children
  B. 5,000 wishes granted in 1995
    1. 500 trips to Disneyland
    2. 1,500 trips to Walt Disney World
    3. 3,000 Christmas in July

FIGURE CLA2-1a

(continued)

COMPUTER LABORATORY ASSIGNMENT 1 (continued)

FIGURE CLA2-1b

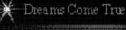

FIGURE CLA2-1c

5. Spell check the presentation by clicking the Spelling button on the Standard toolbar.
6. Apply template sparkles.ppt located in the c:\powerpnt\template\sldshow subdirectory.
7. Save the presentation on your data disk with the filename CLA2-1 using the Save As command in the File menu.
8. Print the presentation slides by selecting the File menu, choosing the Print command, selecting Handouts (2 slides per page) from the Print What drop-down list box, clicking the Pure Black & White check box, and then choosing the OK button in the Print dialog box.
9. Print the presentation outline by selecting the File menu, choosing the Print command, selecting Outline View from the Print What drop-down list box, and then choosing the OK button in the Print dialog box.

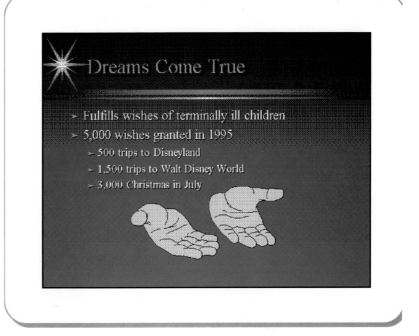

FIGURE CLA2-1d

COMPUTER LABORATORY ASSIGNMENT 2
Adding Clip Art to a Presentation

Purpose: To become familiar with adding clip art to a presentation.

Problem: As the marketing executive for Fly High Golf Ball Company, you have completed the outline for the 1996 Midwest Open Golf Benefit (Figure CLA2-1). You have decided to enhance your presentation by adding clip art. If you did not complete Computer Laboratory Assignment 1, see your instructor for a copy of presentation Figure CLA2-1.

Instructions: Perform the following tasks:

1. Open presentation CLA2-1.PPT from your data disk.
2. Click the Slide view button to display Slide 1.

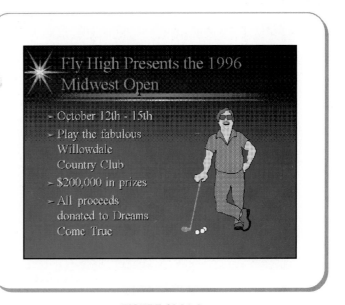

FIGURE CLA2-2a

(continued)

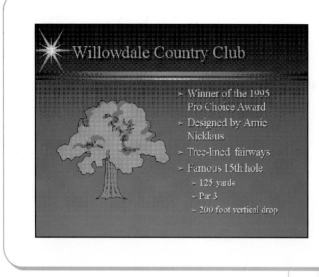

FIGURE CLA2-2b

3. Click the Layout button on the status bar and change the slide layout to Text & Clip Art.
4. Insert clip art, Golfer, from the Sports & Leisure category in the Microsoft ClipArt Gallery to Slide 1.
5. Increase font size of bulleted text to 32 points.

FIGURE CLA2-2c

6. Click the Next Slide button to advance to Slide 2 and change the slide layout to Clip Art & Text.
7. Insert clip art, Summer Tree, from the Backgrounds category in the Microsoft ClipArt Gallery to Slide 2.
8. Click the Next Slide button to advance to Slide 3 and change the slide layout to Text & Clip Art.
9. Insert clip art, Stack of Money, from the Currency category in the Microsoft ClipArt Gallery to Slide 3.

10. Click the Next Slide button to advance to Slide 4 and change the slide layout to Text over Object.
11. Insert clip art Open Hands from the Gestures category in the Microsoft ClipArt Gallery to Slide 4.
12. Save the presentation with the filename CLA2-2 using the Save As command from the File menu.
13. Drag the elevator up the vertical scroll bar to go to Slide 1. View the presentation in Slide Show view.
14. Print the presentation by choosing Slides in the Print dialog box.

FIGURE CLA2-2d

COMPUTER LABORATORY ASSIGNMENT 3
Building a Presentation in Outline View, Selecting a Template, Demoting Paragraphs, Promoting Paragraphs, Changing Slide Order, and Adding Clip Art

Purpose: To become familiar with creating a presentation in Outline view, adding a template, adding clip art, and changing slide order.

Problem: You are a student in Management 583 — Small Business Management. You are to make an on-screen presentation on starting a home-based business. You have researched home-based businesses from information received from the U.S. Small Business Administration. You decide to enhance the presentation by adding a title slide and graphics.

Instructions: Perform the tasks on the next page:

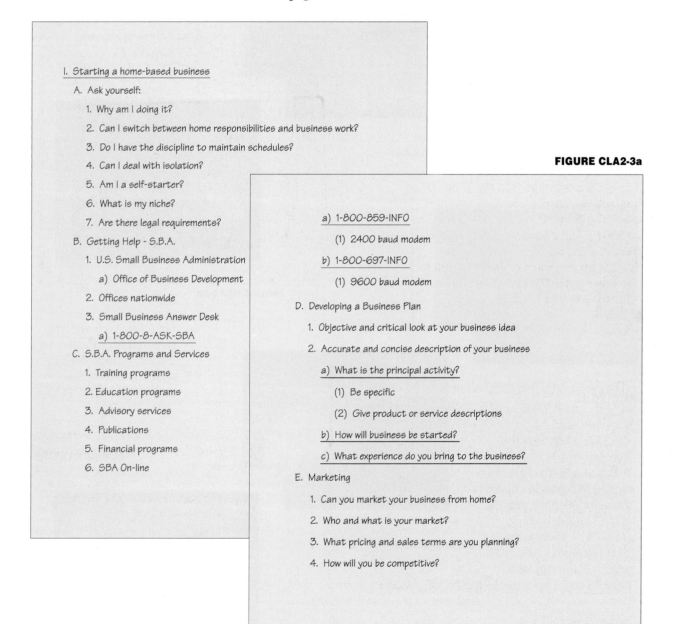

FIGURE CLA2-3a

I. Starting a home-based business

  A. Ask yourself:

    1. Why am I doing it?

    2. Can I switch between home responsibilities and business work?

    3. Do I have the discipline to maintain schedules?

    4. Can I deal with isolation?

    5. Am I a self-starter?

    6. What is my niche?

    7. Are there legal requirements?

  B. Getting Help - S.B.A.

    1. U.S. Small Business Administration

      a) Office of Business Development

    2. Offices nationwide

    3. Small Business Answer Desk

      a) 1-800-8-ASK-SBA

  C. S.B.A. Programs and Services

    1. Training programs

    2. Education programs

    3. Advisory services

    4. Publications

    5. Financial programs

    6. SBA On-line

      a) 1-800-859-INFO

        (1) 2400 baud modem

      b) 1-800-697-INFO

        (1) 9600 baud modem

  D. Developing a Business Plan

    1. Objective and critical look at your business idea

    2. Accurate and concise description of your business

      a) What is the principal activity?

        (1) Be specific

        (2) Give product or service descriptions

      b) How will business be started?

      c) What experience do you bring to the business?

  E. Marketing

    1. Can you market your business from home?

    2. Who and what is your market?

    3. What pricing and sales terms are you planning?

    4. How will you be competitive?

(continued)

FIGURE CLA2-3b

COMPUTER LABORATORY ASSIGNMENT 3 (continued)

1. Use the Pick a Look Wizard option to apply template twinkles.ppt from the template subdirectory sldshow and include your name, the date, and page number on the slides and on the outline.

2. Create a title slide with the following information, replacing Mary Smithson with your name in the subheading.

   Starting a Home-Based
   Business
   Mary Smithson
   Management 583
   Small Business
   Management

FIGURE CLA2-3c

3. Type your presentation on starting a home-based business in Outline view. The outline is shown in Figure CLA2-3a on page PP131.

FIGURE CLA2-3d

FIGURE CLA2-3e

4. On Slide 2, change the bulleted list font size to 24 and change the line spacing to .5 before paragraph.

FIGURE CLA2-3f

FIGURE CLA2-3g

5. On Slide 3, change the slide layout to Clip Art & Text and add the Two Men in Discussion clip art from the People category in the ClipArt Gallery.

6. On Slide 4, change the slide layout to Clip Art & Text and add the Sales Presentation clip art from the People category in the ClipArt Gallery. Adjust the font size so the text fits in the text placeholder.

7. On Slide 5, change the slide layout to Text & Clip Art and add the Hand Writing clip art from the Academic category. Adjust the font size so the text fits in the text placeholder.

8. On Slide 6, change the slide layout to Text over Object and add Business Meeting clip art from the People category. Adjust the font size so the text fits in the text placeholder.

9. Spell check your presentation and then save it with the filename CLA2-3 using the Save As command in the File menu.

10. Print your presentation slides and outline.

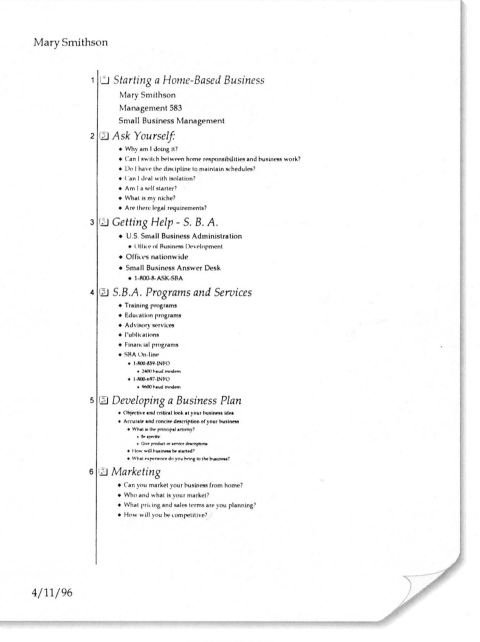

FIGURE CLA2-3h

COMPUTER LABORATORY ASSIGNMENT 4
Designing a Slide

Purpose: To provide practice in planning, designing, and creating a presentation in Outline view.

Problem: Each year, the alumni association offers a discounted travel package to its members. This year, you are the travel director for the alumni association responsible for presenting two travel packages at the alumni association's annual dinner. At the dinner, the members present will vote on the package that will be offered to all alumni association members. You are to scan through the ClipArt Gallery to select appropriate clip art. Then, research the travel packages with your local travel agency.

Instructions: Create a title slide and three informative slides in Outline view. Select an appealing template that fits the theme of your presentation. You should include appropriate clip art on each slide. Be sure to spell check your presentation. Save your presentation with the filename CLA2-4 before printing it. Print the outline with Zoom Control set at 33%. Then, print the slides.

ENHANCING A PRESENTATION AND ADDING GRAPHS AND TABLES

OBJECTIVES   You will have mastered the material in this project when you can:

▸ Modify an Existing Presentation
▸ Save a Presentation with a New Filename
▸ Create a graph using Microsoft Graph 5
▸ Create a table using Microsoft Word 6

▸ Add transitions to a slide show
▸ Apply build effects to a slide
▸ Set slide timing
▸ Run an automatic slide show

▶ INTRODUCTION

I n Projects 1 and 2, you learned how to create a presentation in Slide view and in Outline view. The slides within these presentations contained both text and clip art. PowerPoint has many other presentation features designed to grasp your audience's attention. For example, your slides can contain tables and graphs to pictorially represent data trends and patterns. You can also add special effects to your presentation, such as controlling the motion of one slide exiting the screen and another entering. This project incorporates these features into the slide show you began in Project 2.

▶ PROJECT THREE — SAN BAARBO VACATIONS ENHANCED

P roject 3 enhances the San Baarbo Vacation presentation created in Project 2. The original presentation promoted two vacation packages to San Juan to prospective customers. To better explain the vacation packages, the travel agency has decided to add more detail and pizzazz to the presentation. This includes a list of cabin classes, a graph of cabin fares, a list of San Juan features, and a seasonal temperature table. The travel agency is preparing for a tourism show and wants to automate the slide show to run without human intervention. Additional features are to include a visual effect to smooth the transition from one slide to the next and to build each bulleted slide line-by-line to emphasize the current bulleted paragraph.

Slide Preparation Steps

The following slide preparation steps summarize how to create the slides shown in Figures 3-1a through 3-1i. If you are creating these slides on a personal computer, read these steps without doing them.

1. Start PowerPoint.
2. Open an existing presentation and save it with a new filename.
3. Apply the template TROPICS.PPT to the presentation.
4. Change the Slide 2 slide layout to Object over Text.
5. Add a new bulleted list slide.
6. Add a new graph slide.
7. Add another bulleted list slide and save the presentation.
8. Add a table slide.
9. Add a closing slide.
10. Spell check the presentation and save it.
11. Add transition to the presentation.
12. Add build effects to the presentation and save it.
13. Automate the slide show.
14. Save the presentation and exit PowerPoint.

The following sections describe these steps in detail.

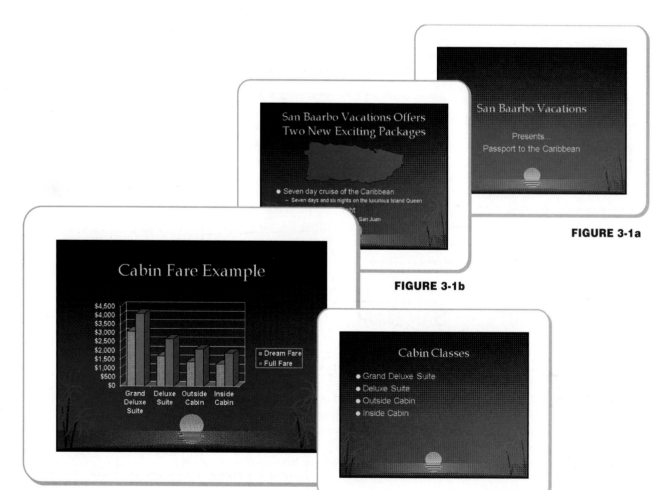

FIGURE 3-1a

FIGURE 3-1b

FIGURE 3-1f

FIGURE 3-1e

▶ MODIFYING AN EXISTING PRESENTATION

Because you are enhancing the presentation you created in Project 2, the first step in this project is to open the PROJ2.PPT file. So that the original Project 2 presentation remains intact, you will save the PROJ2.PPT file with a new filename: PROJ3.PPT. You will then make modifications to the new file's existing slides and add four new slides. The steps on the following pages illustrate these procedures.

Starting PowerPoint

To start PowerPoint, the Windows Program Manager must display on the screen and the Microsoft Office group window must be open. Double-click the Microsoft PowerPoint program-item icon in the Microsoft Office group window. Then, choose the OK button in the Tip of the Day dialog box.

Opening a Presentation

The San Baarbo Vacations presentation was saved in Project 2 using the file-name PROJ2.PPT. Therefore, the first step is to open PROJ2.PPT, as shown below.

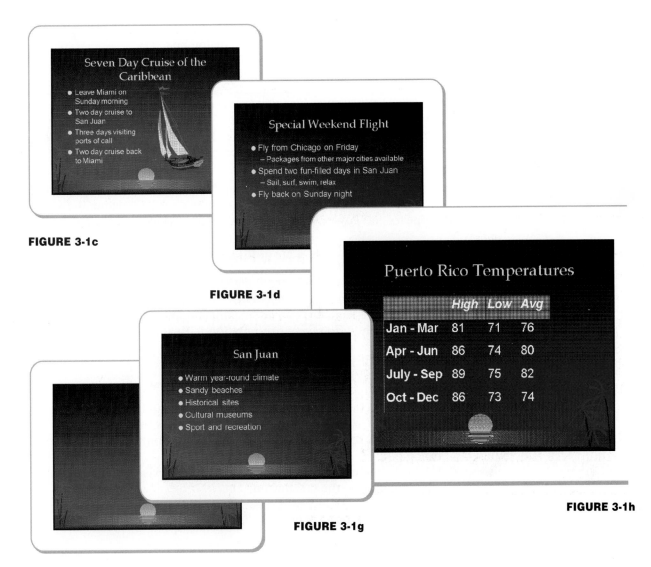

FIGURE 3-1c

FIGURE 3-1d

FIGURE 3-1g

FIGURE 3-1h

FIGURE 3-1i

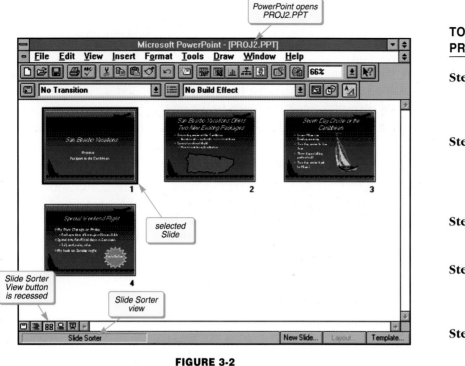

FIGURE 3-2

TO OPEN AN EXISTING PRESENTATION

Step 1: Insert the diskette containing the file PROJ2.PPT into drive A.

Step 2: Select the Open an Existing Presentation option in the PowerPoint startup dialog box.

Step 3: Choose the OK button in the PowerPoint startup dialog box.

Step 4: If necessary, click the Drives box arrow and select drive A in the Open dialog box.

Step 5: Select proj2.ppt by clicking its filename in the File Name list box.

Step 6: Choose the OK button in the Open dialog box.

Step 7: If necessary, click the Maximize button on the PROJ2.PPT title bar to maximize the PowerPoint window.

PowerPoint opens PROJ2.PPT and displays it in Slide Sorter view, which was the view it was in last time you saved it (Figure 3-2). If your screen differs from Figure 3-2, click the Slide Sorter View button at the bottom of the screen. The PowerPoint window is maximzed.

An alternative to using the OK button in Step 6 is to double-click the filename PROJ2.PPT in the File Name list box. When you double-click a filename, the Open dialog box disappears and PowerPoint opens the presentation.

Saving the Presentation with a New Filename

Because you want the PROJ2.PPT presentation to remain unchanged, you should save it with a new filename, such as PROJ3.PPT. Then, make any necessary revisions to the new file. Essentially, you are making a duplicate copy of a file. The following steps illustrate how to save a presentation with a new filename using the Save As command from the File menu.

TO SAVE THE PRESENTATION WITH A NEW FILENAME

Step 1: From the File menu, choose the Save As command.

Step 2: Type proj3 in the File Name box. Do not press the ENTER key.

Step 3: With drive A set as the default, choose the OK button in the Save As dialog box.

Step 4: When the Summary Info dialog box displays, revise the information and then choose the OK button.

The presentation is saved to drive A with the filename PROJ3.PPT (Figure 3-3).

Changing Templates

Because San Baarbo Vacations is modifying the contents of this presentation, the travel agency will also give it a new look by changing the template. Recall from Project 1 that a template may be changed at any time during the development of the presentation. Perform the steps below to change the template from TRAVELS.PPT to TROPICS.PPT.

TO CHANGE TEMPLATES

Step 1: Click the Template button on the status bar.

Step 2: Drag the File Name scroll bar elevator to the bottom of the scroll bar. Then, select the tropics.ppt template in the File Name list box.

Step 3: Choose the Apply button in the Presentation Template dialog box.

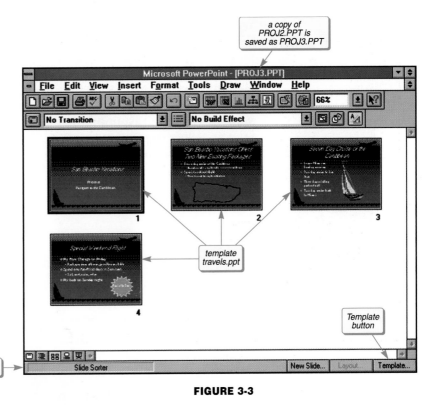

FIGURE 3-3

The slides display with the new template: tropics.ppt (Figure 3-4).

The TROPICS.PPT template places palm trees at the bottom of the slide with the sun rising over the ocean. Changing the template is a quick and easy way to change the focus of a presentation, depending on your target audience.

Changing Slide Layout

Slide 2 in the presentation currently has the Text over Object slide layout; that is, the bulleted list displays above the graphic of Puerto Rico. However, you would prefer that the graphic display above the text. Thus, perform the following steps to change the slide layout to Object over Text. For a detailed explanation of this procedure, refer to pages PP89 and PP90 in Project 2.

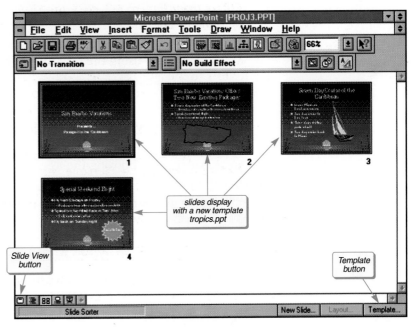

FIGURE 3-4

TO CHANGE SLIDE LAYOUT

Step 1: Click the Slide View button at the bottom of the screen to change views.
Step 2: Click the Next Slide button on the vertical scroll bar one time to display Slide 2.
Step 3: Click the Layout button on the status bar.
Step 4: Select the Object over Text slide layout (▯) by clicking it.
Step 5: Choose the Apply button in the Slide Layout dialog box.

Slide 2 changes to the Object over Text slide layout (Figure 3-5). The clip art map of Puerto Rico displays above the bulleted paragraphs.

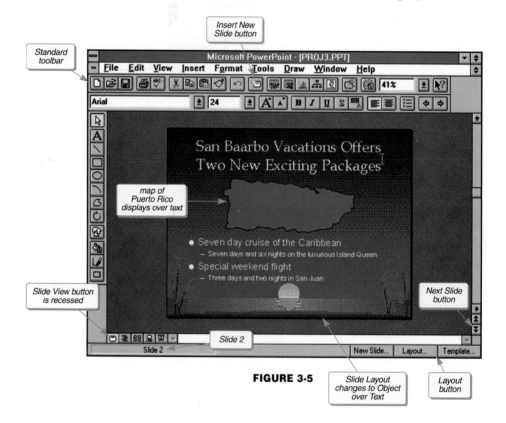

FIGURE 3-5

An alternative to choosing the Apply button in Step 5 is to double-click the slide layout in the Slide Layout dialog box. When you double-click a slide layout, the Slide Layout dialog box disappears, and PowerPoint displays the slide with the new layout.

Deleting an Object

Slide 4 currently has a seal object in its lower right corner. To alter the look of your presentation, you decide to remove this object, as shown in the steps below.

TO DELETE AN OBJECT

Step 1: Click the Next Slide button twice to display Slide 4.
Step 2: Select the seal object by clicking it. Be sure to select the whole object and not just the text within the object.

Step 3: Press the
DELETE key.

The seal object is deleted from Slide 4 (Figure 3-6).

If you accidentally delete text instead of the entire object, click the Undo button on the Standard toolbar. Then, repeat Steps 2 and 3.

Adding a New Slide to the Presentation

The next step is to add a fifth slide to the presentation that outlines the four major types of cabin classes. Recall that you add a new slide by clicking the Insert New Slide button on the Standard toolbar. Perform the following steps to add a bulleted list slide to the presentation.

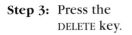

FIGURE 3-6

TO ADD A NEW SLIDE TO THE PRESENTATION

Step 1: Click the Insert New Slide button on the Standard toolbar.
Step 2: Select Bulleted List from the New Slide dialog box by double-clicking it.
Step 3: Type `Cabin Classes` as the title for Slide 5.
Step 4: Select the text object by clicking anywhere inside the text placeholder.
Step 5: Type `Grand Deluxe Suite` and press the ENTER key.
Step 6: Type `Deluxe Suite` and press the ENTER key.
Step 7: Type `Outside Cabin` and press the ENTER key.
Step 8: Type `Inside Cabin`

Slide 5 is complete (Figure 3-7).

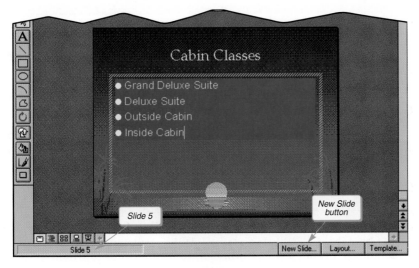

FIGURE 3-7

From the previous steps, you can see that you can add a new slide to the end of a presentation by simply clicking the Insert New Slide button.

▶ USING MICROSOFT GRAPH TO CREATE A COLUMN GRAPH

Graphs are used to display trends and magnitudes to your audience. The next slide in this presentation contains a column graph that compares costs between cabin class fares (Figure 3-8). In the column graph for this project, each column represents the cost of a cabin. Full fares are the usual and customary costs for a room; dream fares are promotional rates, usually lower in cost than the full fare. Full fare columns are a different color from dream fare columns; the respective colors of these two fares are indicated in the **legend** on the graph. A legend is an explanatory table or list of symbols appearing on a graph. By scanning the graph, you can easily see that the highest cabin fare is in the Grand Deluxe Suite.

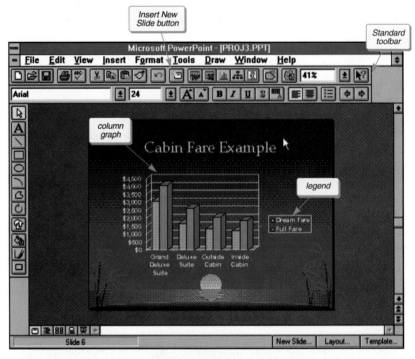

FIGURE 3-8

PowerPoint comes with a **supplementary application** called **Microsoft Graph 5**, which allows you to create graphs within PowerPoint. When you open a supplementary application, its menus, buttons, tools, etc., are available to you directly on the PowerPoint screen. This concept of bringing the application to you is called **OLE**, or **Object Linking and Embedding**. The graph you create is actually an **embedded object** because it is created in another application, Microsoft Graph, and inserted into your presentation.

Creating a graph requires several steps. First, you add a new slide with the graph layout. Next, you open the Graph application into the PowerPoint screen. Then, you decide on the graph type. For example, you can display the data using a bar graph, a column graph, a pie graph, or one of the other fourteen graph types. Table 3-1 summarizes the most often used graph types. Finally, you enter and format the data for the graph.

▶ **TABLE 3-1**

GRAPH ICON	GRAPH TYPE	DESCRIPTION
	Bar Graph	Shows individual figures at a specific time or illustrates comparisons. The categories on a bar graph are organized vertically, and he values are organized horizontally, placing more emphasison comparisons and less emphasis on time. Also available in 3-D (three-dimensional).
	Column Graph	Shows variation over a period of time or illustrates comparisons between items. Although similar to a bar graph, a column graph's categories are organized horizontally, and its values are organized vertically. Also available in 3-D.
	Line Graph	Shows trends or changes in data over a period of time at even intervals. A line graph emphasizes time flow and rate of change, instead of the amount of change.
	Pie Graph	Shows the proportion of parts to a whole. This graph type is useful for emphasizing a significant element. A pie graph always contains one data series. If you select more than one data series, only one will display in your graph. Also available in 3-D.

The steps on the following pages explain in detail how to create the column graph for this project.

Adding a New Slide with the Graph AutoLayout

Because you want the column graph on a new slide, you will select the Graph AutoLayout as shown in these steps.

TO ADD A NEW SLIDE WITH THE GRAPH AUTOLAYOUT

Step 1: Click the Insert New Slide button on the Standard toolbar.
Step 2: Double-click the Graph AutoLayout (▦) in the New Slide dialog box.

Slide 6 displays the graph placeholder (Figure 3-9).

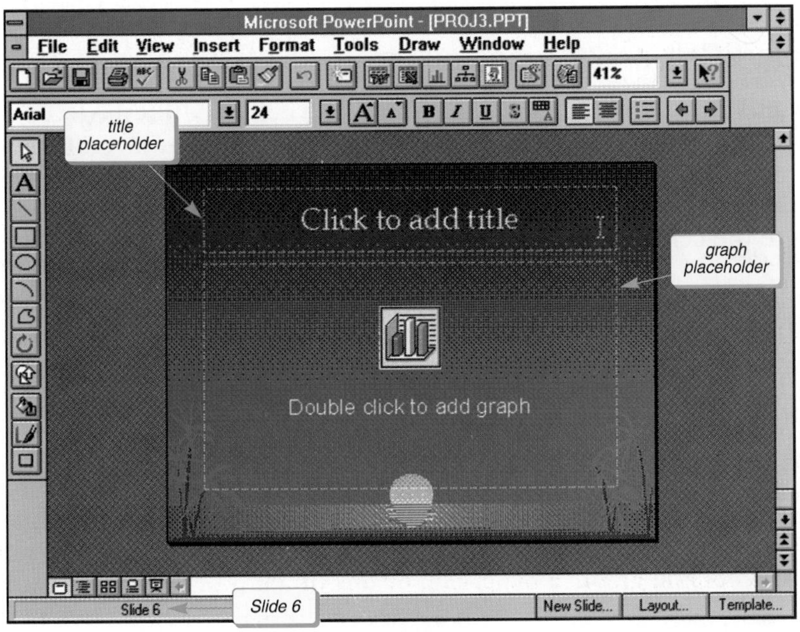

FIGURE 3-9

The Datasheet

The **datasheet** (Figure 3-10), a Microsoft Graph window, is a rectangular grid containing columns (vertical) and rows (horizontal). A column letter above the grid, called the **column heading**, identifies each column. A row number on the left side of the grid, called the **row heading**, identifies each row.

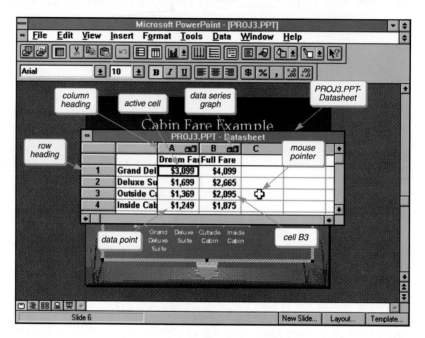

FIGURE 3-10

The datasheet contains numbers, called **data points**, in the rows and columns. Microsoft Graph (referred to as Graph) uses the data points to create the graph that displays in the presentation. Notice in Figure 3-10 that behind the Datasheet window is the column graph that represents the data points in the datasheet. The datasheet can contain a maximum of 4,000 rows and 4,000 columns.

Cell, Active Cell, and Mouse Pointer

The intersection of each column and row is a cell. A **cell** is the basic unit of the datasheet into which you enter data. A cell is identified by its **cell reference**, which is the coordinates of the intersection of a column and a row. To identify a cell, specify the column letter first, followed by the row number. For example, cell B3 refers to the cell located at the intersection of column B and row 3 (Figure 3-10).

One cell on the datasheet, designated the **active cell**, is the one in which you can enter data points. The active cell is identified by a heavy black border surrounding the cell. For example, the active cell in Figure 3-10 is cell A1.

The mouse pointer in Graph becomes one of several shapes, depending on the task you are performing and the pointer's location on the screen. The mouse pointer in Figure 3-10 has the shape of a block plus sign (⊕), which indicates it is positioned on a cell in the datasheet.

Opening the Graph Application into the PowerPoint Window

In order to create the column graph in Slide 6, you must first open the Graph application. Recall that OLE brings this supplementary application to the PowerPoint window and makes the menus, buttons, tools, etc., in the Graph application available on the PowerPoint screen. Once open, Graph displays a Datasheet window in a work area in the middle of the PowerPoint screen, as shown in the steps below.

TO OPEN THE GRAPH APPLICATION INTO THE POWERPOINT WINDOW ▼

STEP 1

Type Cabin Fare Example

PowerPoint displays the title of Slide 6 in the title placeholder.

STEP 2 ▶

Double-click the graph placeholder (see Figure 3-9) in the middle of Slide 6.

Graph displays the PROJ3.PPT — Datasheet window in a work area on the PowerPoint screen (Figure 3-11). Notice that sample data displays in the datasheet in the Datasheet window. The data points in the sample datasheet are plotted in a graph on Slide 6, which is positioned behind the Datasheet window. You can change the data points in the sample datasheet.

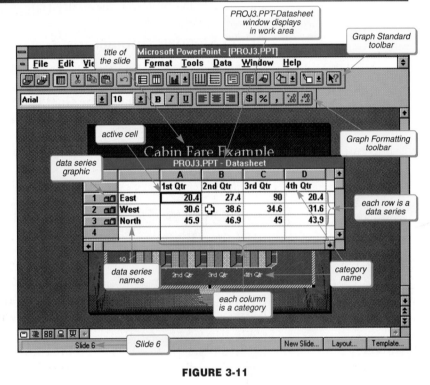

FIGURE 3-11

Graph displays default data in the sample datasheet to help you create your graph. A **data series** is a single row or a single column of data points on the datasheet. Each data series displays as a set of **data markers** on the graph, such as bars, lines, or pie slices.

In Figure 3-11, notice that the default data series is a single row; that is, each row in the datasheet is represented by a cluster of columns in the graph. The **data series names** display in the column to the left of the data points in the datasheet and in a legend in the graph. In the sample datasheet, East, West, and North are the data series names. Because the rows in this datasheet are the data series, each column in the datasheet is called a **category**. In this case, **category names** display in the column above the data points in the datasheet and below the columns in the graph. In the sample datasheet, 1st Qtr, 2nd Qtr, 3rd Qtr, and 4th Qtr are the category names.

Graph plots the data based on the data points you enter and the **orientation** you choose. The default orientation is data series in rows; that is, rows in the datasheet are plotted as columns in the graph. Later in this project, you will change the orientation to data series in columns.

A data series graphic displays to the right of the data series name in the datasheet to indicate the current graph type and the color of the data series. For example, in Figure 3-11 the data series graphic ( ) for East indicates the current graph type is a column graph, and the East data series is colored orange in the graph.

The default graph type is a 3-D column graph. If your graph type differs from the one in Figure 3-11, choose the Chart Type command from the Format menu and select 3-D Column in the Chart Type dialog box.

Graph Standard Toolbar

Notice in Figure 3-11 that the Standard toolbar buttons have changed. This is because you are no longer working in PowerPoint; instead, you are working in Graph. Later, when you exit the Graph application, the PowerPoint Standard toolbar will reappear. The Graph Standard toolbar contains buttons to help you complete the most frequently used actions in Graph. Table 3-2 illustrates the Graph Standard toolbar's buttons and their functions.

▹ **TABLE 3-2**

ICON	NAME	FUNCTION
	Import Data Button	Imports data from another application. The data you import is inserted into the datasheet and displayed graphically in the graph window.
	Import Chart Button	Imports an existing graph from Microsoft Excel.
	View Datasheet Button	Displays the datasheet window, allowing you to edit or format the data.
	Cut Button	Removes the selection and places it on the Clipboard.
	Copy Button	Copies the selection and places it on the Clipboard.
	Paste Button	Pastes the contents of the Clipboard into the selection.
	Undo Button	Reverses the last command you chose, if possible, or deletes the last entry you typed.
	By Row Button	Associates graph data series with rows on the datasheet.
	By Column Button	Associates graph data series with columns on the datasheet.
	Chart Type Button	Displays a palette of fourteen graph types. Clicking any one applies that graph type to active graph.
	Vertical Gridlines Button	Controls whether major vertical gridlines, indicating large groupings of values or categories, are visible on the graph.

ICON	NAME	FUNCTION
	Horizontal Gridlines Button	Controls whether major horizontal gridlines, indicating large groupings of values, are visible on the graph.
	Legend Button	Adds a legend to the right of the plot area and resizes the plot area to accommodate the legend. If the graph already has a legend, clicking the Legend button removes it.
	Text Box Button	Draws a text box in which you can type text on a worksheet; lets you add unattached, or "floating", text to a graph.
	Drawing Button	Displays the Drawing toolbar.
	Color Button	Changes the foreground color of a selected object.
	Pattern Button	Changes the pattern and pattern color of a selected object.
	Help Button	Adds a question mark (?) to the mouse pointer so you can get information about commands or screen elements.

Graph Formatting Toolbar

Like the Standard toolbar, the Formatting toolbar in Graph is different from the Formatting toolbar in PowerPoint. The Formatting toolbar displays directly below the Standard toolbar. If your screen does not display a Formatting toolbar, choose the Toolbars command from the View menu; then, select the Formatting check box in the Toolbars dialog box and choose the OK button. Table 3-3 explains the function of the buttons and boxes on the Graph Formatting toolbar.

▶ **TABLE 3-3**

ICON	NAME	FUNCTION
Arial	Font Box	Lists the available fonts.
10	Font Size Box	Lists the available sizes for the font selected in the Font Box.
B	Bold Button	Applies bold formatting to characters in cells, text boxes, or graph text.
I	Italic Button	Applies italic formatting to characters in cells, text boxes, or graph text.
U	Underline Button	Applies a single underline to characters in cells, text boxes, or graph text.
	Align Left Button	Aligns the contents of text boxes or graph text to the left.
	Center Button	Centers the contents of text boxes or graph text.

(continued)

ICON	NAME	FUNCTION
≡	Align Right Button	Aligns the contents of text boxes or graph text to the right.
$	Currency Style Button	Applies the currently defined Currency style to selected cells.
%	Percent Style Button	Applies the curently defined Percent style to selected cells.
,	Comma Style Button	Applies the currently defined Comma style to selected cells.
.0 .00	Increase Decimal Button	Adds one decimal place to the number format each time you click the button.
.00 .0	Decrease Decimal Button	Removes one decimal place from the number format each time you click the button.

Deleting Data from Columns in the Datasheet

The sample datasheet is a four-column datasheet containing columns A, B, C, and D (see Figure 3-11 on page PP145). San Baarbo Vacations is creating a two-column graph to compare the Dream Fare and the Full Fare (see Figure 3-8 on page PP142). Thus, the next step is to delete the data from columns C and D in the sample datasheet, as shown in the following steps.

TO DELETE DATA FROM COLUMNS IN THE DATASHEET ▼

STEP 1 ▶

Point to the column C heading (Figure 3-12a).

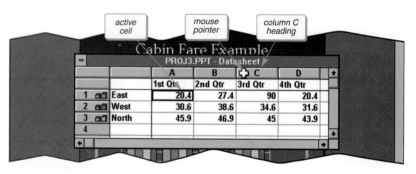

FIGURE 3-12a

STEP 2 ▶

Select columns C and D by dragging the mouse pointer through the column C and D headings.

Columns C and D are selected (Figure 3-12b). Selected columns are highlighted.

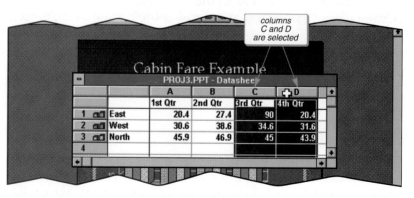

FIGURE 3-12b

STEP 3 ▶

Press the DELETE key.

The data in columns C and D is deleted (Figure 3-13). Notice that the graph behind the Datasheet window changes to reflect the deleted columns; that is, the 3rd Qtr and 4th Qtr columns have been removed from the graph.

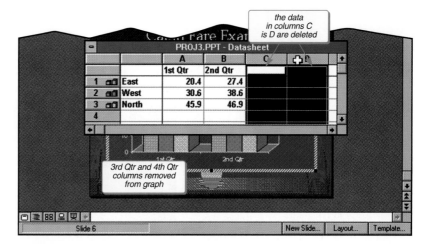

FIGURE 3-13

Selecting a Cell in a Datasheet

In order to enter data into a cell, you must first select it. One way to **select a cell** (make it active) is to use the mouse to move the mouse pointer (the block plus sign) to the active cell and click the left mouse button.

Another method to select a cell is to use the arrow keys that are located to the right of the type-writer area on the keyboard. An **arrow key** selects the cell adjacent to the active cell in the direction of the arrow on the key. The ENTER key selects the cell immediately below the active cell. Table 3-4 summarizes the keys you press to move to various locations in the datasheet.

▶ **TABLE 3-4**

TO MOVE	PRESS
One cell	One of the arrow keys
Down one cell (immediately below an active cell)	ENTER
To beginning of a row	HOME
To first data cell (cell A1)	CTRL+HOME
To end of row (last occupied column)	END
To lower right cell containing data	CTRL+END
Down one window	PAGE DOWN
Up one window	PAGE UP
Right one window	ALT+PAGE DOWN
Left one window	ALT+PAGE UP
Up or down to the edge of the current data region	CTRL+DOWN ARROW or CTRL+UP ARROW
Left or right to the edge of the current data region	CTRL+LEFT ARROW or CTRL+RIGHT ARROW

Pressing the END key moves the insertion point to column D at the end of the current row. This is because you deleted the data in columns C and D, and Graph still recognizes column D as the last occupied column. Until you close the presentation, the graph and corresponding datasheet are not reset. Therefore, if you open the presentation, return to the datasheet, and then press the END key, the insertion point would then move to column B of the current row.

Entering Category Names

Recall that the category names in the sample datasheet display above the data points and below the columns in the graph. The current category names are 1st Qtr and 2nd Qtr. You can change these default category names. To do this, you select the appropriate cell and then enter the text, as described in the steps on the next page.

TO ENTER THE CATEGORY NAMES ▼

STEP 1 ▶

Select the first cell under the column A heading, containing 1st Qtr as the category name, by pointing to the cell and clicking the left mouse button.

The cell becomes the active cell as designated by the heavy border around it (Figure 3-14). The mouse pointer is also in the cell.

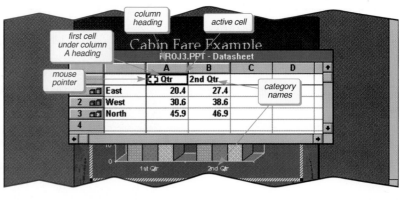

FIGURE 3-14

STEP 2 ▶

Type Dream Fare

When you type the first character, the heavy border disappears and an insertion point displays in the cell. Dream Fare displays left-aligned in the first cell under the column A heading (Figure 3-15). When you enter text into a datasheet cell, Graph automatically left-aligns it within the cell. Notice that the category name, Dream Fare, is too large for the cell and spills into the cell to its immediate right.

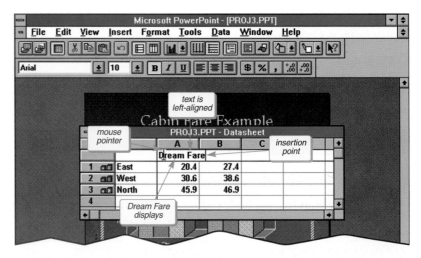

FIGURE 3-15

STEP 3 ▶

Press the RIGHT ARROW key.

*Graph enters the category name, Dream Fare, beneath the column A heading, and the first cell under the column B heading, containing the category name 2nd Qtr, becomes the active cell (Figure 3-16). Because a category name is in the cell to the right of Dream Fare, Graph **truncates**, or chops off, the right-most characters of the category name in the datasheet. The graph, however, displays the category name in its entirety. Notice that the graph changes to reflect the new category name; that is, Dream Fare replaces 1st Qtr.*

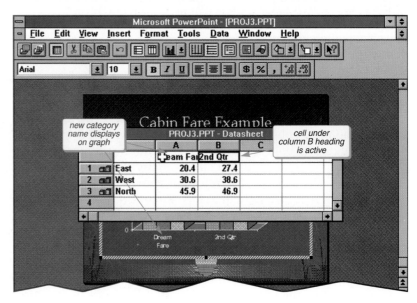

FIGURE 3-16

STEP 4 ▶

Type Full Fare

The category names are now complete (Figure 3-17).

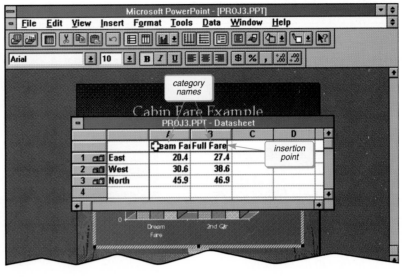

FIGURE 3-17

Although the category names display in the cell as you type them, they are not actually *entered* into the cell until you press an arrow key or the ENTER key, or until you click another cell. (This explains why the category name Full Fare does not yet display on the graph.)

Entering the Data Series Names

The next step in developing the datasheet, and its associated graph, in Project 3 is to enter the data series names in the column to the right of the row headings. Recall that the data series names display to the left of the data points in the datasheet and in the legend on the graph. The default data series names are East, West, and North. The process of changing these default data series names is similar to changing the category names and is described below.

TO ENTER THE DATA SERIES NAMES ▼

STEP 1 ▶

Select the first cell to the right of the row 1 heading, containing East as the data series name.

The cell immediately to the right of the row 1 heading becomes the active cell (Figure 3-18).

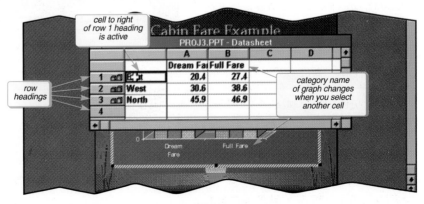

FIGURE 3-18

STEP 2 ▶

Type Grand Deluxe Suite **and press the DOWN ARROW key.**

Graph enters the data series name, Grand Deluxe Suite, in the first cell to the right of the row 1 heading. The first cell to the right of the row 2 heading becomes the active cell (Figure 3-19). Because there is a data point to the right of Grand Deluxe Suite, this data series name is truncated in the cell. The legend, which is hidden behind the Datasheet window, displays the data series in its entirety.

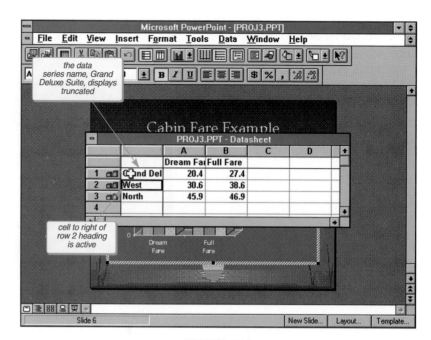

FIGURE 3-19

STEP 3 ▶

Type Deluxe Suite **in the first cell to the right of the row 2 heading and press the DOWN ARROW key. Type** Outside Cabin **in the first cell to the right of the row 3 heading and press the DOWN ARROW key. Type** Inside Cabin **in the first cell to the right of the row 4 heading.**

The data series names are complete (Figure 3-20). Notice that the Inside Cabin data series name displays in its entirety because you did not press an arrow key or the ENTER key after typing it.

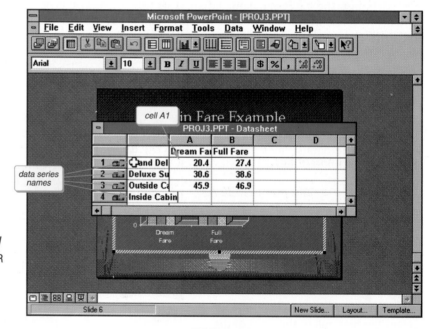

FIGURE 3-20

Entering the Data Points

In Graph, you can enter data points into cells to represent amounts. Recall that a cell containing a data point is referenced by its column and row coordinates. For example, the first cell containing a data point in Figure 3-20 is cell A1. Again, Graph displays default data points in these cells. Perform the following steps to change the default data points in the datasheet.

TO ENTER THE DATA POINTS ▼

STEP 1 ▶

Select cell A1, which contains the default data point 20.4.

Cell A1 becomes the active cell (Figure 3-21).

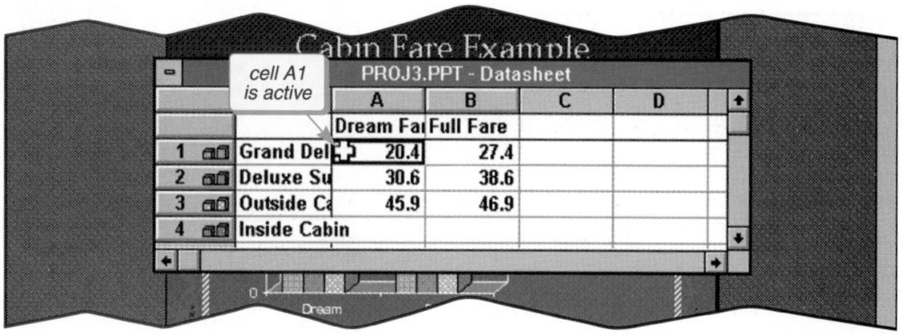

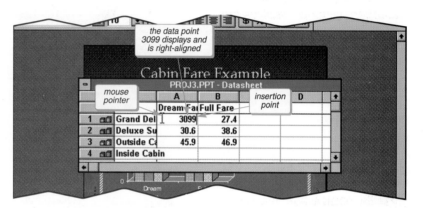

FIGURE 3-21

STEP 2 ▶

Type 3099

The data point 3099 displays in the active cell, which is cell A1 (Figure 3-22). (Data points are entered without using a dollar sign. The data points on the datasheet are formatted with a dollar sign later in this project.)

FIGURE 3-22

STEP 3 ▶

Press the RIGHT ARROW key.

Graph enters the data point 3099 in cell A1, and cell B1 becomes the active cell (Figure 3-23). Notice that data points are right-aligned in a cell.

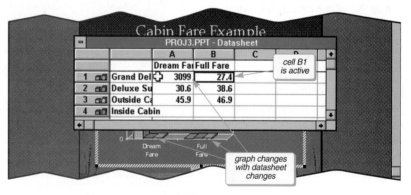

FIGURE 3-23

STEP 4 ▶

Type 4099

The data point 4099 displays in the active cell B1 (Figure 3-24).

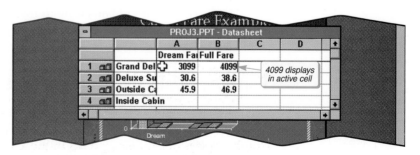

FIGURE 3-24

STEP 5 ▶

Select cell A2 by clicking it.

Cell A2 becomes the active cell (Figure 3-25).

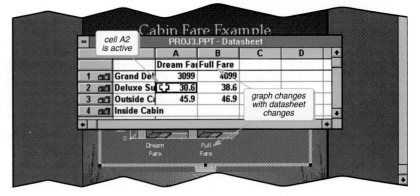

FIGURE 3-25

STEP 6 ▶

Enter 1699 **in cell A2,** 2665 **in cell B2,** 1369 **in cell A3,** 2095 **in cell B3,** 1249 **in cell A4, and** 1875 **in cell B4. Do not press an arrow key or the ENTER key after typing cell B4's entry.**

The datasheet entries are complete (Figure 3-26).

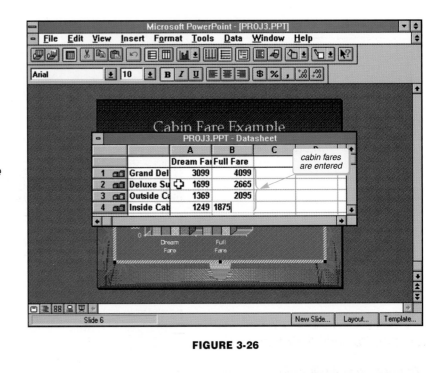

FIGURE 3-26

If your screen scrolls up at the end of Step 6, click the up arrow on the Datasheet window vertical scroll bar to bring the entire datasheet back into view.

If you need to modify the contents of a cell, click the cell and type the correct name or data point.

The next section explains how to format the datasheet using the Graph Formatting toolbar. For a detailed explanation of the Graph Formatting toolbar, see Table 3-3 on page PP147.

Formatting Data Points on the Datasheet

Changing the format of the data points on the datasheet allows you to represent currency and percentages, insert commas, and increase or decrease the number of positions after the decimal point. Perform the following steps to format the data points on the datasheet to represent dollar amounts.

TO FORMAT DATA POINTS ON THE DATASHEET ▼

STEP 1 ►

Select columns A and B by dragging the mouse pointer through the column A and B headings.

Columns A and B are selected (Figure 3-27).

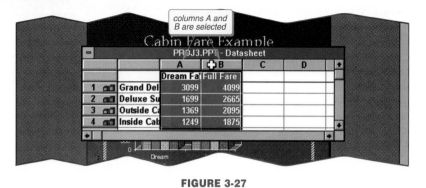

FIGURE 3-27

STEP 2 ►

Point to the Currency Style button ($) on the Formatting toolbar (Figure 3-28).

Recall that the PowerPoint window is displaying the Graph Formatting toolbar, not the PowerPoint Formatting toolbar.

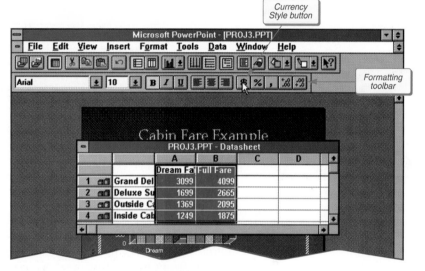

FIGURE 3-28

STEP 3 ►

Click the Currency Style button.

The currency style is applied to the data points in the selected cells (Figure 3-29). That is, the data points display with dollar signs, commas, and two decimal positions.

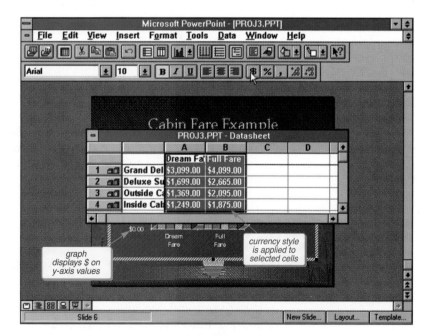

FIGURE 3-29

STEP 4 ▶

Click the Decrease Decimal button (□) on the Formatting toolbar two times.

The decimal points are removed from the data points in the selected cells (Figure 3-30). Thus, the data points display as whole numbers. Each time you click the Decrease Decimal button, one decimal position is removed from the data points in the selected cells.

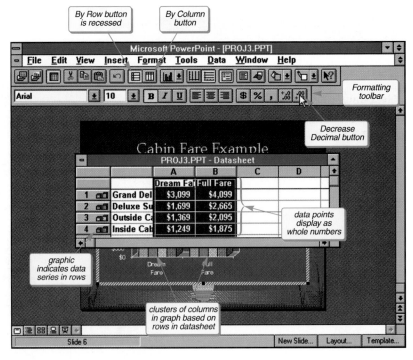

FIGURE 3-30

Changing Graph's Orientation

Recall that Graph plots the data based on the data points you enter and the orientation you choose. Recall also that the default orientation is data series in rows; that is, rows in the datasheet are plotted as clusters of columns in the graph. However, you want the data series in columns. That is, columns in the datasheet should be plotted as columns in the graph.

Currently, the By Row button (□) on the Standard toolbar is recessed, indicating the data series is in rows. The By Column button (□) on the Standard toolbar associates the data series plotted on the graph with columns on the datasheet. Perform the following steps to change the graph's orientation from data series in rows to data series in columns.

TO CHANGE A GRAPH'S ORIENTATION ▼

STEP 1 ►

Click the By Column button on the Standard toolbar.

The data series are now based on the columns in the datasheet (Figure 3-31).

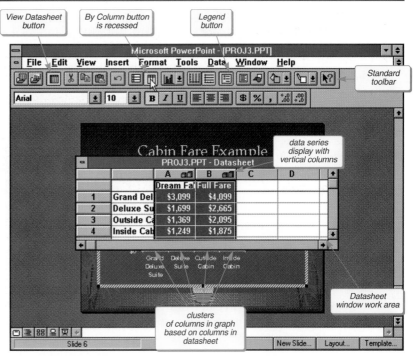

FIGURE 3-31

STEP 2 ►

Click outside the Datasheet window work area.

The Graph application closes and the PowerPoint application reappears. The Cabin Fare Example graph displays in the PowerPoint window (Figure 3-32). A legend displays to the right of the graph to identify the different data series displayed.

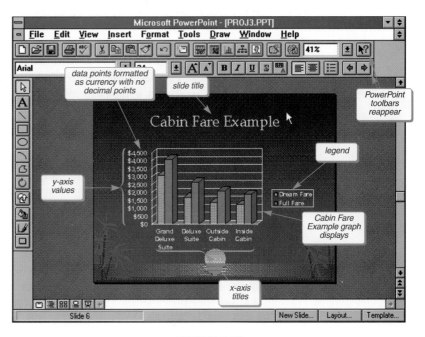

FIGURE 3-32

Several major changes occur on the datasheet when you click the By Column button in Figure 3-31 on the previous page. First, the By Column button is recessed. Second, the data series names and category names are swapped; that is, the names beneath the column headings become the data series names, and the names to the right of the row headings become the category names. Third, because the data series and category names have switched, the words beneath the columns in the graph change to the new data series names, and the legend changes to the new category names. Instead of two data series names, the graph has four data series names. Finally, the data series graphic displays in the column header above the data series, instead of the row heading to left of the data series.

If, for some reason, you want to edit the graph, simply double-click it to open the Graph application. If you need to modify the contents of the datasheet, you can display it again by clicking the View Datasheet button (▦) on the Graph Standard toolbar. If you accidentally delete the legend from an existing graph, you can add it again by clicking the Legend button on the Graph Standard toolbar. Then, to return to PowerPoint, simply click anywhere outside the Datasheet window work area.

Changing Graph Types

Recall from Table 3-1 on page PP143 that the four most common graph types are bar graph, column graph, line graph, and pie graph. Project 3 uses the column graph to compare costs between cabin class fares.

If, for some reason, you wanted to change the graph type, you would click the Chart Type button on the Graph Standard toolbar. When the Chart Type drop-down list displays, select one of the graph types. To help you determine what the graph will look like, the Chart Type drop-down list displays a graphic of each of the fourteen graph types.

When you select a new graph type, several changes occur. First, the graph displays as the new graph type. Second, depending on the graph type selected, names beneath the column and row headings may switch position with each other. Finally, the data series graphic in the datasheet displays reflecting the new graph type.

Adding Data Labels

Data labels add detail to the graph by placing a label on the graph for a data series, an individual data point, or for all the data points in the graph. Data for the data label comes directly from the datasheet. Thus, if a data point value changes, so does the data label.

It is sometimes useful to add the actual number value of the data point onto the chart. For example, in a column graph with wide value ranges between data points, placing the actual value next to the column eliminates the guessing of the data point. This is because the data point value would display on the graph.

Another purpose of data labels is to show percentages. For example, in a pie graph you are illustrating one data series as the whole pie. Each pie wedge represents one data point in the datasheet. Therefore, displaying data labels as a percentage on the pie graph shows the exact contribution of the data point to the data series. This is often useful when making budget presentations.

To add data labels to a graph, you must be in Microsoft Graph 5 and the menu bar must display. From the Insert menu, choose the Data Labels command. When the Data Labels dialog box displays, select the option button for the type of data label you wish to display. Then, choose the OK button.

Adding Another Slide to the Presentation

You want to add another slide to your presentation that describes the climate and attractions at San Juan, as shown in these steps.

**TO ADD ANOTHER SLIDE
TO THE PRESENTATION**

Step 1: Click the Insert New Slide button on the Standard toolbar.

Step 2: Double-click the Bulleted List AutoLayout in the New Slide dialog box.

Step 3: Type `San Juan` as the title for Slide 7.

Step 4: Select the text object by clicking anywhere inside the text placeholder.

Step 5: Type `Warm year-round climate` and press the ENTER key.

Step 6: Type `Sandy beaches` and press the ENTER key.

Step 7: Type `Historical sites` and press the ENTER key.

Step 8: Type `Cultural museums` and press the ENTER key.

Step 9: Type `Sport and recreation`

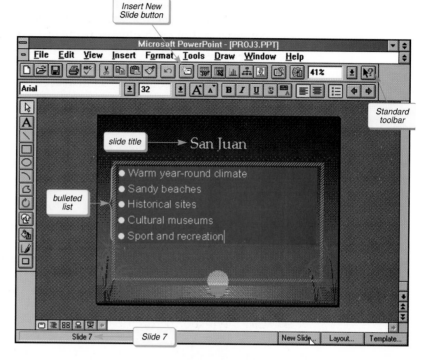

FIGURE 3-33

Slide 7 displays as shown in Figure 3-33.

Saving the Presentation

Because several changes have been made since your last save, you should save the presentation again with the same filename by clicking the Save button on the Standard toolbar.

▶ ADDING A TABLE

The next slide in this presentation contains a table that shows the temperatures for Puerto Rico (Figure 3-34). The rows in the table display each quarter in a year, and the columns display high, low, and average temperatures. Including the headings, the table contains four columns and five rows.

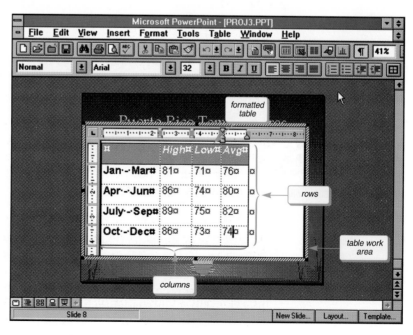

FIGURE 3-34

A **table** is a collection of columns and rows. Similar to a datasheet, the intersection of a column and a row on a table is called a cell. Cells are filled with data. The major difference between a table and a datasheet is that a graph is generated from data points on a datasheet; that is, the datasheet does not display on the slide, whereas, the data in a table displays on the slide in its column-row format. Another difference between a table and a datasheet is that the data you enter within a cell of a table wordwraps just as the text does between the margins of a document, instead of being truncated as in a cell in a datasheet.

Like the graph, a table is actually an embedded object because it is created in Microsoft Word 6. When you instruct PowerPoint to insert a table on a slide, Word opens and its menus, buttons, tools, etc., are available to you directly on the PowerPoint screen.

Creating a table requires several steps. First, you add a new slide with the table layout. Next, you open the Word application into the PowerPoint screen. Then, you enter headings and data into the table. Finally, you format the table so it looks more professional. The following pages contain a detailed outline of these steps.

Adding a Slide with the Table AutoLayout

Because you want the table on a separate slide, you add a new slide with the Table AutoLayout, as shown in these steps.

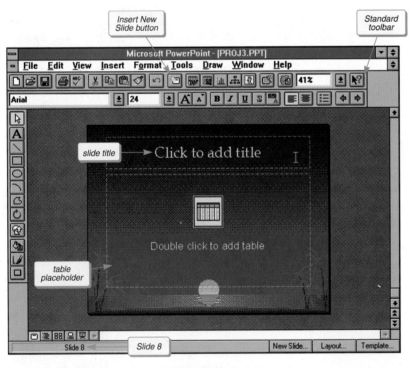

FIGURE 3-35

TO ADD A NEW SLIDE WITH THE TABLE AUTOLAYOUT

Step 1: Click the Insert New Slide button on the Standard toolbar.

Step 2: Double-click the Table AutoLayout (▦) in the New Slide dialog box.

Slide 8 displays the table placeholder (Figure 3-35).

Opening the Word Application and Inserting a Table

In order to create the table in Slide 8, you must first open the Word application. Recall that OLE brings this supplementary application to the PowerPoint window and makes the menus, buttons, tools, etc., from the Word application available on the PowerPoint screen. Once open, Word displays an Insert Word Table dialog box in a work area in the middle of the PowerPoint screen. You establish the number of columns and rows in the dialog box to insert a table, as shown in the steps below.

TO OPEN THE WORD APPLICATION AND INSERT A TABLE ▼

STEP 1

Type Puerto Rico Temperatures

PowerPoint displays the title of Slide 8 in the title placeholder.

STEP 2 ▶

Double-click the table placeholder in the Table AutoLayout.

Word displays the Insert Word Table dialog box on the PowerPoint screen (Figure 3-36). The table is currently set to display two columns and two rows. Your table should have four columns and five rows.

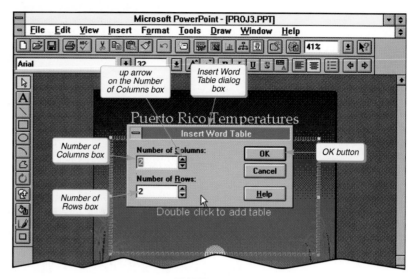

FIGURE 3-36

STEP 3 ▶

Click the up arrow next to the Number of Columns box two times.

The number 4 displays in the Number of Columns box, which indicates four columns are in this table (Figure 3-37).

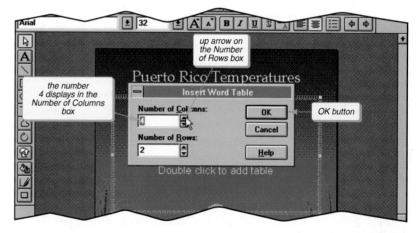

FIGURE 3-37

STEP 4 ▶

Click the up arrow next to the Number of Rows box three times.

The number 5 displays in the Number of Rows box, which indicates are five rows are in this table (Figure 3-38).

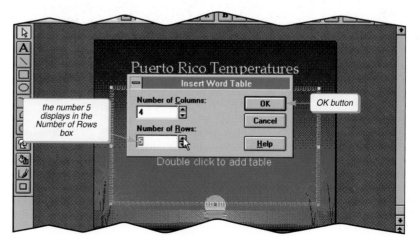

FIGURE 3-38

STEP 5 ▶

Choose the OK button.

Word inserts an empty table containing four columns of equal width and five rows of equal height (Figure 3-39). The insertion point is in the first cell (column 1, row 1) of the table.

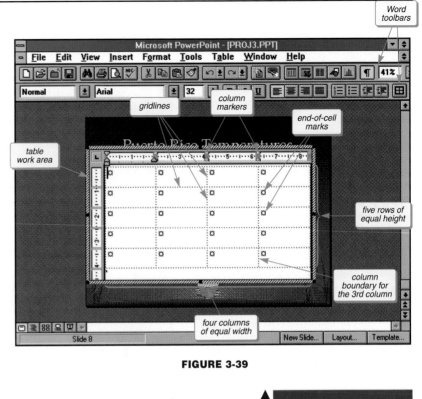

FIGURE 3-39

Notice in Figure 3-39 that the PowerPoint toolbars and menus have been replaced with the Word toolbars and menus.

The table displays on the screen with dotted **gridlines**. If your table does not have gridlines, choose the Gridlines command from the Table menu. Word does not print the table with gridlines; instead, the gridlines display to help you identify in which row and column you are working.

The vertical gridline immediately to the right of a column is called the **column boundary**. You decrease the width of a column by dragging the column boundary to the left. You increase the width of the column by dragging the column boundary to the right. You can also change column widths by dragging the **column markers** on the horizontal ruler.

Each cell has an **end-of-cell mark**, which is used to select a cell; that is, you point to the end-of-cell mark and click it to select a cell. The end-of-cell marks are currently left-aligned within each cell, indicating the data will be left-aligned. The alignment buttons on the Formatting toolbar change the alignment of a cell's contents.

To advance from one cell to the next, press the TAB key. To advance from one row to the next, also press the TAB key or click in the cell; do not press the ENTER key. The ENTER key is used to begin new paragraphs within a cell.

Adding Column Headings

Each column containing data should be identified with a heading. Perform the following steps to add column headings to the table.

TO ADD COLUMN HEADINGS ▼

STEP 1 ►

Click the cell located in column 2, row 1. Type High

The word High displays left-aligned in the cell (Figure 3-40). Recall that the alignment of cell data is controlled by the alignment of the end-of-cell marks.

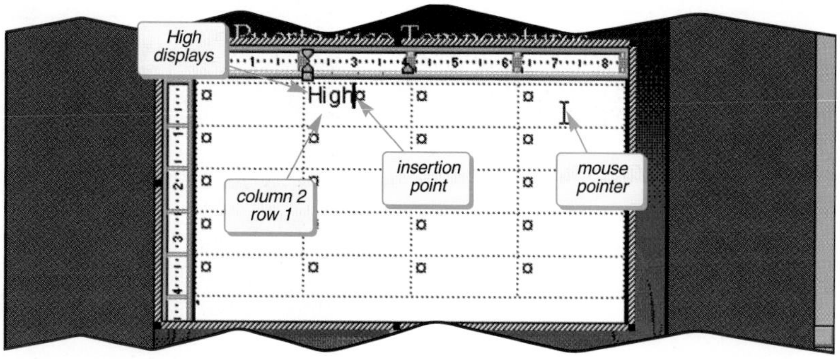

FIGURE 3-40

STEP 2 ►

Press the TAB key. Type Low **and press the TAB key. Type** Avg

The table displays three column headings (Figure 3-41).

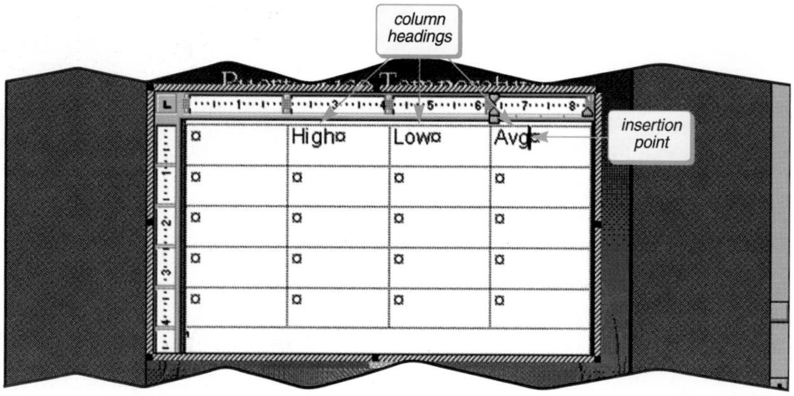

FIGURE 3-41

The column headings are complete. The next step is to fill in the rows of the table.

Filling in the Rows

As you fill in each row of the table, you should first label the row with a row heading. Then, complete the row with the data in the appropriate column. Perform the following steps to fill in the rows for the Puerto Rico Temperature table.

TO FILL IN THE ROWS ▼

STEP 1 ►

Click the cell in column 1, row 2. Type Jan - Mar **(Be sure to press the SPACEBAR before and after the hyphen.)**

The row heading is left-aligned in the cell (Figure 3-42).

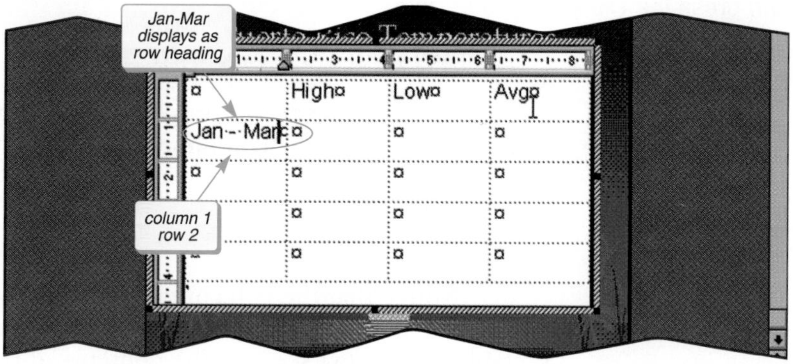

FIGURE 3-42

STEP 2 ▶

Press the TAB key and type 81

The high temperature for January through March displays left-aligned in the cell (Figure 3-43).

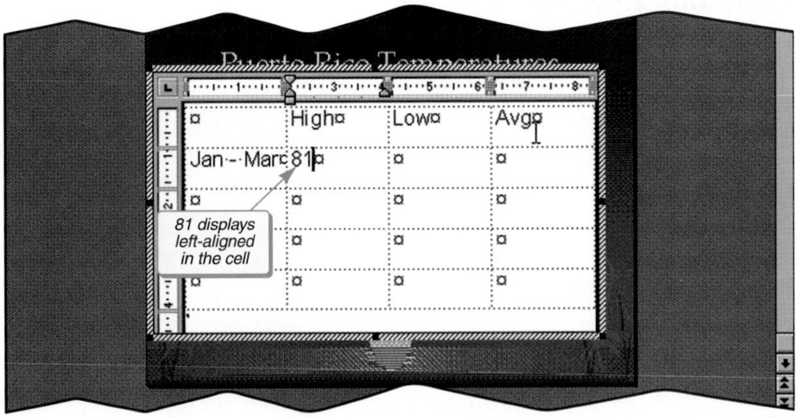

FIGURE 3-43

STEP 3 ▶

Press the TAB key. Type 71 **and press the TAB key. Type** 76

The high, low, and average temperatures for the months of January through March are entered (Figure 3-44).

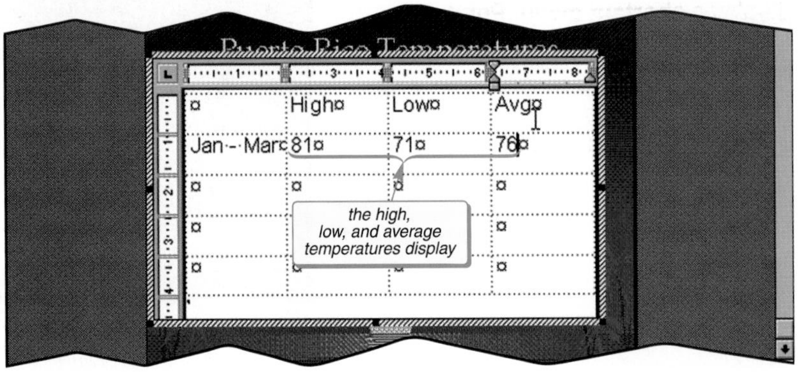

FIGURE 3-44

STEP 4 ▶

Press the TAB key. Type Apr - Jun **and press the TAB key. Type** 86 **and press the TAB key. Type** 74 **and press the TAB key. Type** 80 **and press the TAB key. Type** July - Sep **and press the TAB key. Type** 89 **and press the TAB key. Type** 75 **and press the TAB key. Type** 82 **and press the TAB key. Type** Oct - Dec **and press the TAB key. Type** 86 **and press the TAB key. Type** 73 **and press the TAB key. Type** 74

The table is complete (Figure 3-45).

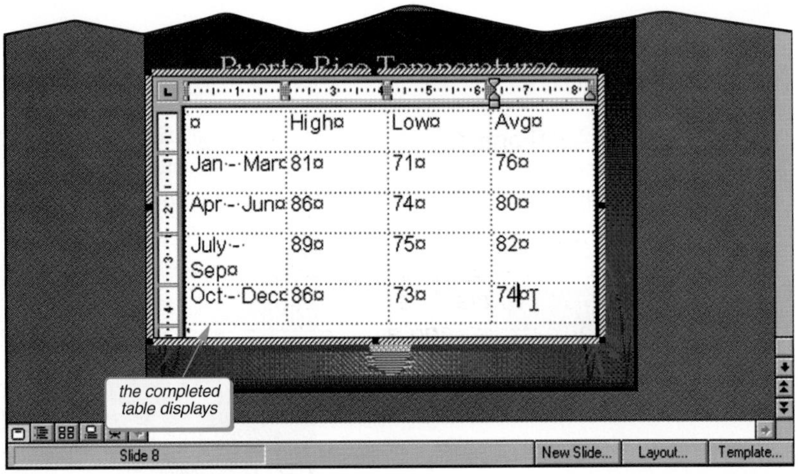

FIGURE 3-45

Notice that the cell containing the row heading July – Sep wrapped in the cell because the heading is too long to fit on one line in the cell. When you format the table in the next section, the contents of this cell will no longer wordwrap.

Formatting the Table

Because PowerPoint creates tables using Microsoft Word, the table may be automatically formatted using Word's Table AutoFormat command, which provides thirty-four predefined formats for tables. These predefined formats vary the borders, shading, colors, and fonts for the cells within a table. Perform the following steps to format the table with the Table AutoFormat command.

TO FORMAT THE TABLE ▼

STEP 1 ▶

With the insertion point and mouse pointer somewhere in the table, click the right mouse button to display a shortcut menu. Point to the Table AutoFormat command in the shortcut menu.

Word displays a shortcut menu for tables (Figure 3-46).

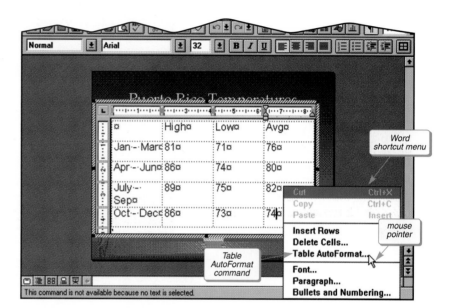

FIGURE 3-46

STEP 2 ▶

Choose the Table AutoFormat command.

The Table AutoFormat dialog box displays (Figure 3-47). The first pre-defined table format, Simple 1, is selected in the Formats list, and a preview of the selected format displays in the Preview area.

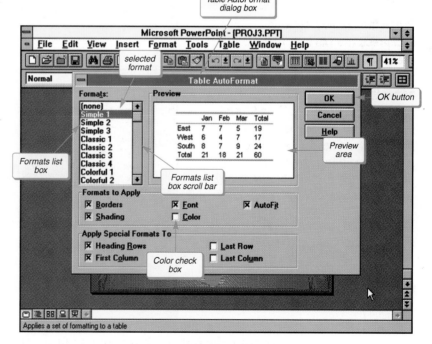

FIGURE 3-47

STEP 3 ▶

Select Classic 4 in the Formats list box by clicking it.

Word displays a preview of the Classic 4 format (Figure 3-48).

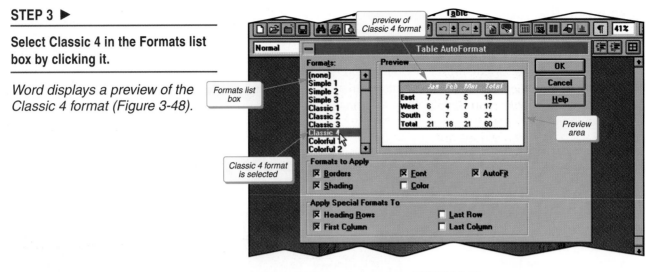

FIGURE 3-48

STEP 4 ▶

If it is not already selected, click the Color check box in the Formats to Apply area.

The table displays in color because the Color check box is selected (Figure 3-49).

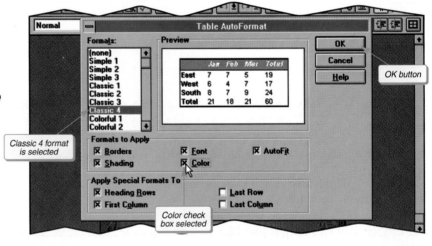

FIGURE 3-49

STEP 5 ▶

Choose the OK button.

The Table AutoFormat dialog box closes and the table displays with the Classic 4 format (Figure 3-50). Notice that the cell containing the July - Sep heading no longer word-wraps. Because the AutoFit check box was selected in the Table Auto-Format dialog box, Word redefines the column width based on the cell containing the longest data item.

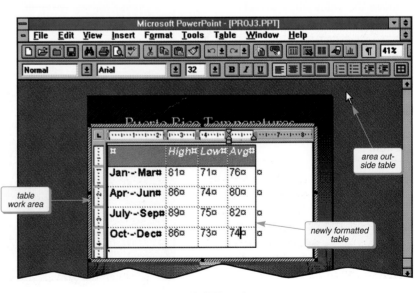

FIGURE 3-50

STEP 6 ▶

Click outside the table work area.

The Word application closes and the PowerPoint application reappears. The table displays on Slide 8 in the PowerPoint window (Figure 3-51). Because the table does not fill the table placeholder, it appears to be left-aligned on the slide.

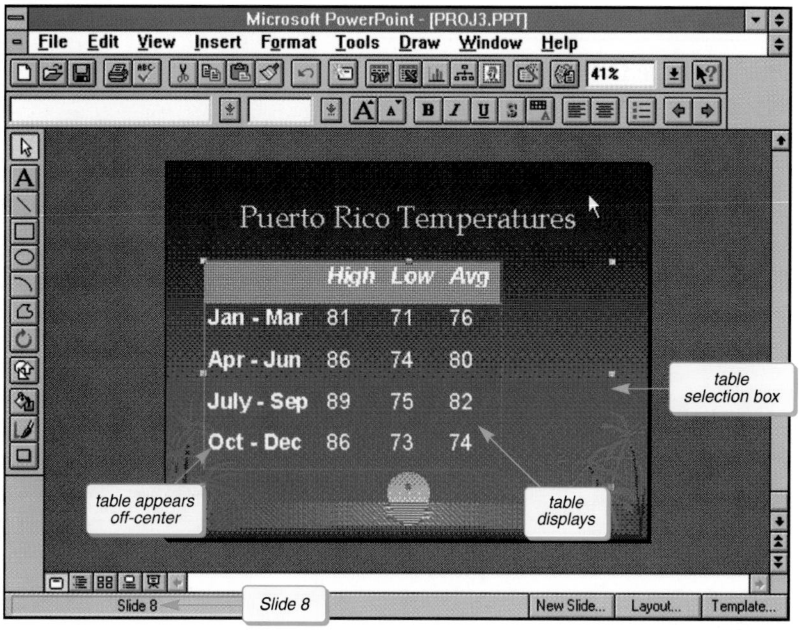

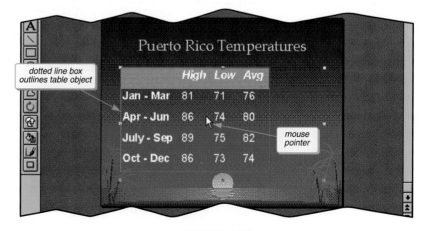

FIGURE 3-51

If, at a later time, you want to edit the table, simply double-click it to open the Word application. When your revisions are complete, click outside the table work area to return to PowerPoint.

Moving the Table Object

You want the table to begin directly beneath the letter P in the Puerto Rico Temperatures title object. Thus, you want to move the table. Because the table is an object, you can drag it just like you do any other object, as shown in these steps.

TO MOVE THE TABLE OBJECT ▼

STEP 1 ▶

Point to the center of the table. Then, press and hold the left mouse button.

When you press and hold the left mouse button, a dotted box outlines the table object (Figure 3-52). As you move, the outline box follows your pointer to show you where the table will be placed when you release the mouse button.

FIGURE 3-52

STEP 2 ▶

Drag the table to the right until the left edge of the outline box aligns with the letter P in Puerto Rico (Figure 3-53).

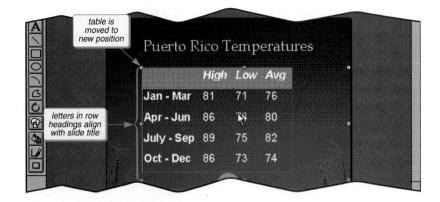

FIGURE 3-53

STEP 3 ▶

Release the left mouse button.

Word drops the table into place on Slide 8 (Figure 3-54). Recall that the procedure of moving an object with the mouse is called dragging and dropping.

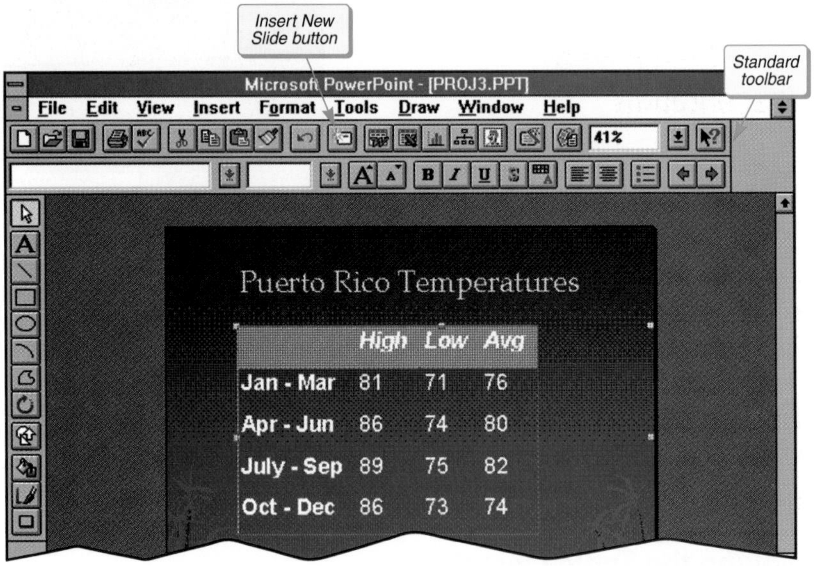

FIGURE 3-54

The revisions to the San Baarbo Vacations presentation are complete. However, the travel agency has decided to end the presentation with a blank slide, instead of returning to the PowerPoint screen. Thus, the next section adds a blank slide to the end of the presentation.

Adding a Blank Slide to End the Presentation

Recall that when you advance past the last slide in Slide Show view, PowerPoint returns to the PowerPoint screen. To prevent the audience from seeing the PowerPoint screen, it is a good practice to end your presentation with a **closing slide**.

 PRESENTATION TIP

The last slide of your presentation should be a closing slide, which may be a summary, a closing thought, or simply a blank slide. Using a blank slide to end an on-screen presentation gives the presentation a clean ending.

Perform the following steps to add a blank slide to the end of the presentation.

TO ADD A BLANK SLIDE

Step 1: Click the Insert New Slide button on the Standard toolbar.

Step 2: Double-click the Blank AutoLayout (☐) in the New Slide dialog box.

Slide 9 displays only the tropics template (Figure 3-55).

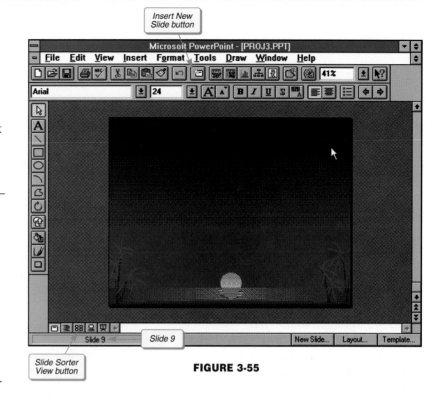

FIGURE 3-55

Spell Checking a Presentation

You should spell check your presentation before saving it again by clicking the Spelling but-ton on the Standard toolbar. For a detailed explanation of spell checking a pre-sentation, refer to pages PP44 and PP45 in Project 1.

Saving the Presentation

Because several changes have been made since your last save, you should save the presentation again with the same filename by clicking the Save button on the Standard toolbar.

▶ ADDING SPECIAL EFFECTS

PowerPoint provides many special effects to make your slide show presen-tation look professional. Two of these special effects are called transition and build. With these special effects, you control how slides enter and exit the screen and how the contents of a bulleted slide display. The following pages discuss each of the special effects in detail.

Adding Transitions to a Slide Show

PowerPoint allows you to control the way you advance from one slide to the next by adding transitions to an on-screen slide show. **Transitions** are special visual effects that display when you move one slide off the screen and bring on the next one. PowerPoint has over forty different transitions. The transition name char-acterizes the visual effect that displays.

You set slide transitions through the Transition Effects box or the Transition button on the Slide Sorter toolbar, which displays when you are in Slide Sorter view.

Slide Sorter Toolbar

In Slide Sorter view, the Slide Sorter toolbar displays beneath the Standard toolbar — in place of the Formatting toolbar. The Slide Sorter toolbar contains tools to help you quickly add special effects to your slide show. Table 3-5 explains the function of the buttons and boxes on the Slide Sorter toolbar.

▸ **TABLE 3-5**

ICON	NAME	FUNCTION
	Transition Button	Displays the Transition dialog box, which lists special effects used for slide changes during a slide show.
No Transition	Transition Effects Box	Displays a list of transition effects. Selecting a transition effect from the list applies it to the selected slide(s) and demonstrates it in the preview box.
	Build Button	Displays the Build dialog box which contains special effects to apply to a slide series. For example, building a slide on the screen, one bulleted paragraph at a time.
No Build Effect	Build Effects Box	Displays a list of build effects.
	Hide Slide Button	Excludes a slide from the presentation without deleting it.
	Rehearse Timings Button	Records the amount of time spent on each slide during a presentation rehearsal.
	Show Formatting Button	Displays or hides character formatting attributes.

In the San Baarbo Vacations presentation, you want the Strips Right-Down transition between slides; that is, all slides begin stacked on top of one another, like a deck of cards. As you click the mouse to view the next screen, the current slide exits the screen by shrinking down toward the bottom right corner of the screen until it is gone. Perform the following steps to add the Strips Right-Down transition to the San Baarbo Vacations presentation.

TO ADD TRANSITIONS TO A SLIDE SHOW ▼

STEP 1 ▶

Click the Slide Sorter View button at the bottom of the PowerPoint screen. Select Slide 9 by clicking it.

PowerPoint displays the presentation in Slide Sorter view (Figure 3-56). Depending on the last slide you viewed, your screen may display differently. Slide 9 is selected. Slide 9 currently does not have a transition effect, as noted in the Transition Effects box on the Slide Sorter toolbar.

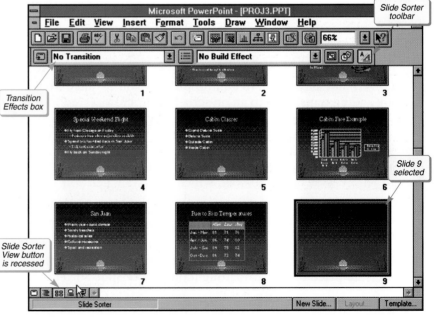

FIGURE 3-56

STEP 2 ▶

Select the Edit menu and point to the Select All command (Figure 3-57).

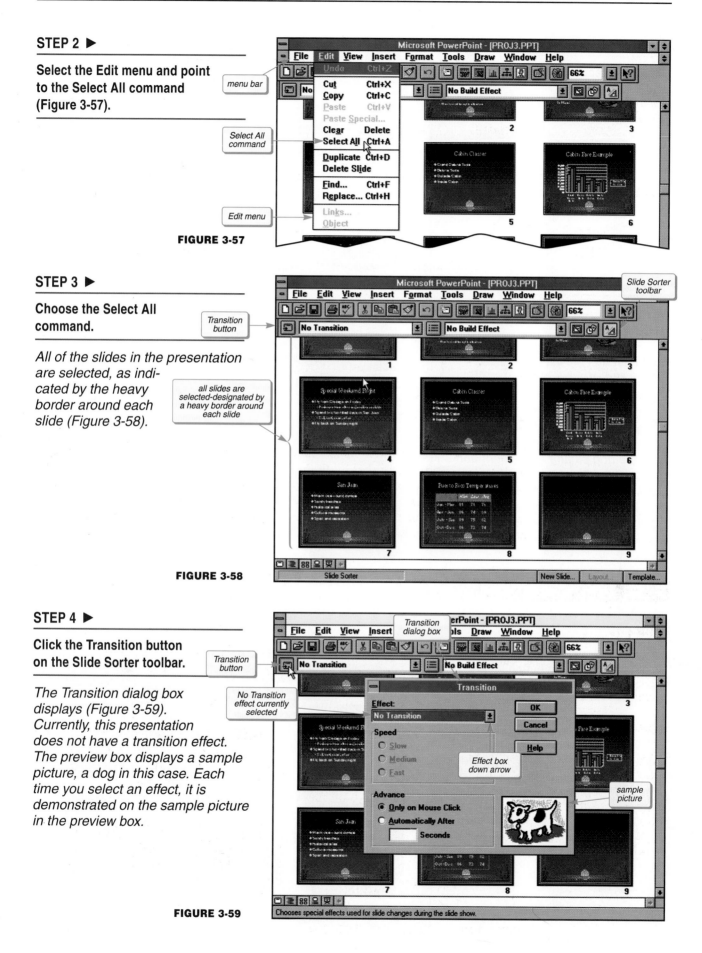

FIGURE 3-57

STEP 3 ▶

Choose the Select All command.

All of the slides in the presentation are selected, as indicated by the heavy border around each slide (Figure 3-58).

FIGURE 3-58

STEP 4 ▶

Click the Transition button on the Slide Sorter toolbar.

The Transition dialog box displays (Figure 3-59). Currently, this presentation does not have a transition effect. The preview box displays a sample picture, a dog in this case. Each time you select an effect, it is demonstrated on the sample picture in the preview box.

FIGURE 3-59

STEP 5 ▶

Click the Effect box arrow.

A list of transition effects displays (Figure 3-60).

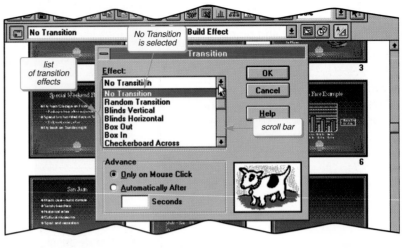

FIGURE 3-60

STEP 6 ▶

Scroll through the list of transition effects and click the Strips Right-Down effect.

The preview box demonstrates the Strips Right-Down effect by stripping the dog picture to the right and down off the preview box and then displaying a key picture (Figure 3-61). To see the demonstration again, simply click the picture in the preview box.

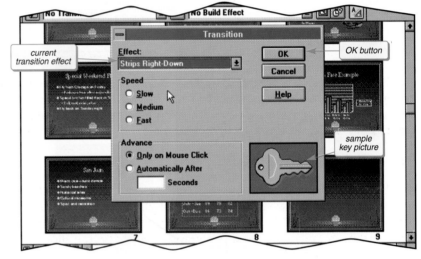

FIGURE 3-61

STEP 7 ▶

Click the Slow option button in the Speed box.

When you click the Slow option button, the preview box demonstrates the effect and speed of the transition (Figure 3-62). The key picture slowly moves down and to the right of the preview box as the dog picture displays.

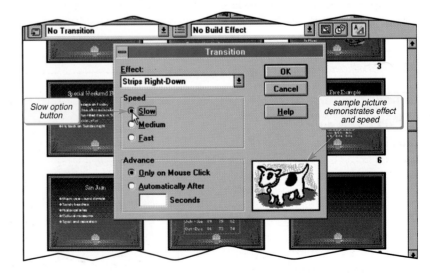

FIGURE 3-62

STEP 8 ▶

Choose the OK button.

PowerPoint displays the presentation in Slide Sorter view (Figure 3-63). A transition icon (▢) displays under each slide, which indicates that transition effects have been added to the slides. The transition effect currently applied to the selected slide(s) displays in the Transition Effects box.

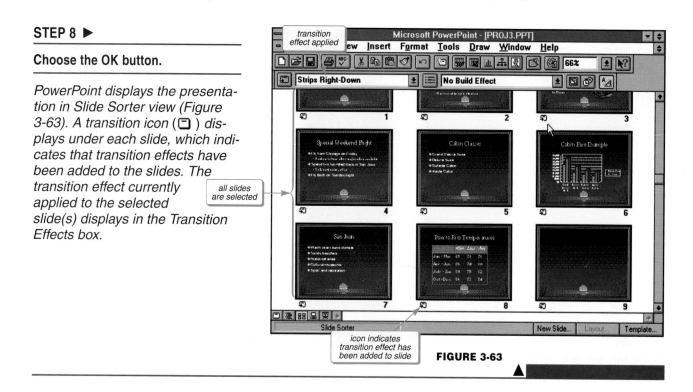

FIGURE 3-63

Transition has been applied to the entire presentation. When you have finalized your presentation, you should select the Fast option button in the Transition dialog box because you do not want to emphasize the transition. The next step in creating this slide show is to add special effects to individual slides.

Applying Build Effects

Build effects are applied to bulleted slides. This special effect instructs PowerPoint to progressively disclose each bulleted paragraph, one at a time, during the running of a slide show. PowerPoint has thirty build effects and the capability to dim the other bulleted paragraphs already on the slide when a new paragraph is displayed.

On Slide 1, you want to apply the Fly From Left effect. When you display a slide with this effect, bulleted paragraph *flies* in from the left edge of the screen to its proper location on the slide each time you click the mouse. Perform the following steps to apply build effects to an existing bulleted slide.

TO APPLY BUILD EFFECTS ▼

STEP 1 ▶

If Slide 1 does not currently display, drag the elevator to the top of the vertical scroll bar to display it.

This presentation currently does not have any build effects, as designated in the Build Effects box (Figure 3-64). All slides in the presentation are currently selected. You need to deselect the slides before you select Slide 2.

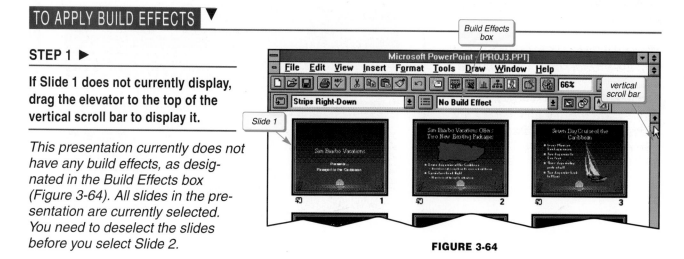

FIGURE 3-64

STEP 2 ▶

Click between Slide 1 and Slide 2.

No slides in the presentation are selected and the insertion point is between Slides 1 and 2 (Figure 3-65). (Clicking anywhere outside the selected slides deselects the slides in the presentation.)

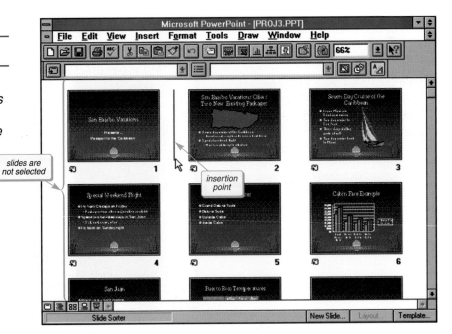

FIGURE 3-65

STEP 3 ▶

Select Slide 2 by clicking it.

Slide 2 is the only selected slide in the presentation (Figure 3-66). Slide 2 currently does not have any build effects.

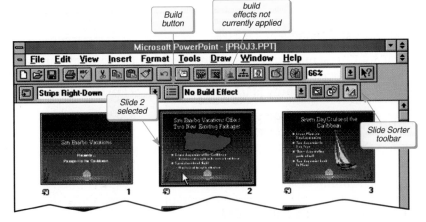

FIGURE 3-66

STEP 4 ▶

Click the Build button on the Slide Sorter toolbar.

The Build dialog box displays (Figure 3-67). PowerPoint displays the defaults for the Dim Previous Points and Effect boxes. The default color is controlled by the color scheme of the template. The defaults are not used in the slide until their check boxes are selected.

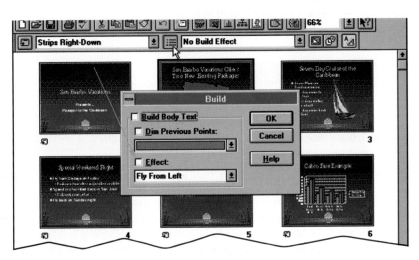

FIGURE 3-67

STEP 5 ▶

Click the Effect check box.

The Effect check box is selected (Figure 3-68) The Build Body Text check box is automatically selected when either the Dim Previous Points or Effect check box is selected. Fly From Left, the default effect, displays in the Effect box.

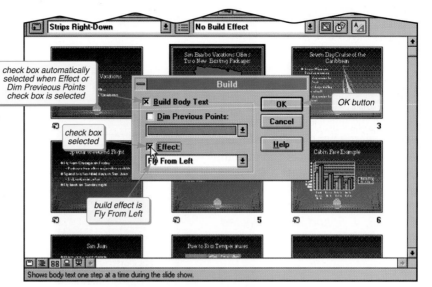

FIGURE 3-68

STEP 6 ▶

Choose the OK button in the Build dialog box.

A build icon ( ) displays under Slide 2 and to the right of the transition icon, which indicates that build effects have been applied to the slide (Figure 3-69).

STEP 7

Click between Slide 1 and Slide 2.

No slides in the presentation are selected and the insertion point is between Slides 1 and 2 (Figure 3-65 above).

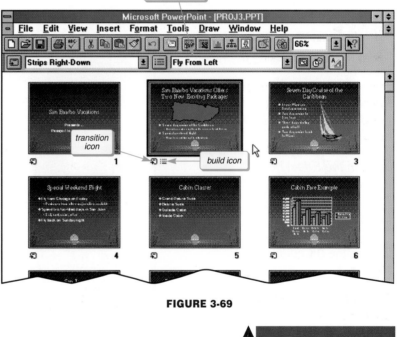

FIGURE 3-69

The Fly From Left build effect has been applied to Slide 2. The next section applies this same build effect to the remaining bulleted slides in the presentation.

Applying a Build Effect to the Remaining Bulleted Slides

The next step is to apply the Fly From Left build effect to Slides 3, 4, 5, and 7 in the San Baarbo Vacations presentation. These slides are **noncontiguous**; that is, not consecutive. To select noncontiguous slides, you press and hold the SHIFT key while clicking each slide, then release the SHIFT key called (**SHIFT+click**). Use the SHIFT+click technique to apply the build effect to the remaining bulleted slides in the presentation as shown in these steps.

TO APPLY A BUILD EFFECT TO THE REMAINING BULLETED SLIDES ▼

STEP 1 ▶

Press and hold the SHIFT key and click Slide 3, Slide 4, and Slide 5. Release the SHIFT key. Drag the vertical scroll bar elevator until Slide 7 displays. Then, press and hold the SHIFT key and click Slide 7. Release the SHIFT key.

Slides 3, 4, 5, and 7 are selected (Figure 3-70).

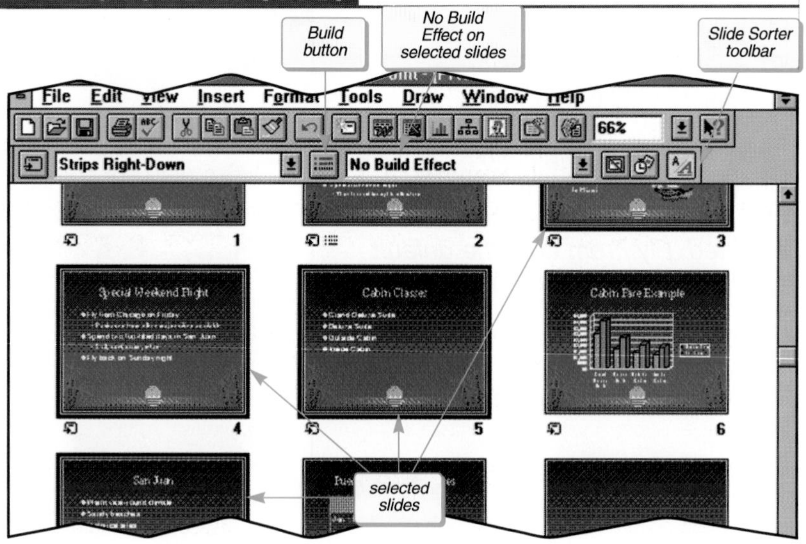

FIGURE 3-70

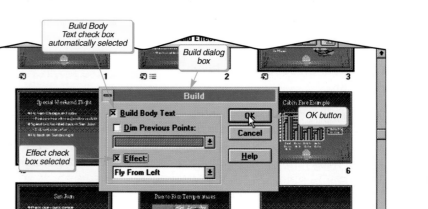

STEP 2 ▶

Click the Build button on the Slide Sorter toolbar. When the Build dialog box displays, click the Effect check box.

PowerPoint automatically selects the Build Body Text check box when the Effect check box is selected (Figure 3-71). Fly From Left displays in the Effect box.

FIGURE 3-71

STEP 3 ▶

Choose the OK button.

The Fly From Left build effect is applied to the selected slides (Figure 3-72).

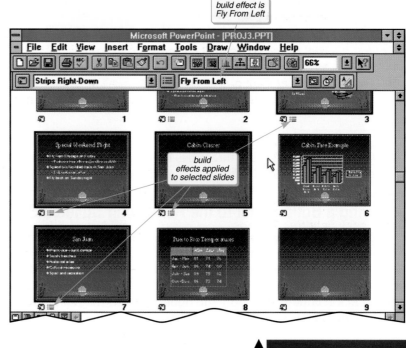

FIGURE 3-72

The revisions to the San Baarbo Vacations presentation are complete.

Dim Previous Points

When you added the Fly From Left build effect, you selected the Effect check box in the Build dialog box. You could have also selected the Dim Previous Points check box, which tells PowerPoint to change the color of the previous bulleted paragraph as a new one displays on the screen. You can accept the default dim color displayed in the Dim Previous Points color box, or you can click the box arrow and select a different dim color. Because of the many color choices, you should experiment with your presentation to decide the color best suited for your presentation. Many times, you will decide not to select the Dim Previous Points check box because you could not find a dim color to enhance your presentation, as is the case in the San Baarbo Vacation presentation.

Saving the Presentation Again

Because several changes have been made since your last save, you should save the presentation again with the same filename by clicking the Save button on the Standard toolbar.

▶ RUNNING AN AUTOMATIC SLIDE SHOW

 n Project 1, you were introduced to using Slide Show view to look at your presentation one slide at a time. You will now use Slide Show view to run an **automatic slide show**. The automatic slide show will display each slide for a period of time. The time is set using the **Rehearse Timings button**. The Rehearse Timings button, found on the Slide Sorter toolbar, allows you to run a slide show and rehearse your presentation. While you are running the slide show, PowerPoint keeps track of the length of time each slide is displayed and then sets the timing accordingly. Once timings are set, you must tell PowerPoint to use these times to run the automatic slide show.

> **PRESENTATION TIP**
> Allow an average of two minutes for each slide in your presenta-
> tion. Some slides will take longer to explain, while others will take
> less. Rehearsing your presentation will help you determine the
> proper amount of time for each slide. Allow at least two to three
> minutes for the closing slide to wrap up your presentation.

TO SET SLIDE TIMINGS ▼

STEP 1 ▶

Point to the Rehearse Timings button on the Slide Sorter toolbar (Figure 3-73).

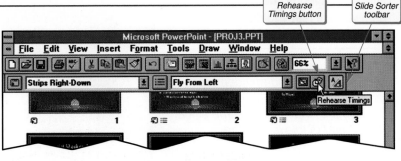

FIGURE 3-73

STEP 2 ▶

Click the Rehearse Timings button on the Slide Sorter toolbar.

PowerPoint begins the slide show and displays Slide 1 (Figure 3-74). A timer box displays at the lower left of the slide. The timer accumulates until you click the left mouse button.

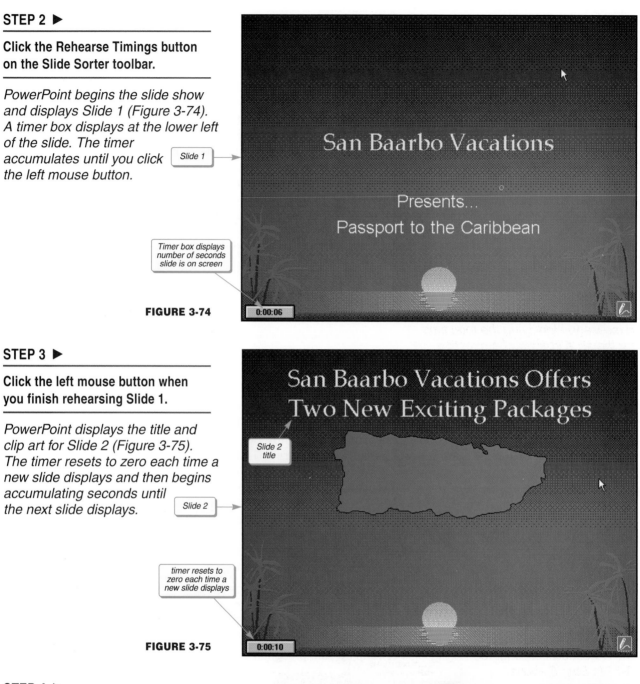

Slide 1

Timer box displays number of seconds slide is on screen

FIGURE 3-74

STEP 3 ▶

Click the left mouse button when you finish rehearsing Slide 1.

PowerPoint displays the title and clip art for Slide 2 (Figure 3-75). The timer resets to zero each time a new slide displays and then begins accumulating seconds until the next slide displays.

Slide 2 title

Slide 2

timer resets to zero each time a new slide displays

FIGURE 3-75

STEP 4 ▶

Click the left mouse button when you are ready to display the first bulleted paragraph.

PowerPoint displays the first bulleted paragraph and any demoted paragraphs (Figure 3-76). The timer displays the total elapsed time since Slide 2 first displayed on the screen.

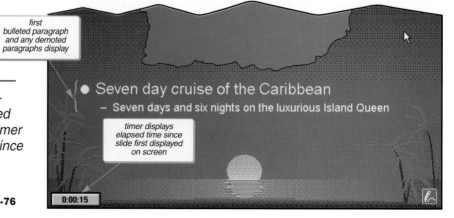

first bulleted paragraph and any demoted paragraphs display

timer displays elapsed time since slide first displayed on screen

FIGURE 3-76

STEP 5 ▶

Click the left mouse button to display each of the remaining bulleted paragraphs on Slide 2. When you finish rehearsing Slide 2, click the left mouse button to rehearse Slide 3. Continue rehearsing your presentation until you reach Slide 9, the slide that displays only the tropics template. When Slide 9 displays, allow the timer to accumulate for two to three minutes. Click the left mouse button.

PowerPoint returns to Slide Sorter view and displays the Microsoft PowerPoint information box (Figure 3-77). The information box displays a message identifying the total time for the slide show and a question asking to record the slide timings in Slide Sorter view. In this figure, the total time used during the presentation rehearsal was 9 minutes and 10 seconds. Depending on your rehearsal, your time will differ.

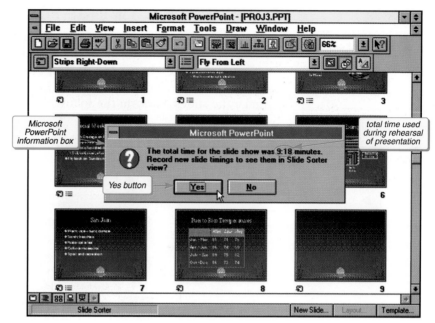

FIGURE 3-77

STEP 6 ▶

Choose the Yes button.

PowerPoint displays the amount of time each slide displays before the next slide replaces it (Figure 3-78). The time is listed as minutes and seconds. If you wanted to run the rehearsal again before setting the timings, you would choose the No button from Figure 3-77 in Step 5 above.

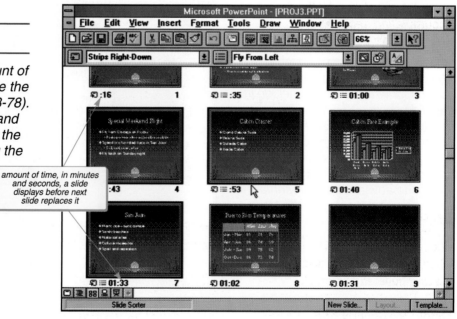

FIGURE 3-78

The timings for each slide have been established during the rehearsal. The next step is to activate the automatic slide show.

▶ USING SLIDE TIMINGS FOR AUTOMATIC SLIDE SHOW

By default, PowerPoint manually advances slides in a slide show. Recall in Projects 1 and 2 that you clicked the mouse pointer to move through your presentation. In order for PowerPoint to automatically run your presentation based on your rehearsal timings, you need to change the option to advance the slides. Perform the following steps to change the advance option.

TO CHANGE THE ADVANCE OPTION FROM MANUAL TO SLIDE TIMINGS ▼

STEP 1 ▶

Select the View menu and point to the Slide Show command (Figure 3-79).

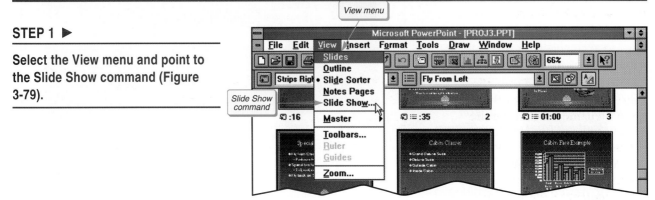

FIGURE 3-79

STEP 2 ▶

Choose the Slide Show command. When the Slide Show dialog box displays, select the Use Slide Timings option button. Then, point to the Show button (**Show**).

The Slide Show dialog box contains options for which slides to include in the slide show and options for how to advance the slides in the slide show (Figure 3-80). The default settings are for all slides and manual advance. You are using the slide timings to advance your presentation so you have selected the Use Slide Timings option. The Show button will activate the automatic slide show so you can test your timings.

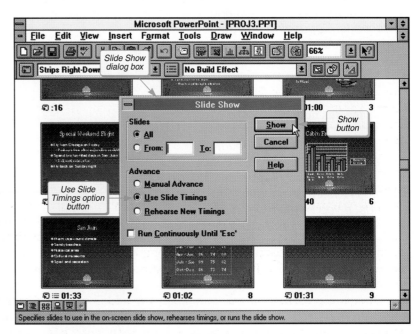

FIGURE 3-80

STEP 3

Choose the Show button.

PowerPoint begins the automatic slide show with the timings you used in your rehearsal.

PowerPoint moves through the slide show. To interrupt or exit the slide show, press the ESC key. Table 3-6 contains slide show shortcuts.

PRESENTATION TIP
Practice running your automatic slide show several times before presenting it to an audience.

Saving the Presentation and Exiting PowerPoint

The presentation is complete. Because several changes have been made since your last save, you should save the presentation again with the same filename by clicking the Save button on the Standard toolbar.

You may now exit PowerPoint by choosing the Exit command from the File menu.

▶ TABLE 3-6

TASK	SHORTCUT
Go to slide <number>	<Number>+ENTER
Black/unblack screen	B, . (period)
White/unwhite screen	W, , (comma)
Show/hide pointer	A, = (equal)
Stop/restart automatic show	S, + (plus)
End show	ESC, CTRL+Break, - (hyphen)
Erase screen annotations	E
Use new time	T
Use original time	O
Advance on mouse click	M
Advance to hidden slide	H
Go to Slide 1	Press and hold both mouse buttons for two seconds
Advance to next slide	Click mouse button, SPACEBAR, N, RIGHT ARROW, DOWN ARROW, PAGE DOWN
Return to previous slide	Click right mouse button, BACKSPACE, P, LEFT ARROW, UP ARROW PAGE UP

▶ PROJECT SUMMARY

Project 3 enhanced the San Baarbo Vacations presentation started in Project 2. The first step was to save the presentation with a new name so as to preserve the original Project 2 presentation. You then changed templates to give the presentation a new look. Next, you deleted the seal object on Slide 4 because it was no longer applicable to the presentation. You then added a new bulleted list to explain available cabin classes. Next, you added a graph to illustrate the differences in cabin fares. To create the graph, you used Microsoft Graph 5 and completed a datasheet. Next, you added a bulleted list to explain the many features of San Juan. To further support the presentation, you added a temperature table using Microsoft Word 6.

Once the presentation was complete, you added special effects to the slide show. First, you added a transition effect to strip the current slide off the screen down and to the right. Then, you created build effects to display each bulleted paragraph independently of the others. At the end of the project, you rehearsed your presentation to establish timings to run an automatic slide show. Finally, you changed the PowerPoint advance option to allow PowerPoint to run your slide show automatically.

▶ KEY TERMS AND INDEX

In PowerPoint, you can accomplish a task in a number of ways. The following table provides a quick reference to each task in this project with its available options. The commands listed in the Menu column can be executed using either the keyboard or mouse.

Task	Mouse	Menu	Keyboard Shortcuts
Add a Legend	Click Legend button on Graph Standard toolbar	From Graph Data menu, choose Legend	
Add a Transition	Click Transition button on Slide Sorter toolbar	From Tools menu, choose Transition	
Change the Graph Orientation	Click By Row or click By Column button on Graph Standard toolbar	From Graph Data menu, choose Series in Rows or choose Series in Columns	
Clear Cell(s)		From Edit menu, choose Clear	Press DELETE
Create a Build Slide	Click Build button on Slide Sorter toolbar	From Tools menu, choose Build	
Delete a Datasheet Cell		From Graph Edit menu, choose Delete	
Delete a Database Column			Press CTRL+HYPHEN
Delete a Database Row			Press CTRL+HYPHEN
Delete a Table Column		From Word Table menu, choose Delete Cells	
Delete a Table Row		From Word Table menu, choose Delete Cells	

Task	Mouse	Menu	Keyboard Shortcuts
Insert a Graph	Double-click in graph placeholder of click Insert Graph button or double-click in empty object placeholder	From Insert menu, choose Microsoft Graph	
Insert a Table	Double-click in table placeholder or click Insert Table button or double-click in empty object placeholder	From Insert menu, choose Microsoft Word Table	
Save a Presentation with a Different Filename		From File menu, choose Save As	Press F12
Select All Cells in Tables		From Word menu, choose Select All	Press CTRL+A
Select All Slides (Slide Sorter		From Edit menu, choose Select All	Press CTRL+A
Select a Cell	Click in cell		
Select a Database Column	Click in column heading		
Select a Database Row	Click in row heading		
Select a Graph Type	Click Chart Type button on Graph Standard toolbar	From Format menu, choose Chart Type	
Select Noncontiguous Slides	SHIFT+click slide		
Choose Slide Sorter view	Click Slide Sorter View button	From View menu, choose Slide Sorter	Press CTRL+ALT+P
Start Slide Show	Click Slide Show View button on View Button bar	From View menu, choose Slide Show	
View a Datasheet	Click View Datasheet button on Graph Standard toolbar	From View menu on Graph menu, choose Datasheet	

STUDENT ASSIGNMENTS

STUDENT ASSIGNMENT 1
True/False

Instructions: Circle T if the statement is true or F if the statement is false.

T F   1. Double-clicking the graph placeholder closes PowerPoint and opens Microsoft Graph.

T F   2. In a datasheet, pressing the ENTER key selects the cell adjacent to the active cell.

T F   3. A legend is an explanatory table or list of symbols appearing on a graph.

T   F   4. Clicking the Currency button on the Graph Formatting toolbar inserts dollar signs and two decimal positions to the selected data points.

T   F   5. A cell is the basic unit of the datasheet.

T   F   6. A data series is a single row or a single column of data points on the table.

T   F   7. A column heading is a letter identifying a column in a table.

T   F   8. Microsoft Word truncates category names to fit in the datasheet cell.

T   F   9. In a datasheet, a row number on the left side of the grid is called the row heading.

T   F   10. Clicking the By Row button on the Graph Formatting toolbar changes the orientation to associate the chart data series with horizontal rows on the datasheet.

T   F   11. When you open a supplementary application, such as Microsoft Graph, its menus, buttons, and tools are available to you directly on the PowerPoint screen.

T   F   12. You change the width of a table column by dragging the column boundary or by dragging a column marker on the horizontal ruler.

T   F   13. In a table, each cell has an end-of-cell mark, which is used to select a cell.

T   F   14. Transitions are special visual effects that emphasize the current bulleted paragraph by building a slide one bulleted paragraph at a time.

T   F   15. A cell is identified by its cell reference, which is the coordinates of the intersection of a column and a row.

T   F   16. Once applied, build effects instruct PowerPoint to progressively disclose each bulleted paragraph, one at a time, during the running of a slide show.

T   F   17. The datasheet is a rectangular grid containing horizontal columns and vertical rows.

T   F   18. A table is actually an embedded object because it is created in Microsoft Word 6.

T   F   19. The numbers representing data in a datasheet are called data points.

T   F   20. Microsoft Word wordwraps text entries to fit into a cell.

STUDENT ASSIGNMENT 2
Multiple Choice

Instructions: Circle the correct response.

1. Microsoft Graph uses the data points to create the _____ that displays in the presentation.
   a. graph   b. datasheet   c. table   d. all of the above

2. To identify a cell, specify the _____ first, followed by the _____ .
   a. row letter, column number   c. column number, row letter
   b. column letter, row number   d. row number, column letter

3. To select noncontiguous slides, hold down the _____ key while clicking each slide.
   a. SHIFT   b. ALT   c. TAB   d. CTRL

4. The datasheet uses the _____ toolbars.
   a. PowerPoint   b. Word 6   c. Graph 5   d. Office

5. A cell is _____ .
   a. a basic unit of a datasheet   c. the intersection of each column and row   d. all of the above

6. When entering data into a table, press the _____ key to advance to the next cell.
   a. SHIFT   b. ENTER   c. TAB   d. both b and c

7. The _____ toolbar displays buttons for adding transition and build effects to slides in a slide show.
   a. Special Effects   b. Formatting   c. Standard   d. Slide Sorter

8. Click the _____ button to create a slide that progressively discloses each bulleted paragraph.
   a. Transition   b. Build   c. Rehearse Timings   d. both a and b

9. To add a new slide, click the _____ .
   a. Insert New Slide button on the Standard toolbar
   b. AutoLayout button on the status bar
   c. New Slide button on the Formatting toolbar
   d. both a and c

10. When designing a presentation, allow an average of _____ minutes for each slide.
    a. two   b. five   c. one   d. ten

STUDENT ASSIGNMENT 3
Understanding the Datasheet Window

Instructions: Arrows in Figure SA3-3 point to the major components of a Graph Datasheet window. Identify the various parts of the window in the spaces provided.

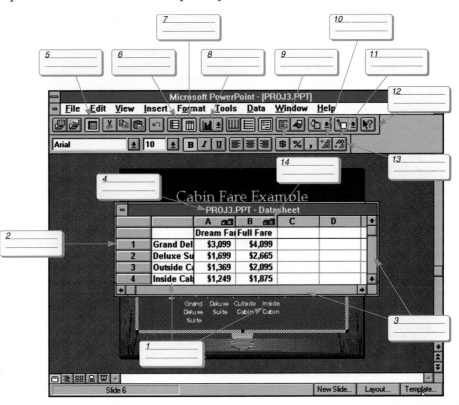

FIGURE SA3-3

STUDENT ASSIGNMENT 4
Understanding the Slide Sorter Toolbar

Instructions: Arrows in Figure SA3-4 point to buttons on the Slide Sorter toolbar. In the spaces provided, identify and briefly explain the purpose of each button and box.

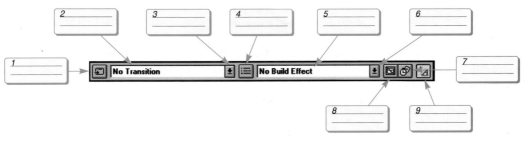

FIGURE SA3-4

STUDENT ASSIGNMENT 5
Understanding How to Add a Graph

Instructions: Assume you are in Slide view and are adding a graph to the end of a presentation. Fill in the step numbers below to indicate the sequence necessary to add the graph shown in Figure SA3-5.

Step ____: Click Decrease Decimal button.
Step _3_: Type the slide title.
Step ____: Click outside the Datasheet window work area to display graph in slide.
Step _4_: Double-click the graph placeholder.
Step ____: Delete data in columns C and D.
Step _1_: Click the Insert New Slide button on the Standard toolbar.
Step ____: Select data points.
Step ____: Type column headings, data series names, and data points into datasheet.
Step _2_: Double-click the Graph AutoLayout in the New Slide dialog box.
Step ____: Click Currency Style button.

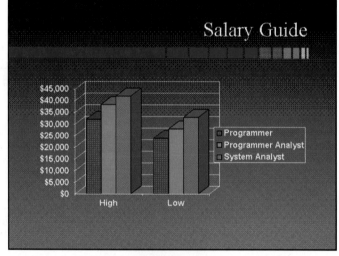

FIGURE SA3-5

STUDENT ASSIGNMENT 6
Understanding How to Add Build Effects

Instructions: Assume you are in Slide view and are adding build effects to all bulleted list slides in your presentation. Fill in the step numbers below to indicate the sequence necessary to add build effects.

Step ____: Click between any two slides to deselect the bulleted list slides.
Step ____: Click the Effect check box.
Step ____: Click the Slide Sorter View button.
Step ____: Choose the OK button in the Build dialog box.
Step ____: Select all bulleted list slides in the presentation.
Step ____: Click the Build button on the Slide Sorter toolbar.

COMPUTER LABORATORY EXERCISES

COMPUTER LABORATORY EXERCISE 1
Using PowerPoint Help

Instructions: Start PowerPoint. Open a blank presentation and choose the Title Slide AutoLayout. Perform the following tasks:

1. From the Help menu, choose the Search for Help on command. Type slide show when the Search dialog box displays, . Choose the Show Topics button. If it is not already selected, select About Creating and Running Slide Shows. Choose the Go To button. Read the information. From the File menu, choose the Print Topic command.

2. Scroll down the screen until the See also section displays. Jump to Running a slide show by clicking it. Read and print the information on running a slide show. Click the Tip button (**Tip**) at the top of the screen. Read the tip. Click the Back button (**Back**) to return to About Creating and Running Slide Shows.

3. Jump to Setting slide timings by clicking it. Read and print the information on setting slide timings.

4. Scroll until the See also section displays. Jump to Hints for creating and running slide shows. Read and print the information on hints for creating and running slide shows. Click the Back button.

5. Exit Help by choosing the Exit command from the File menu.

COMPUTER LABORATORY EXERCISE 2
Adding a Table to a Presentation

Instructions: Start PowerPoint. Open the presentation CLE3-2.PPT from the PPOINT4 subdirectory on the Student Diskette that accompanies this book. Perform the following tasks to add a table so the presentation looks like the one in Figures CLE3-2a through CLE3-2c.

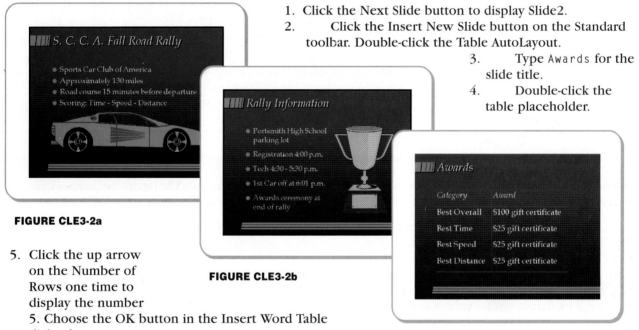

1. Click the Next Slide button to display Slide2.
2. Click the Insert New Slide button on the Standard toolbar. Double-click the Table AutoLayout.
3. Type Awards for the slide title.
4. Double-click the table placeholder.

FIGURE CLE3-2a

FIGURE CLE3-2b

FIGURE CLE3-2c

5. Click the up arrow on the Number of Rows one time to display the number 5. Choose the OK button in the Insert Word Table dialog box.

6. Type Category and press the TAB key. Type Award and press the TAB key. Type Best Overall and press the TAB key. Type $100 gift certificate and press the TAB key. Type Best Time and press the TAB key. Type $25 gift certificate and press the TAB key. Type Best Speed and press the TAB key. Type $25 gift certificate

7. With the insertion point and mouse pointer somewhere in the table, click the right mouse button to display a shortcut menu. Point to the Table AutoFormat command.

8. Select Classic 1 in the Formats list box. Choose the OK.

9. Click outside the table window work area to close Word and to display the table in Slide 3.

10. Save the presentation with the filename CLE3-2 on your data disk.

11. Print the presentation by selecting Slides in the Print What box and by selecting the Pure Black & White check box.

12. From the File menu, choose the Close command to close the presentation.

COMPUTER LABORATORY EXERCISE 3
Converting a Presentation into an Automatic Slide Show

Instructions: Start PowerPoint. Open the presentation CLA2-2.PPT from your data disk. If you did not complete Computer Laboratory Assignment 2 in Project 2, see your instructor for a copy. Perform the following tasks to change the presentation to an automatic slide show.

1. If the presentation is not in Slide Sorter view, click the Slide Sorter View button.
2. SHIFT+click all slides in the presentation.
3. Click the Transition button on the Slide Sorter toolbar.
4. Click the down arrow on the Effect box. Select Checkerboard Across from the Effect drop-down list box. Select the Automatically After option button. Type 20 in the Automatically After text box. Choose the OK button.
5. Click the Build button on the Slide Sorter toolbar.
6. Select the Dim Previous Points check box. Select Cyan (light blue-green), which is located in column 2 row 2 in the Dim Previous Points color drop-down list box.
7. Select the Effect check box. Click the arrow on the Effect box. Scroll down and select Wipe Right from the Effect drop-down list box. Choose the OK button.
8. From the View menu, choose the Slide Show command. Select the Use Slide Timings option button in the Slide Show dialog box. Choose the Show button.
9. Watch the presentation.
10. Save the presentation with the filename CLE3-3.
11. Print the presentation by selecting Slides (with Builds) in the Print What box and by selecting the Pure Black & White check box.
12. From the File menu, choose the Close command to close the presentation.

C O M P U T E R   L A B O R A T O R Y   A S S I G N M E N T S

COMPUTER LABORATORY ASSIGNMENT 1
Building a Presentation with a Graph

Purpose: To become familiar with creating a presentation in Outline view, adding clip art, and inserting a graph.

Problem: You are the Director of Safety for Intergalactic Pipeline. You are to present the annual safety review to all department managers tomorrow afternoon. You have established your agenda. After reviewing the accident statistics, you decide a graph would best represent the five-year accident history. You decide to emphasize the company's safety goal and objectives. You also decide on a plan of action to meet the company's goal.

FIGURE CLA3-1a

I.   **Annual Safety Review**
   A.   T. P. Hamilton
   B.   Director of Safety
   C.   Intergalactic Pipeline
II.   **Agenda**
   A.   Accident history
   B.   Safety goal & objectives
   C.   Plan of action
III.   **Accident History**
IV.   **Safety Goal & Objectives**
   A.   Goal
      1.   Accident-free work place
   B.   Objectives
      1.   Reduce accidents by 20% per year
      2.   Eliminate preventable accidents
V.   **Plan of Action**
   A.   Pre-plan every job
      1.   Job safety analysis sheet
      2.   Material safety data sheet
   B.   Train employees
      1.   Proper use of tools and equipment
   C.   Inspect equipment
      1.   Repair or replace damaged equipment

1. Create the presentation in Figures CLA3-1b through CLA3-1e using the outline in Figure CLA3-1a. Substitute your name for T. P. Hamilton on the title slide.

Year	Total Accidents	Chargeable	Non-Chargeable	Preventable
1991	399	187	214	67
1992	357	148	209	52
1993	323	153	170	65
1994	306	106	200	68
1995	300	89	211	77

2. Click the Template button on the status bar. Double-click the BLUEBOXS.PPT template.
3. Select Slide 2 by clicking it. Click the Slide View button to switch to Slide view. Double-click the Object over Text slide layout. From the Microsoft ClipArt Gallery, choose the People category, and insert the Group Meeting clip art.
4. Click the Next Slide button to display Slide 3. Click the Layout button on the status bar. Double-click the Graph slide layout.
5. Open Graph by double-clicking the graph placeholder. Complete the datasheet using the data in the table below.
6. Click outside the Datasheet window work area to close Graph and to display Slide 3.
7. Click the Next Slide button to display Slide 4. Double-click the Text and Clip Art slide layout. Double-click the clip art placeholder. From the Microsoft ClipArt Gallery, choose the People category, and insert Construction Worker clip art.
8. Save the presentation on your data disk with the filename CLA3-1.
9. Print the presentation using the Pure Black & White option in the Print dialog box.

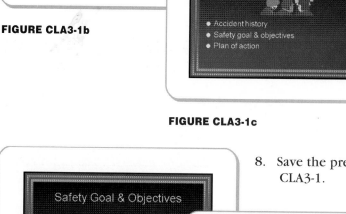

FIGURE CLA3-1b

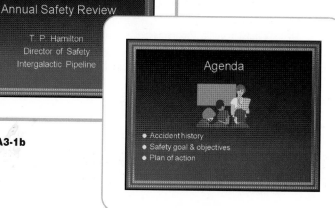

FIGURE CLA3-1c

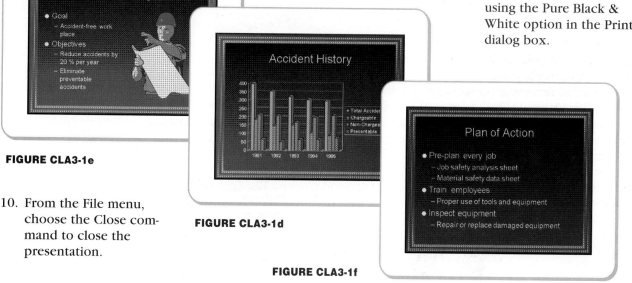

FIGURE CLA3-1e

FIGURE CLA3-1d

FIGURE CLA3-1f

10. From the File menu, choose the Close command to close the presentation.

COMPUTER LABORATORY ASSIGNMENT 2
Building a Presentation with a Table

Purpose: To become familiar with adding a table into a presentation.

Problem: You are the public relations officer for Metropolitan Transportation. Recently, your company re-evaluated all of its service areas. In order to improve community relations, you are speaking at a town hall meeting to announce the increases in service.

Instructions: Perform the following tasks:

1. Create the presentation in Figures CLA3-2b through CLA3-2e using the outline in Figure CLA3-2a.
2. Click the Template button on the status bar. Double-click the TOPLINES.PPT template.
3. Click the Slide View button and display Slide 1. Substitute your name for Linda Johnson on the title slide. Reduce the font size of Presented by to 24 points.
4. Click the Next Slide button to display Slide 2. Click the Layout button on the status bar. Double-click the Text & Clip Art slide layout.
5. Double-click the clip art placeholder. From the Microsoft ClipArt Gallery, choose the Transportation category, and insert the Bus clip art.
6. Click the Next Slide button to display Slide 3. Click the Layout button on the status bar. Double-click the Table slide layout.
7. Open the table work area by double-clicking the table placeholder. Create a table that has five columns and seven rows. Complete the table using the data below.
8. Spell check the contents of the table by clicking the Spelling button on the Word Standard toolbar.

I. **Metropolitan Transportation**
   A. Presented by:
   B. Linda Johnson
   C. Public Relations Officer
II. **Improved Services**
   A. Revised bus schedule
      1. Increased routes
      2. More bus stops
   B. Clean buses
   C. Friendly drivers
   D. No rate increase
III. **Bus Schedule**
IV. **Community Programs**
   A. Senior citizen discount - 5%
   B. Children under 12 ride free with paid adult
   C. Discounted weekend fares
   D. Discounted commuter fares

FIGURE CLA3-2a

Bus Number	502	504	506	509
1st & Maple	6:40	7:40	8:40	9:40
1st & Elm	6:50	7:50	8:50	9:50
2nd & Oak	7:00	8:00	9:00	10:00
2nd & Pine	7:15	8:15	9:15	10:15
3rd & Water	7:30	8:30	9:30	10:30
4th & College	7:45	8:45	9:45	10:45

9. Point to the center of the table and click the right mouse button to display a shortcut menu. Choose the Table AutoFormat command. Select the Classic 1 format. Choose the OK button.
10. Click outside the table to close Word and display the table in Slide 3.
11. Spell check the presentation in PowerPoint by clicking the Spelling button on the Standard toolbar.
12. Save the presentation on your data disk with the filename CLA3-2.
13. Print the presentation.
14. From the File menu, choose the Close command to close the presentation.

FIGURE CLA3-2b

FIGURE CLA3-2c

FIGURE CLA3-2d

FIGURE CLA3-2e

COMPUTER LABORATORY ASSIGNMENT 3
Adding Special Effects into a Presentation and Running a Slide Show

Purpose: To become familiar with adding transition effects, build effects, and running an automatic slide show.

Problem: Your instructor was so impressed with your presentation on starting a home-based business, he invited you to present it again at the Management Department's annual recognition dinner. You want to improve the presentation by adding slide transitions and build effects. You also decide to make the presentation an automatic slide show.

Instructions: Open CLA2-3 from your data disk. If you did not complete Computer Laboratory Assignment 3 in Project 2, see your instructor for a copy.

Instructions: Perform the following tasks:

1. Save the presentation with the filename CLA3-3 on your data disk.
2. If not already in Slide Sorter view, click the Slide Sorter View button.
3. From the Edit menu, choose the Select All command.
4. Click the Transition button. Select Random Transition from the Effect drop-down list. Choose the OK button.
5. Click the Build button. Select the Dim Previous Points check box. Select fuchsia from the Dim Previous Points color drop-down list. Fuchsia is the color sample in column 3, row 1. Select the Effect check box. Select Random Effects from the Effect drop-down list. Choose the OK button.
6. Click the Rehearse Timings button. When the title slide displays, click the left mouse button to display the rest of the slide. Rehearse the entire presentation to set slide timings. When the Microsoft PowerPoint information box displays, click the Yes button.
7. From the View menu, choose the Slide Show command. Select the Use Slide Timings option. Choose the Show button in the Slide Show dialog box.
8. Print the presentation by selecting Slides (with Builds) in the Print What box and by selecting the Pure Black & White check box.
9. From the File menu, choose the Close command to close the presentation.

COMPUTER LABORATORY ASSIGNMENT 4
Designing, Creating, and Running a Slide Show

Purpose: To become familiar with designing, creating, and running an automatic slide show.

Problem: You have been invited to speak to students enrolled in a personal finance course at the local community college. You are presenting information about the different types of mortgage loans and the costs associated with owning a home. Design and create an automatic slide show. Select an appropriate template. The presentation should consist of at least six slides, of which four should include a title slide, a table, a graph, and a closing slide. Use clip art where appropriate. Obtain the following information about mortgage loans from at least four lending institutions: institution name, loan type (fixed or variable), term (length of loan in years), interest rate, and points. Create a table to organize the mortgage loan information. Obtain a list of average home costs for the current year and previous four years. Create a bar graph illustrating the annual fluctuation in the average cost of a home. Add transition and build effects to the slide show. Set timings and run the automatic slide show. Be sure to spell check the presentation before saving it with the filename CLA3-4 on your data disk. Submit a copy of the automatic slide show on disk saved as CLA3-4 along with printouts of the slides using Slides (with Build) in pure black and white. From the File menu, choose the Close command to close the presentation.